IMAGES
of America

Community Boating, Inc.

ON THE COVER: Joseph Lee Jr. walks proudly along the wood boat dock at Community Boating in 1937, the year he started the Community Boat Club, which offered "Boating for All." Lee was to introduce to the youth of Boston's West End the joys of sailing in boats they made themselves and sail on the Charles River Basin in Boston.

IMAGES
of America

Community Boating, Inc.

Anthony M. Sammarco and
Community Boating, Inc.

ARCADIA
PUBLISHING

ISBN 978-1-4671-2809-4

Published by Arcadia Publishing
Charleston, South Carolina

Printed in the United States of America

Library of Congress Control Number: 2018948867

For all general information, please contact Arcadia Publishing:
Telephone 843-853-2070
Fax 843-853-0044
E-mail sales@arcadiapublishing.com
For customer service and orders:
Toll-Free 1-888-313-2665

Visit us on the Internet at www.arcadiapublishing.com

This book is written in honor of Joseph Lee Jr., Leo and Audrey Manfredi, and the past, present and future members of Community Boating, Inc.

Contents

ACKNOWLEDGMENTS

I am indebted to many people for their reminiscences, stories, and suggestions about Community Boating, from its early years in the late 1930s to today. Each person has helped to create a veritable archive of shared history to preserve it for the future. I would like to especially thank Daniel and Deborah Manfredi Winkler for loaning many of the photographs used in the book and for sharing their family stories about their involvement with Community Boating. I would also like to thank the members of Community Boating board and the stalwart staff:

Board members of Community Boating, Inc.: Karyn Brudnicki, president; Brian McManus, vice president; Chip Gaysunas, treasurer; Scott Kline, secretary; and the Directors at Large: John Bates; Lauren Graber; Gus Simiao; Catie O'Sullivan; and Dana Robinson.

The staff of Community Boating: Charlie Zechel, executive director; Andrew Alletag; Sidaulia Benson; Alex Catullo; Paul Gammons; and Ying Chen.

I would also like to thank the following for advice, counsel and encouragement: Susan Agaman; Stacia Bannerman, my editor; Boston Public Library, David Leonard and Henry Scannell (BPL); Hutchinson and Pasqualina Cedmarco; Cesidio "Joe Cedrone; Edie Clifford; Colortek, Jackie Anderson; Gary Dougherty; Daniel and Marilyn Farren; Sean M. Fisher, Commonwealth of Massachusetts, Department of Conservation and Recreation Archives (DCR); John Goode; Edward Gordon; Andrew Griesinger; Helen Hannon; Edward Jacoby; Patricia Kelleher; Stephen M. Kelleher; Jay Kronfeld; the late Ariel Foley Duff Lee; Douglas and Kenwyn Lee; the late George Manfredi; the late Leo and Audrey Manfredi; the Massachusetts Institute of Technology (MIT); Frank Norton; Brendan and Maryann Dworetzky O'Brien; Orleans Camera; Isaac Pato; Lilian M.C. Randall; the late Sylvia Sandeen; Jenney Szeto; Anita Samartino Tekle; Kenneth Turino and Chris Matthias; David Viera; Steve Winkler; West End Branch, Boston Public Library, Helen Bender.

Unless otherwise noted, all photographs are from the archives of Community Boating, Inc.

INTRODUCTION

Boston's Community Boating, now in its seventh decade as a public community sailing program, has introduced generations of the city's youth to the joy of sailing as well as the acquired skill of handling a sailboat on the Charles River Basin.

Community Boating was founded in 1937 by Joseph Lee Jr. (1901–1991), a proponent for outdoor recreation. Lee, who dedicated his entire life to public service, espoused the idea that all children—not just those of the wealthy—should learn to sail, enjoy themselves, and learn skills such as cooperation and joint responsibility.

The sleek sailboats that glide along the Charles River Basin have become an iconic symbol of the city of Boston, much like the swan boats in the Boston Public Garden and the weather beacon atop the John Hancock Building. The sailboats offered enthusiastic youths the opportunity to learn to sail.

It has been said that "public sailing in Boston began largely as a result of Joe Lee's vision." By utilizing his political skill, knowledge of sailing, coupled with his deep and committed interest in the youth of Boston, Joseph Lee began a project that was supported by his family, friends, neighbors, and a group of interested Bostonians to start a small fleet of hand-built sailboats on the Charles River Basin.

Boating on the Charles River in the decade prior to World War II was, as a general rule, limited to members of the Union Boat Club, a private rowing club. As a public sailing program, Community Boating offered something that was more common to summer resort communities, where one would see white sails on the water.

Joseph Lee was one who tested tradition and was considered a revolutionary, a maverick hell-raiser. He was a born-and-bred Boston Brahmin who realized that by offering sailing opportunities to the children of Boston's West End, they would experience a sporting activity usually reserved for a select few.

Joseph Lee founded the Community Boat Club in 1937. Along with his two nephews Kenny and Donny Robertson, he constructed two boats on the roof of his third-floor apartment over what is now the Hilltop Market at the corner of Anderson and Myrtle Streets on Beacon Hill. These first boats reportedly cost $20 each for supplies. Upon their completion, the trio carried their newly built boats down Beacon Hill to the Charles River, where they were launched and sailed, despite repeated warnings to cease from the Boston Police Department.

Lee later received a patent on the "simple method of boat construction, within the capacity of inexperienced builders." Assisted by Arthur E. Peterson, Lee continued building boats, often enlisting the help of local youths from the West End Community House. He said, "It was worthwhile for me to build more boats . . . when I thought of the children living in congested areas nearby, some streets that didn't even get sun. Sailing is just the thing for these children. You're all alone in your boat, a master of your own world."

Within a few years, Lee was overseeing a cadre of determined and enthusiastic youths who built seven boats. The Community Boat Club had grown to 100 members and a fleet of boats along with assistants who oversaw safety rules as well as instruction for sailing and swimming.

Lee and his group of young sailing enthusiasts were a persistent thorn in the side of the Metropolitan District Commission (MDC) and Eugene Hultman, its commissioner. The MDC operated the Charles River Basin and its riverbank parkland known as the Esplanade. Through the considerable influence of his aunt Helen Osborne Storrow, Joseph Lee was able to persuade many elected officials, including his cousin Gov. Leverett Saltonstall, to support the fledgling boat club and allow it to build a boathouse on the river that would serve the needs of the club members. Though there was tremendous political intrigue, haranguing and difficulties with various parties, the club was eventually reformed in 1941 as the Community Sailing Association, with college men hired as sailing instructors to serve adults, juniors, and organizations at very reasonable membership dues. William Roger Greeley, of the Boston architectural firm of Kilham, Hopkins & Greeley, designed the one-story boathouse and extended the docks into the Charles River.

In 1942, adults were permitted to join the club as "cooperative" members if they performed 50 hours or more of volunteer service at Community Boating Inc. The club was officially reorganized in 1946 and, since that time, has continuously offered sailing to people of all ages, abilities, and financial means throughout the Greater Boston area. Community Boating has long promoted an accessible and welcoming environment that encourages learning, volunteerism, and community spirit.

From the 1940s through the early 1970s, Leo and Audrey Manfredi were a vital part of Community Boating who introduced many adults and young adults to the joys of sailing on the Charles River Basin. Leo Manfredi, along with the late Lorna Slocomb, a longtime Beacon Hill resident and member of the board of directors, established an active outreach program that attracted boys and girls from the inner city, the Boys' Clubs of Boston, and the Perkins School for the Blind—a program that was initiated long before the terms "adaptive sports" and "universal access" came into popular use. He was welcoming and inclusive of all and continued the vision of Joseph Lee.

The Community Boating boathouse expanded into a second floor in 1987. Its fleet currently consists of 66 Centerboard Cape Cod Mercuries, 14 Keel Cape Cod Mercuries, 2 Universal Access Program (UAP) Keel Cape Cod Mercuries, 5 Rhodes 19s, 6 Sonars, 2 Ideal 18s, 13 Lasers, 18 420s, more than 30 sit-on-top single/double kayaks, and 20-plus Windsurfers—a veritable league away from the small hand-built sailboats Lee and his nephews built in 1937. Today, there are thousands of members, including young members of the Junior Program who pay nominal dues for a summer of sailing and learning the skills necessary, as Joseph Lee said, to be "a master of your own world."

Asked why he founded the boat club, Lee said, "Yankee thrift, I guess it was. There was the wind blowing over the river and not pushing any boats at all. I couldn't see it going to waste."

As it is stated, the mission of Community Boating, Inc., is to enable "Sailing for All." The corporation offers sailing and other water sports to people of all ages, abilities, and means in the Greater Boston area. The center promotes an accessible and welcoming environment that encourages learning, volunteerism, and community spirit.

One

Boston's West End

The only way that decay and blight may be uprooted . . . is by a complete physical change in the affected neighborhood or area.

—Mayor John B. Hynes

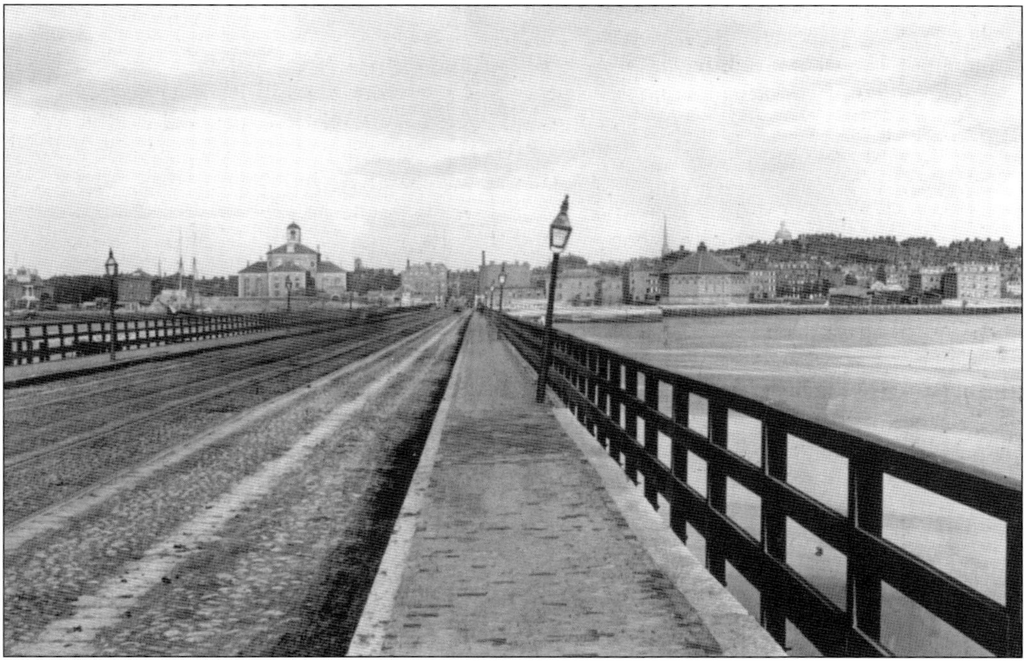

The West Boston Bridge crossed the Charles River, connecting the cities of Cambridge and Boston at Cambridge Street, now known as Charles Circle. This c. 1880 photograph shows the Massachusetts General Hospital and the Charles Street Jail on the left and the dome of the Massachusetts State House rising above the roof lines of Beacon Hill houses on the right. Roughly where the octagonal gasometer is to the right of the gas lamp is the future site of the boathouse of Community Boating. (Author's collection.)

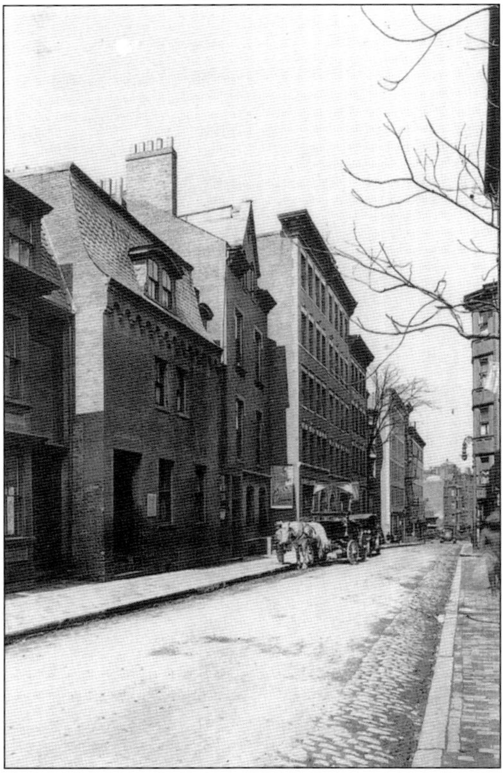

This photograph of nos. 16 to 26 Staniford Street, looking north from Cambridge Street toward Green Street, shows that there were charming early and mid-19th-century houses throughout the West End of Boston. These small houses, especially the mansard roofed house in the center, were comfortable middle-class residences near to downtown but convenient to Cambridge Street and Beacon Hill.

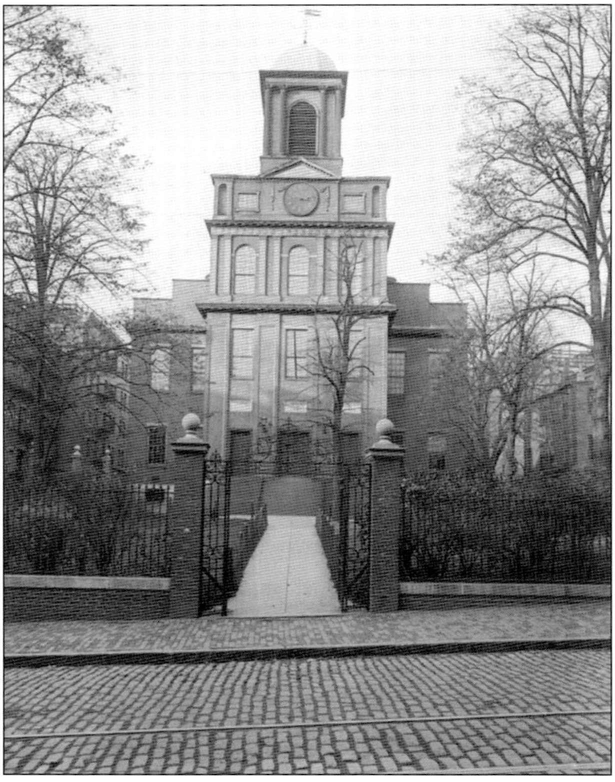

The Old West Church was designed by Asher Benjamin and built in 1806 on Cambridge Street between Lynde and Staniford Streets. The original church, which dated to 1737, was destroyed by the British during the American Revolution; it was to become a fashionable church with the Reverend Cyrus A. Bartol serving as minister. The changing aspect of the West End by immigrants impacted the congregation, and in 1892, the last service was held, and the church was subsequently used as the West End Branch of the Boston Public Library from 1896 to 1940. Since 1964, a Methodist congregation has worshipped here and has restored the church.

The Charles Street Jail was designed by Gridley J. Fox Bryant and built in 1851 at the entrance to the West Boston (now Longfellow) Bridge. It became an anchor in the West End. Designed with four wings of solid Quincy granite, radiating from an octagonal cupola, the wings allowed segregation of prisoners by sex and category of offense, and thirty arched windows, each 33 feet high, provided ventilation and natural light. The original jail contained 220 cells, and today, the jail has been renovated as the Liberty Hotel with the popular Clink Restaurant.

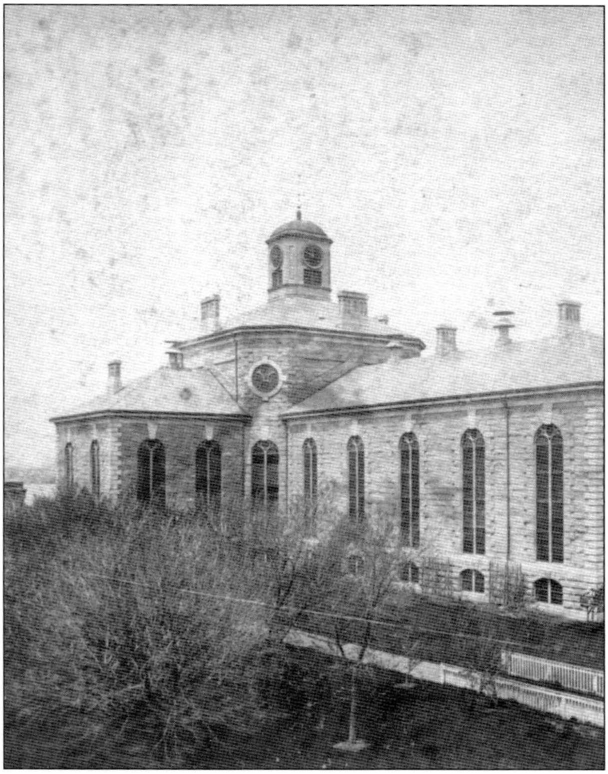

The widening of Cambridge Street in the 1930s was a years-long effort by the determined residents of the West End and Beacon Hill to get both Charles and Cambridge Streets widened and a subway station on the Red Line at Charles Circle. It became a reality in 1932.

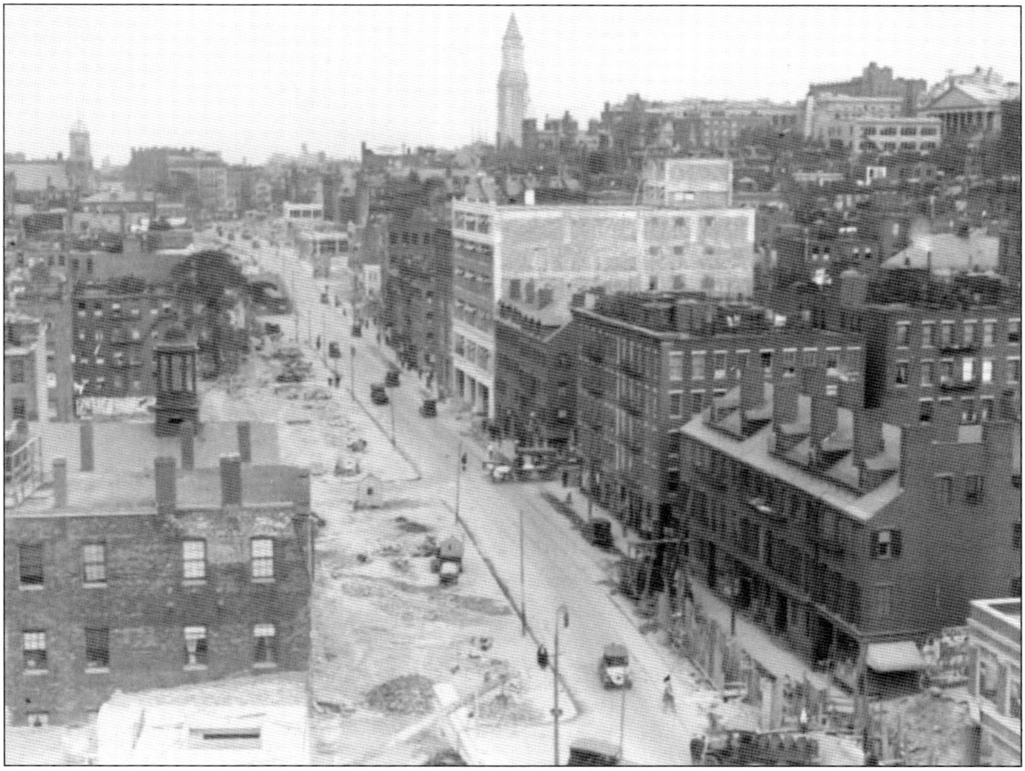

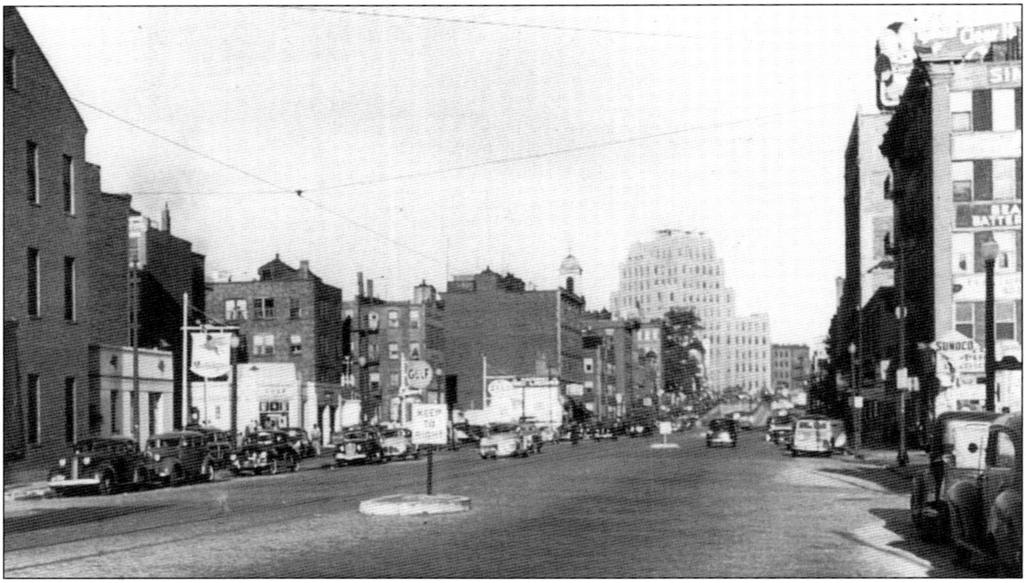

Cambridge Street, looking toward Bowdoin Square in the distance, had 19th- and early-20th-century residences and commercial buildings that lived both sides of the street. The street was really the main thoroughfare in the West End and linked Scully and Bowdoin Squares to the Longfellow Bridge linking Boston and Cambridge. In the center is the New England Telephone and Telegraph Building that was designed by Densmore, LeClear & Robbins and constructed in 1930.

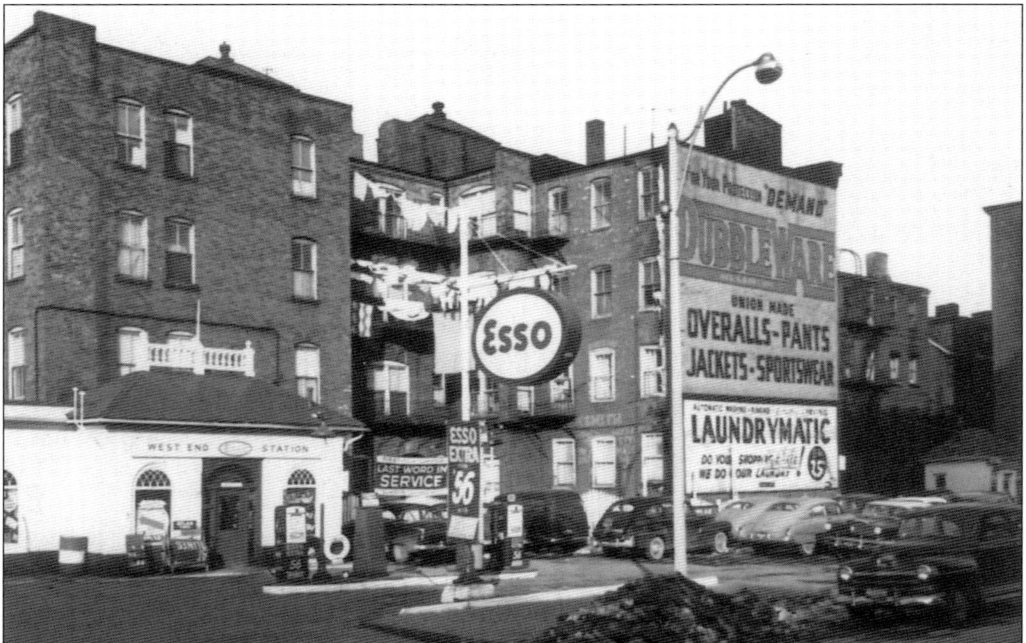

The West End Esso Station was a small Colonial Revival automobile and gasoline station that dated from the early 1920s. Seemingly plunked down on Cambridge Street, the impressive gas station, with its classical arched windows and roof balustrade, gave a distinctly classical feeling to the rear of the apartment buildings rising behind it.

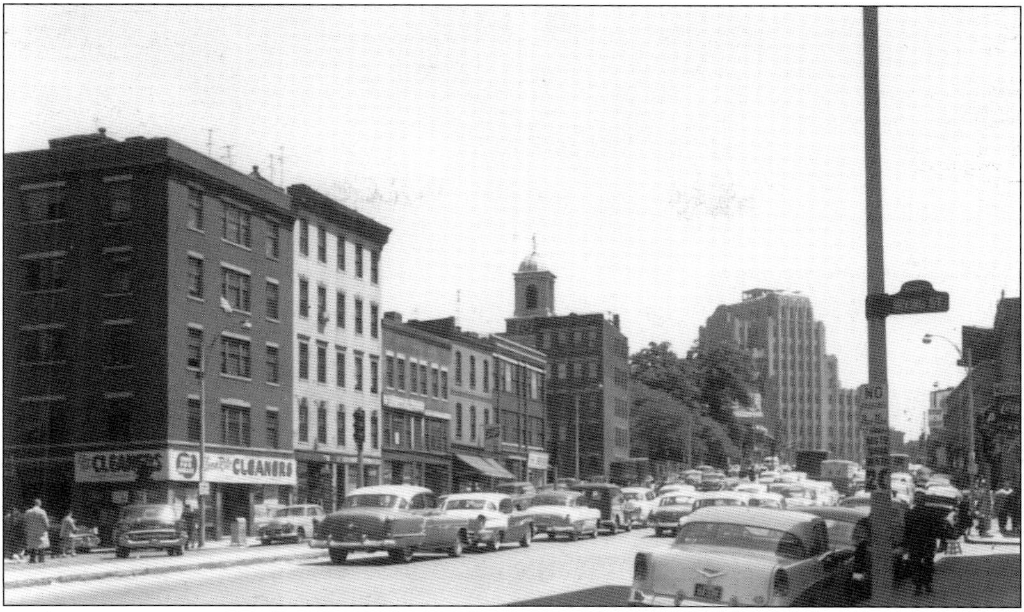

Looking east on Cambridge Street, the belfry of the Old West Church can be seen rising above the roofs of the buildings that would eventually be demolished for a mall with ample parking spaces. As few residents of the West End or on the north slope of Beacon Hill kept automobiles, the parking lot had become a necessity for a 1960s strip mall at the time of urban renewal.

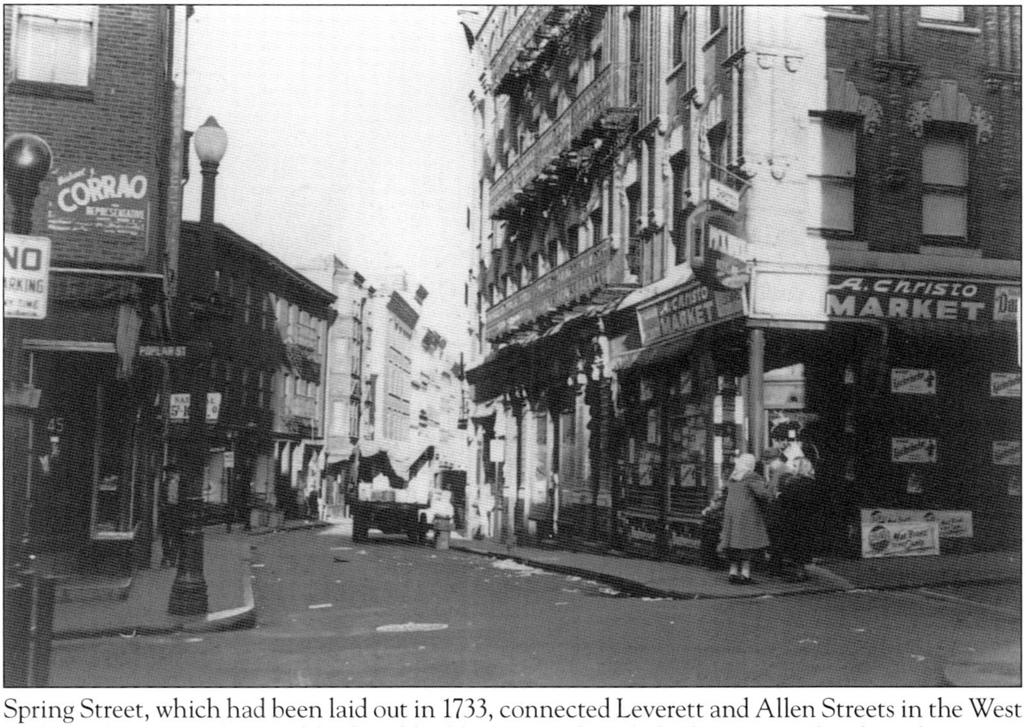

Spring Street, which had been laid out in 1733, connected Leverett and Allen Streets in the West End. By the 1940s, the neighborhood had become a densely built-up area of early-19th-century houses overshadowed by tenements of the late 19th and early 20th century and walk-up apartment and tenement buildings of five floors.

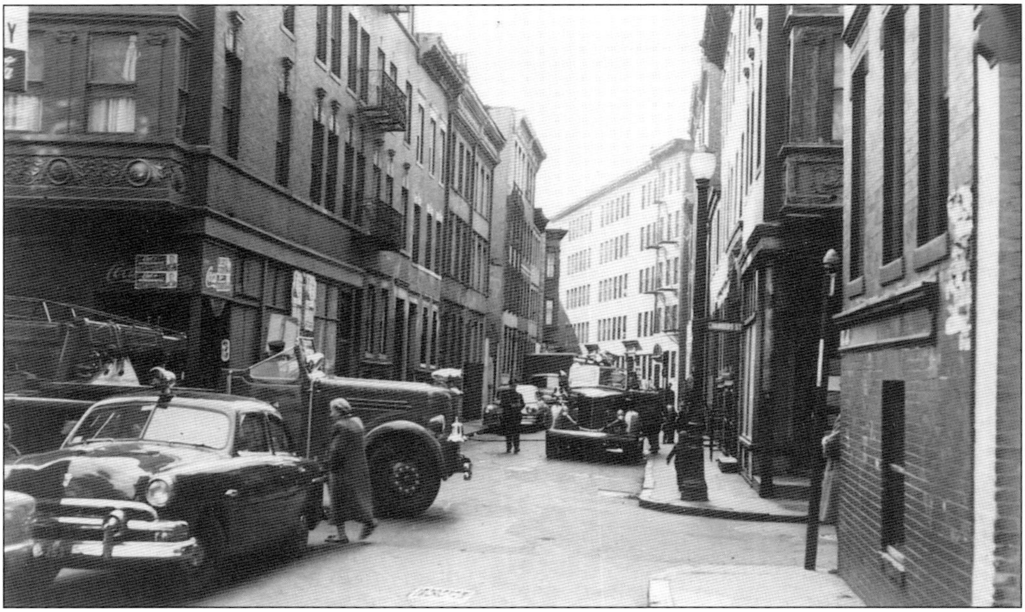

The narrow 19th-century streets of the West End were never more hazardous than when fire apparatus had to be summoned. Here, at the corner of Auburn and Chambers Streets, two Boston Fire Department engines are seen at the intersection, unable to move with automobiles parked on the narrow streets. The density of the West End was a major factor for urban renewal.

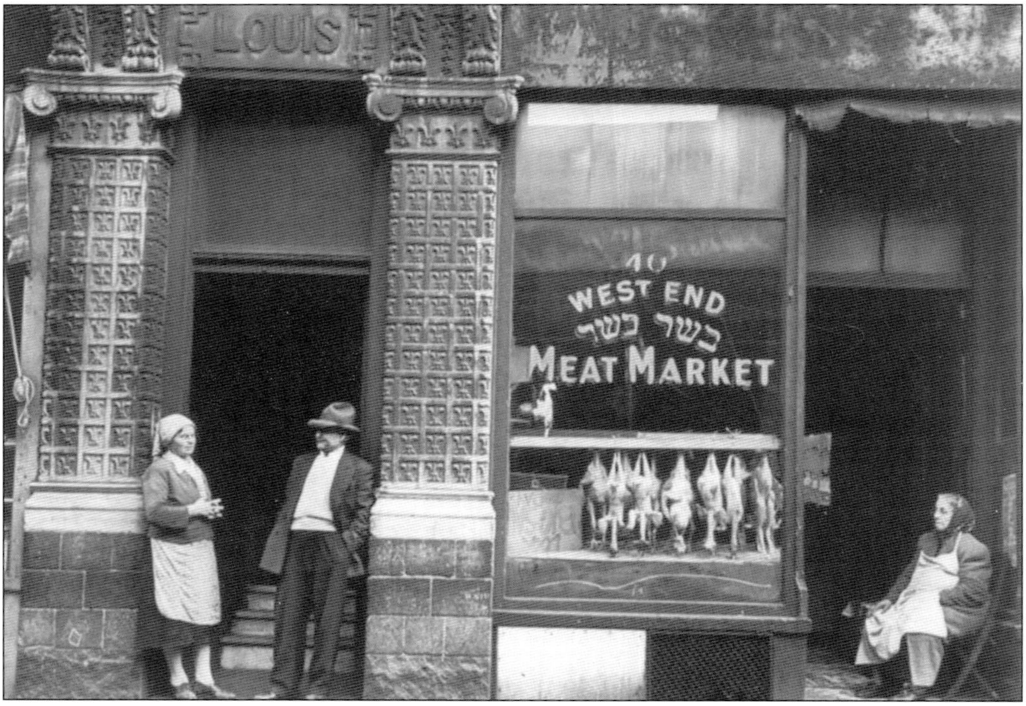

The West End Meat Market was at 40 Spring Street and offered properly prepared kosher meats and poultry. An apron-clad woman sits in the doorway beside a display window with hanging chickens awaiting customers as two neighbors chat at the Ionic pilastered entrance to the *Louis*, an apartment building to the left. (Courtesy of the Boston Public Library)

Cambridge Street looking west in the early 20th century was lined with bars, shops, and rooms, as seen on the sign in the distance to let "by the day or week." This block was a virtual streetscape of signs, placards, and advertisements showing the bustle of the West End. In the distance is Bowdoin Square, named for Gov. James Bowdoin, and the belfry of the Old West Church seen on the far left.

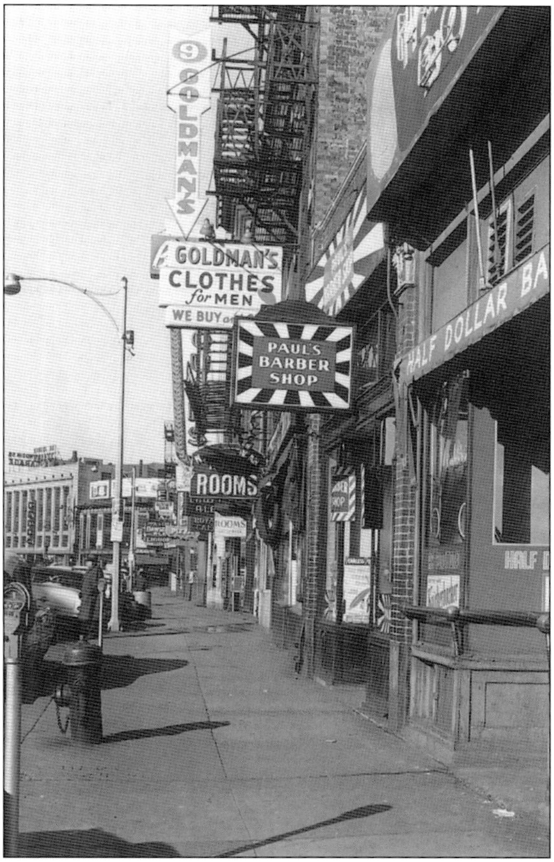

St. Joseph Catholic Church is at the corner of Blossom and McLean Streets. Designed as a Greek Revival church by Alexander Parris, the church was originally built in 1834 for the Twelfth Congregational Society and said to be "the most elegant Church in Boston." As the neighborhood changed with successive waves of immigration in the mid-19th century, it was purchased by the Boston Roman Catholic Diocese in 1862 and dedicated to St. Joseph. Today, it is one of the few buildings to have survived urban renewal of the West End in the early 1960s.

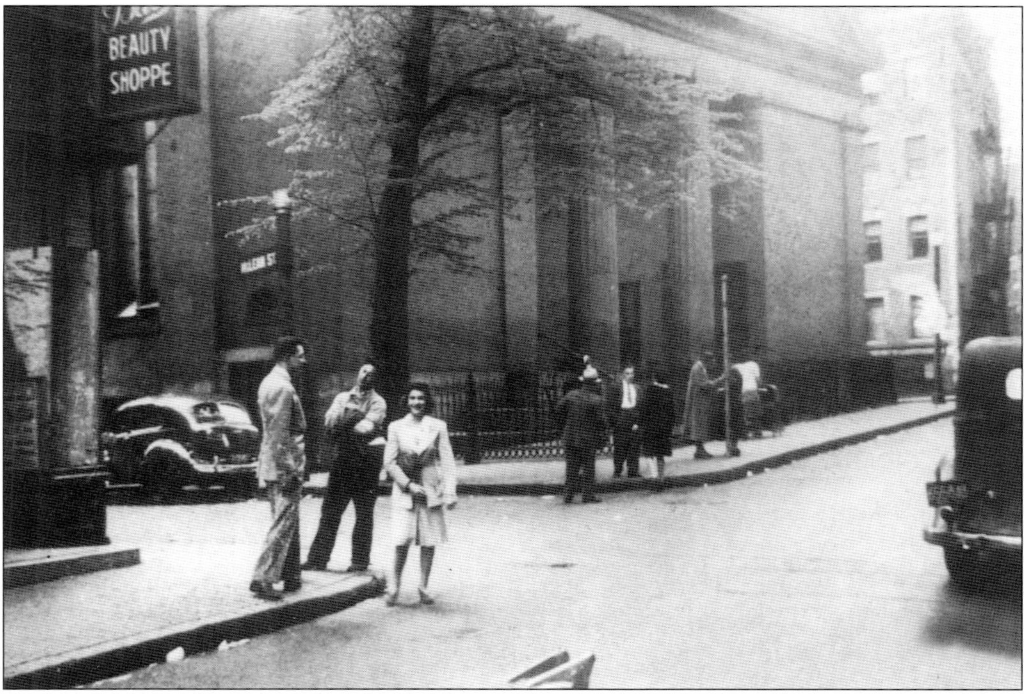

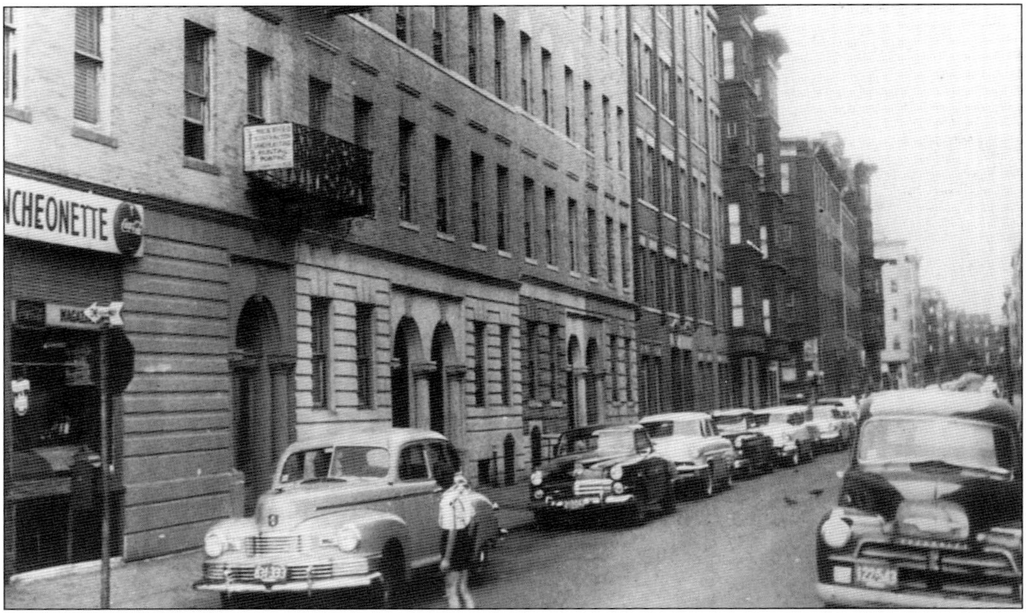

Near the corner of Allen and Charles Streets, the streetscape was composed of five-story tenements and apartment buildings that created a densely built up urban neighborhood with residents of all walks of life, races, and ethnicity. These buildings were lived in by people who had lived in the West End for generations and knew it as an embracing and welcoming neighborhood.

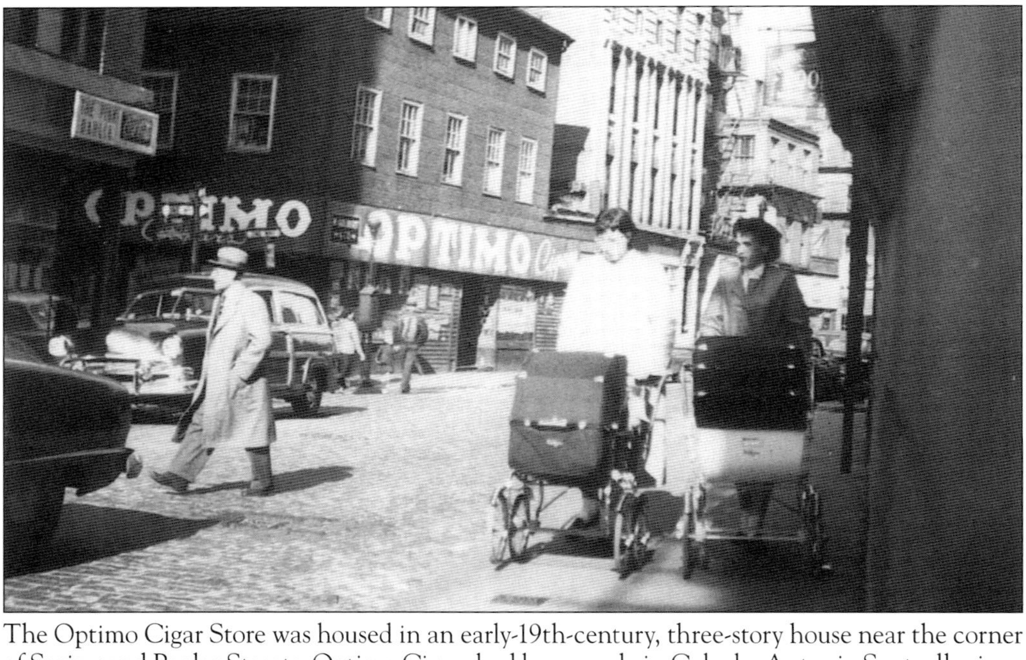

The Optimo Cigar Store was housed in an early-19th-century, three-story house near the corner of Spring and Poplar Streets. Optimo Cigars had been made in Cuba by Antonio Santaella since 1898, and the popular brands of A. Sanataella & Co. included Florida Girl, Flora Mia, Centropolis, Optimo, Marquette Club, Reformador, and Flor de Cervera, of which the Optimo brand was the favorite cigar of Babe Ruth. The company was sold to the Universal Cigar Corporation in 1955. On the left is the Pink Dahlia, a popular West End spa. The women on the right push baby carriages, showing that this was truly a family neighborhood with people of all ages.

James Jackson Storrow (1864–1926) and his wife, Helen Osborn Storrow (1864–1944), were wealthy Bostonians who would be instrumental in the founding of the West End House, a settlement house in Boston's West End that assisted the youth of the neighborhood. Residents of the Back Bay, with an estate in Lincoln, Massachusetts, the Storrows were well known and respected philanthropists who saw the West End House as an important part of the fabric of life of the neighborhood, and they fostered the youth of the West End through their generosity.

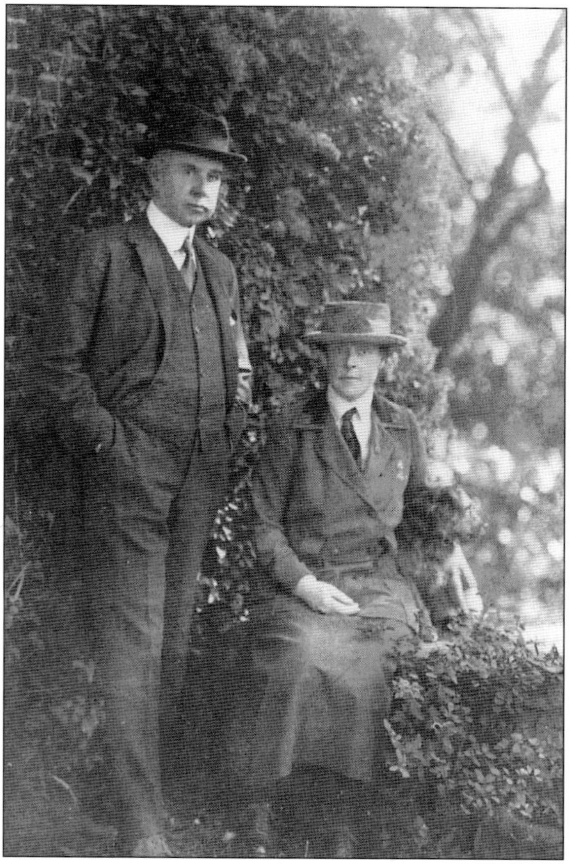

These young boys were playing on a makeshift gymnasium at the West End House after school. The enjoyment of these young children was obvious, but it was indoors, and the concept of offering them the ability to sail in a boat in the open air that they had made themselves was Joseph Lee's idea of how they should spend their free time.

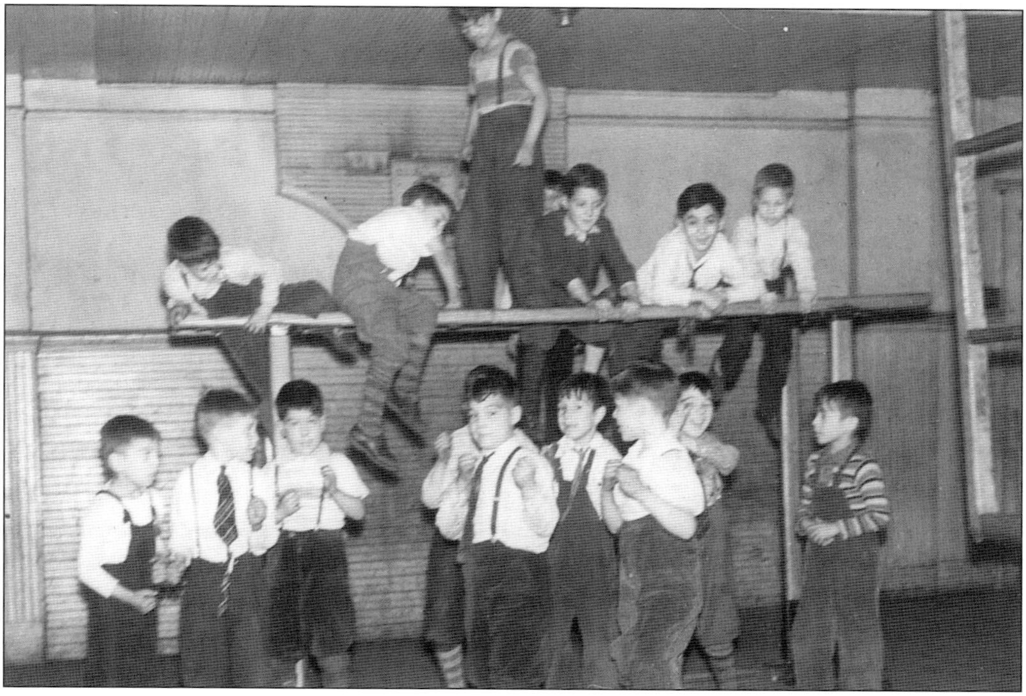

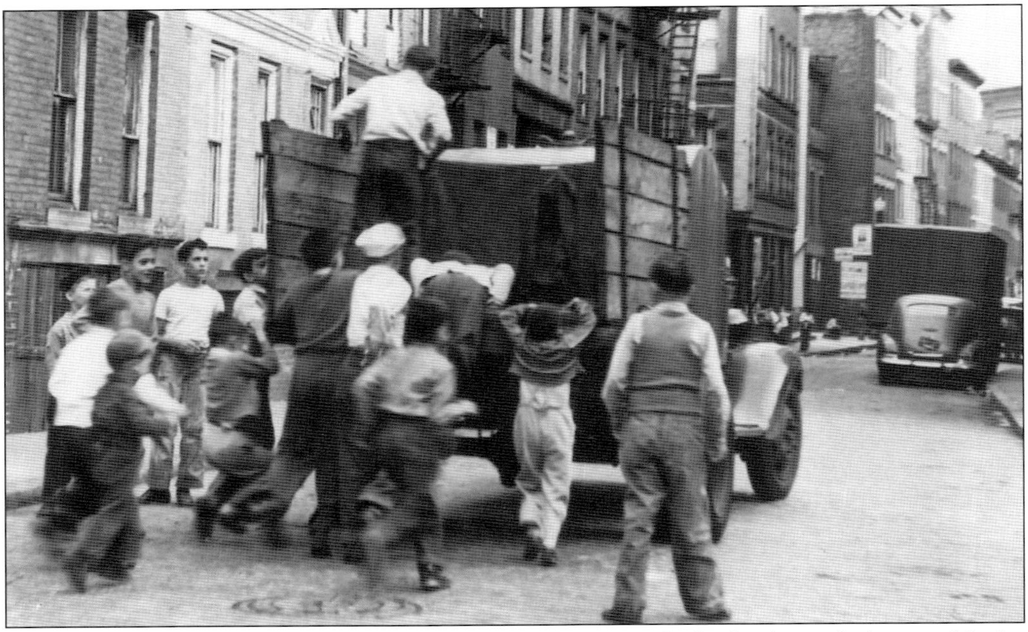

These young boys from the West End House eagerly jump on the back of a truck that would take them for a week at a summer camp in the 1940s. A week in the country was a great change from the densely settled West End, and one can imagine how eagerly it was awaited by the children every summer. By the late 1930s, the boys of the West End were helping Joseph Lee to not just build new sailboats but also learn to sail them on the Charles River Basin.

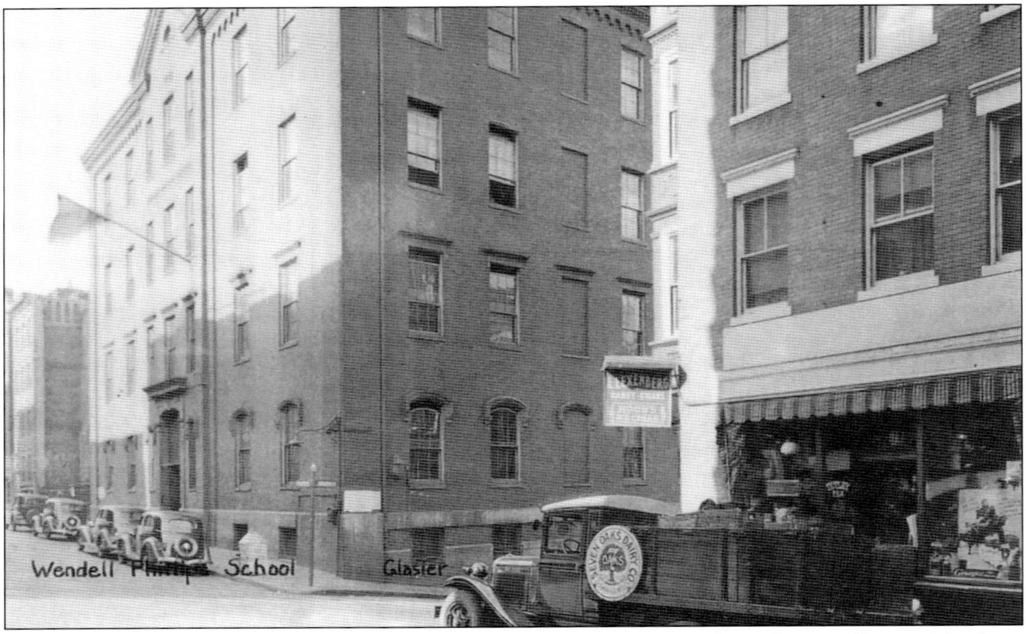

The Wendell Phillips School was designed by noted architect Nathaniel J. Bradlee and built in 1861. The school was named after the great abolitionist and publisher of the *Liberator,* the voice piece of abolitionism in Boston from 1831 to 1863. The school was located at the corner of Phillips and Anderson Streets, and it was closed in 1940; the building converted for use as a technical school. In 1977, the former place of education was converted to housing.

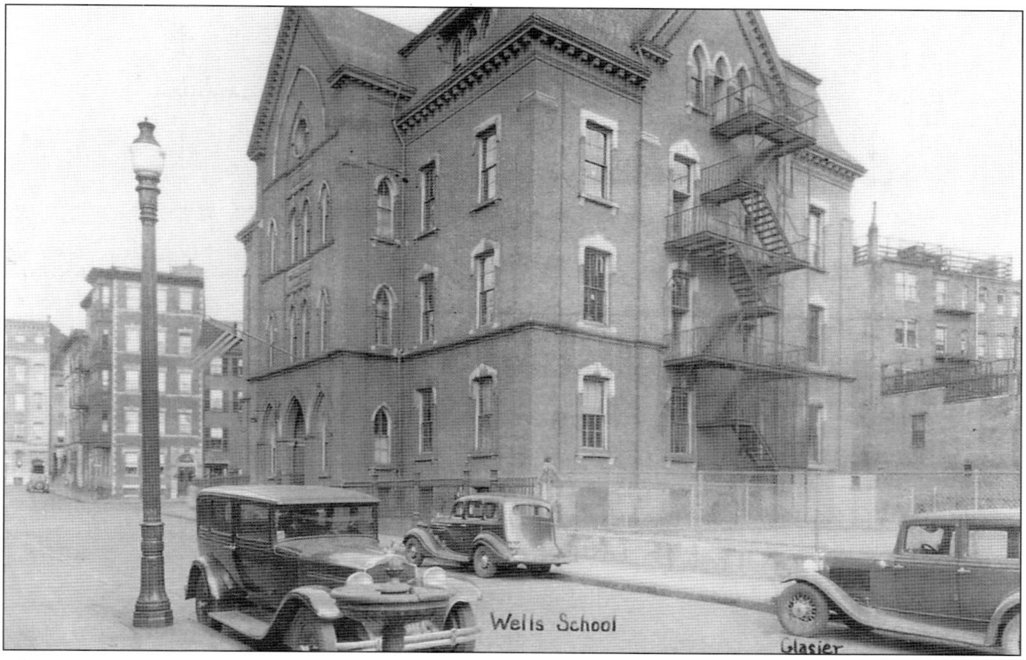

The Wells School was designed by Richards and Park and built in 1868. Named for Charles Welles, the fourth mayor of Boston and president of the Massachusetts Charitable Mechanic Association; the school was at McLean and Blossom Streets. An annex was built in 1914 to accommodate the large number of children from the West End, but the school was closed in 1947 and sold to St. Joseph's Church.

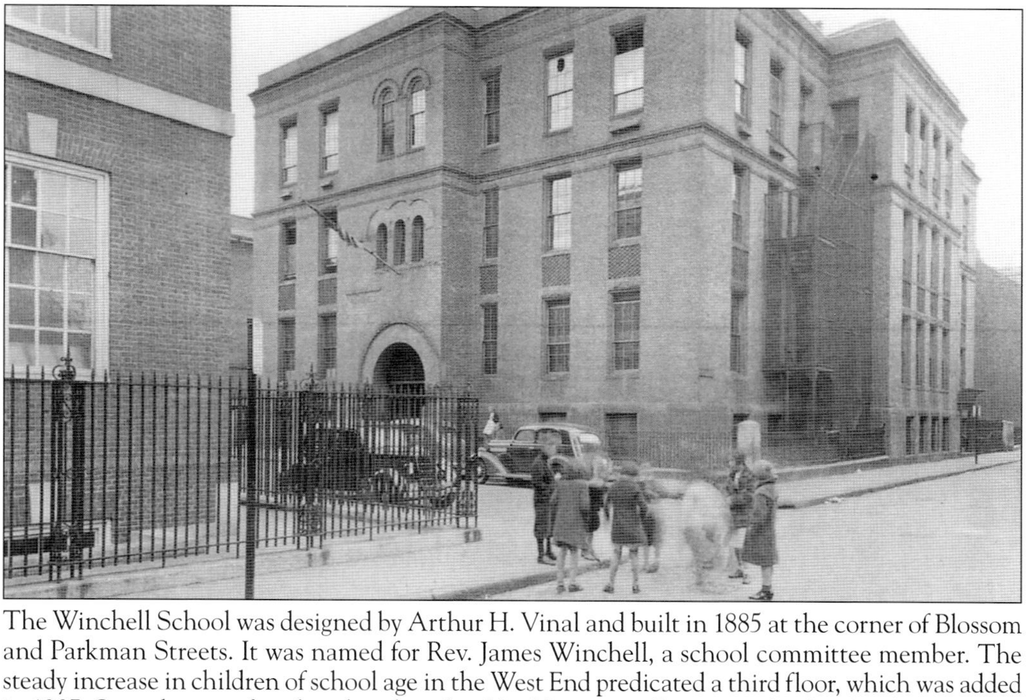

The Winchell School was designed by Arthur H. Vinal and built in 1885 at the corner of Blossom and Parkman Streets. It was named for Rev. James Winchell, a school committee member. The steady increase in children of school age in the West End predicated a third floor, which was added in 1907. Over the next five decades, the school had large enrollments as the families living in the West End were often large. The school was closed in 1960 at the height of the urban renewal.

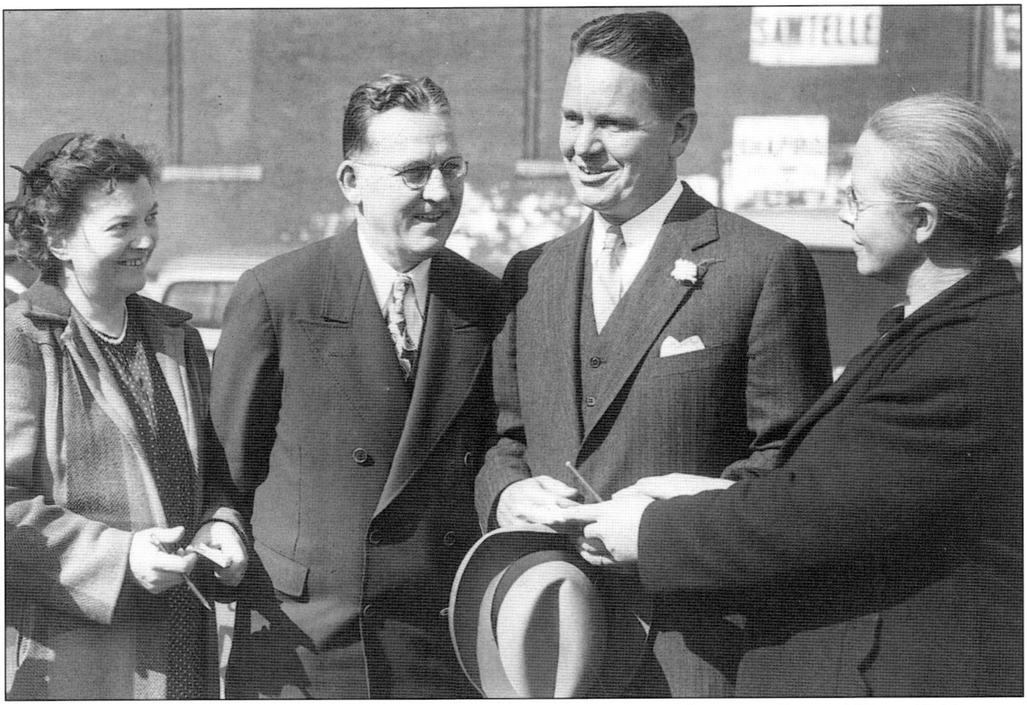

Greeting Maurice J. Tobin (third from left), who served as mayor of Boston from 1938 to 1944, upon his visit to the West End of Boston just after his election is Mrs. Naples (right). Accompanying the mayor was John B. Hynes (left, wearing glasses), who would later serve as mayor of Boston from 1950 to 1959 and declared the West End a slum in order to obtain federal funds necessary for urban renewal.

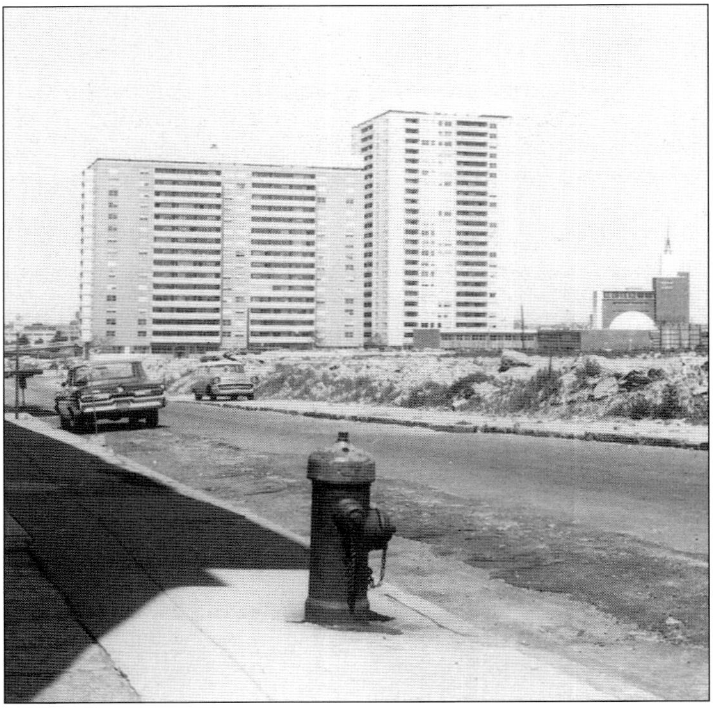

The urban renewal of the West End of Boston would see the neighborhood swept away and rebuilt with luxury high-rise apartment buildings. Seen here are the Charles River Apartments, which were sleek and modern, could boast of city and Charles River views, and were in close proximity to downtown Boston. As Lee said of this urban renewal in a reinterpretation of the Sermon on the Mount, "Blasted be the poor, for theirs is the kingdom of nothing, blasted be they that mourn, for they shall be discomforted. Blasted be the meek, for they shall be kicked off the earth."

Two

THE CHARLESBANK, STORROW DRIVE, AND THE HATCH SHELL

The Hatch Shell is an iconic Boston landmark that unites and enriches the Boston community with vital arts, culture, and much needed green space.

—The Esplanade Association

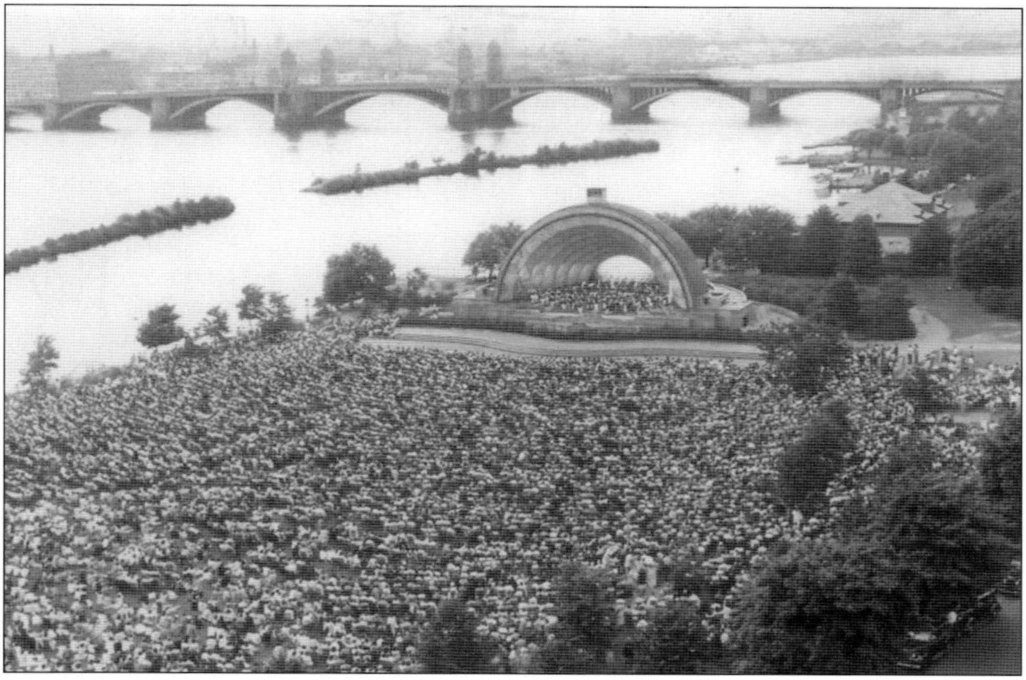

Seen from the air, the Hatch Shell on the Esplanade has become part of a tradition in Boston, with popular open-air concerts as well as the patriotic and rousing concert on the Fourth of July, when the Boston Pops plays the rousing "1812 Overture" to the accompaniment of cannonade and fireworks, thrilling and mesmerizing the audience not only seated on the lawns and in their boats on the Charles River but also those watching from televisions in the comfort of their own homes. Community Boating can be seen on the upper right.

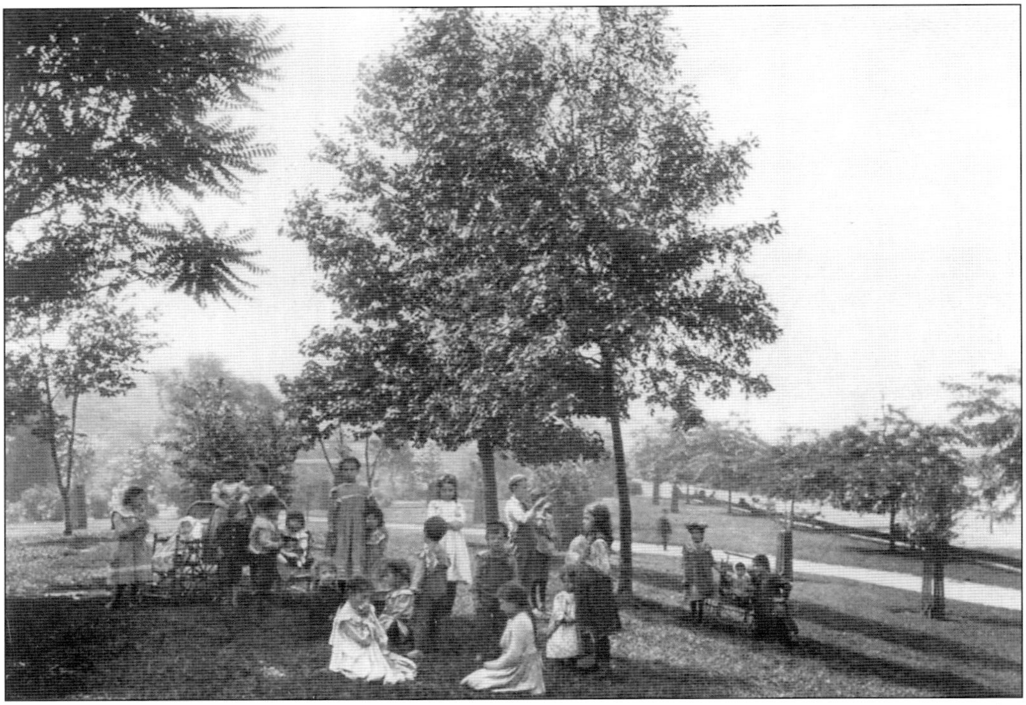

The Charlesbank was created at the turn of the 20th century on the flats of land along the Charles River. Frederick Law Olmsted Sr. designed a park here in the 1880s and 1890s that included a promenade along the river as well as landscaped grounds for active and passive recreation. These children play on the lush green lawns with newly planted trees shading the area that was created as a part of the new park system in and around the city of Boston. This urban park was on a strip of land between Cambridge and Leverett Streets, with the Charles River seen to the right.

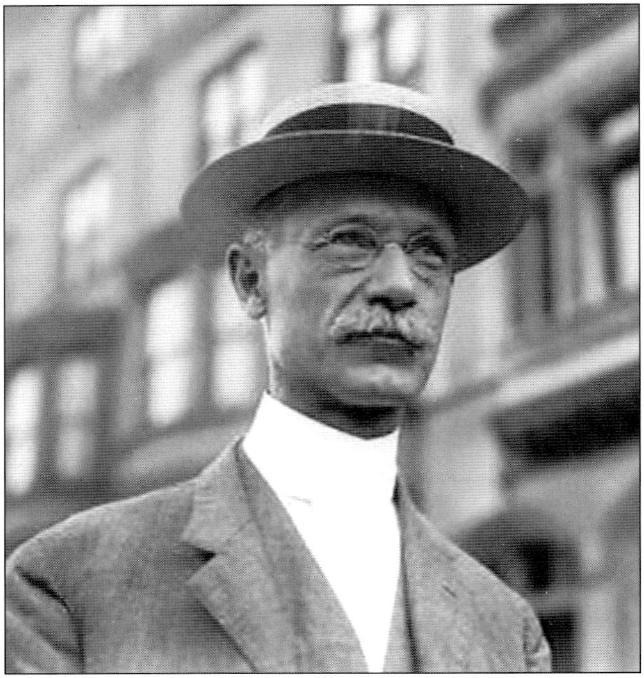

Joseph Lee Sr. (1862–1937) was a resident of Mount Vernon Street on Beacon Hill and the epitome of a Boston Brahmin. He was educated at Harvard and Harvard Law School but never practiced law; he is considered to be the "founder of the playground movement," as he believed that community life could be strengthened by playgrounds and play. Lee founded the Massachusetts Civic League and served as its president from 1897 to 1937. He was an active officer in the Immigration Restriction League from 1905 until his death in 1937, as well as serving as the president of the National Recreation Association from 1910 until the time of his death.

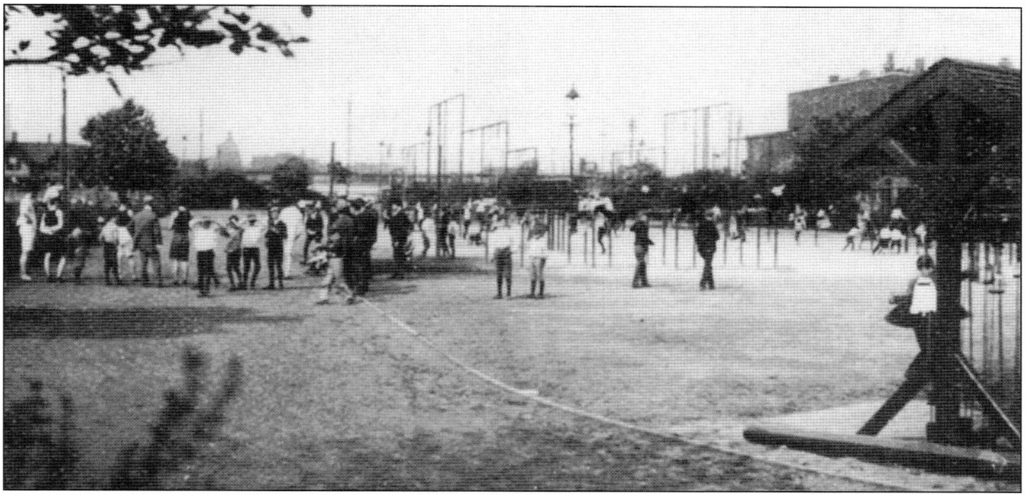

The Charlesbank Gymnasium was an outdoor playground of the children of the West End and Beacon Hill. Its rules enforced the segregation of boys and girls—the boys had their gymnasium near the West Boston (now known as the Longfellow) Bridge, and the girls had their gymnasium near the Craigie Bridge opposite Chambers Street. This outdoor exercise area was strongly supported by Joseph Lee and offered recreation along the riverbank for the neighborhood children.

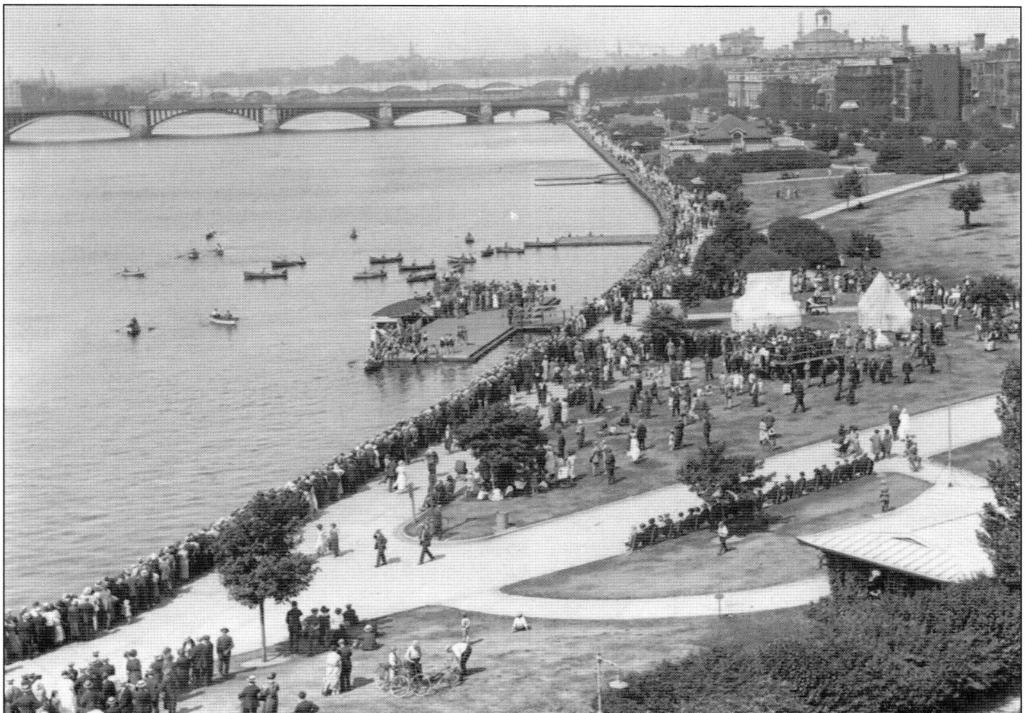

The Esplanade, which was developed along the Charles River as a pleasure park, had a wood boat launch in the center with rowboats as well as small sailboats on the Charles River Basin, with many Bostonians lining the walkways watching the race. On the upper right, the cupola of the Charles Street Jail rising above the rooftops of the Beacon Street houses can be seen. The West Boston Bridge crosses the Charles River, connecting Boston and Cambridge. (Courtesy of the DCR.)

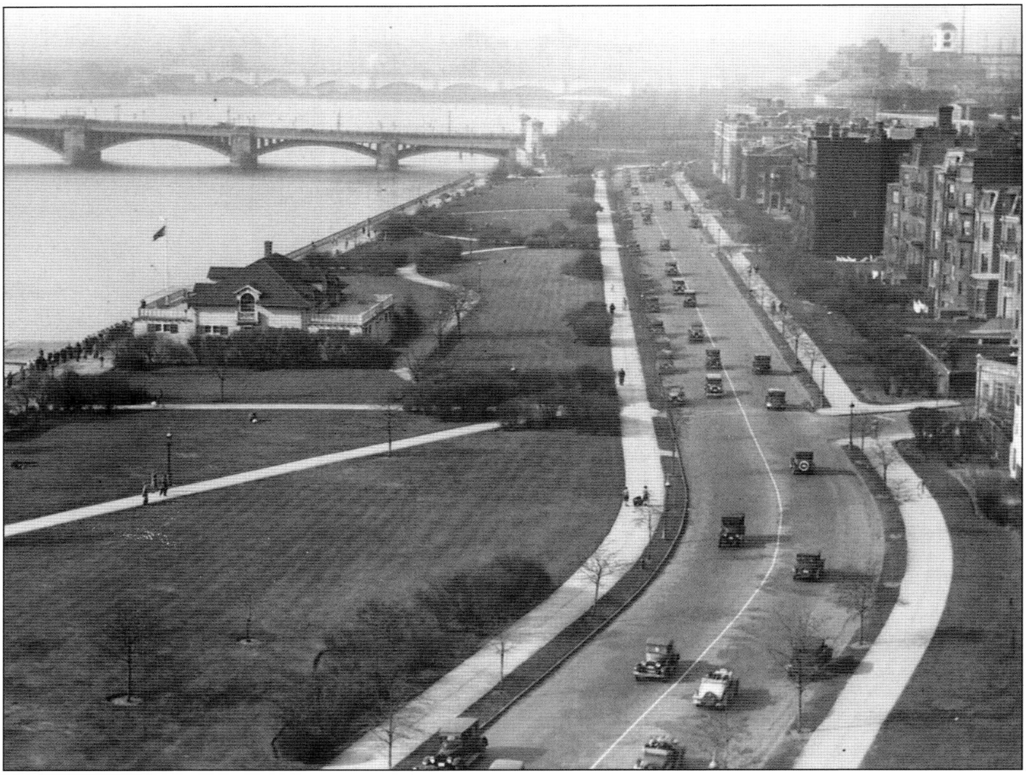

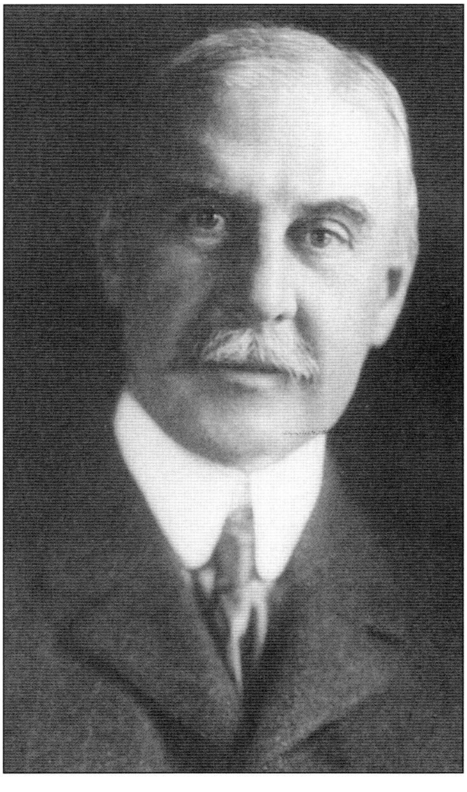

Storrow Drive, a sleek new automobile road, was laid along the contours of the Charles River, seen on the left, and the Flat of Beacon Hill, on the right. Linking the edge of the West End to Cambridge, it was a major improvement of travel through Boston with the ascendancy of the automobile. The building on the left is the Union Boat Club, which had been founded in 1851 and had the distinction of introducing the style of rowing without a coxswain on the Charles River. The Community Boating site would be in the distance when founded in 1937. (Courtesy of the DCR.)

James Jackson Storrow was for whom Storrow Drive was named. A partner in the venerable banking house of Lee, Higginson & Company, he was dedicated to the well-being of Bostonians, having served on the Boston School Committee and the Boston Chamber of Commerce. After his death, his widow, Helen O. Storrow, donated $1 million in his memory to be used to create a pleasure park along the Charles River that enhanced the outdoor recreation for city residents along with walkways and seating areas to enjoy the panoramic views.

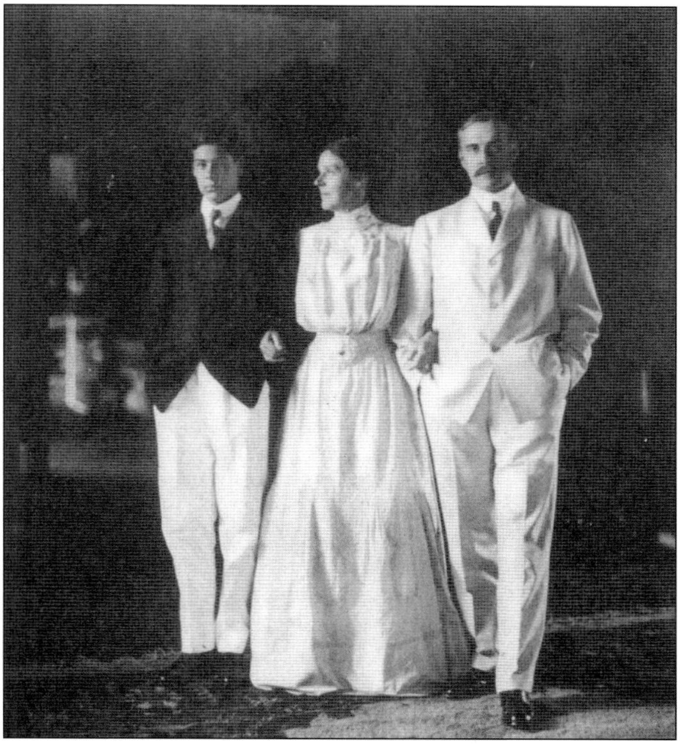

Pictured in 1909, from left to right are James J. Storrow III, Helen Osborn Storrow, and James Jackson Storrow Jr. The Storrows, who lived at 417 Beacon Street in Boston's Back Bay, were distinguished Boston philanthropists who founded the West End House in 1906 through the Storrow Trust. It was largely through the foresight and financial generosity of Helen that the Charles River Basin was landscaped and opened for recreation in the 1930s as well as the construction of the original boathouse of Community Boating.

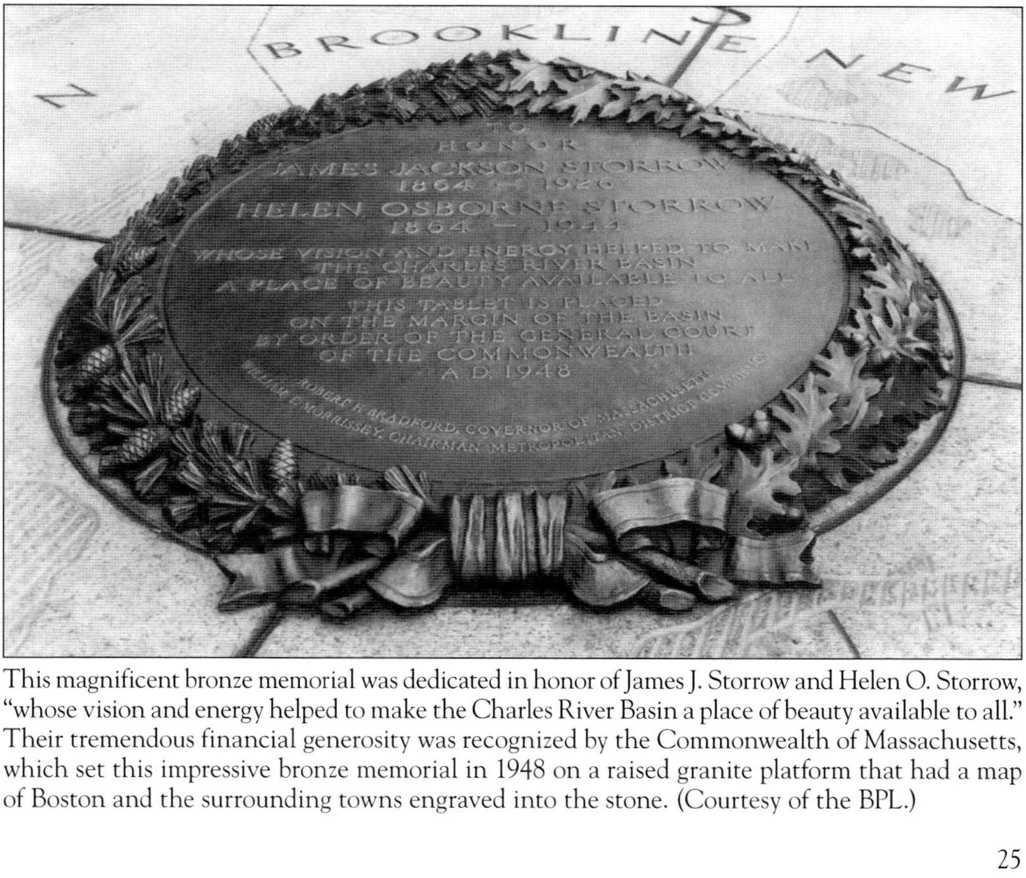

This magnificent bronze memorial was dedicated in honor of James J. Storrow and Helen O. Storrow, "whose vision and energy helped to make the Charles River Basin a place of beauty available to all." Their tremendous financial generosity was recognized by the Commonwealth of Massachusetts, which set this impressive bronze memorial in 1948 on a raised granite platform that had a map of Boston and the surrounding towns engraved into the stone. (Courtesy of the BPL.)

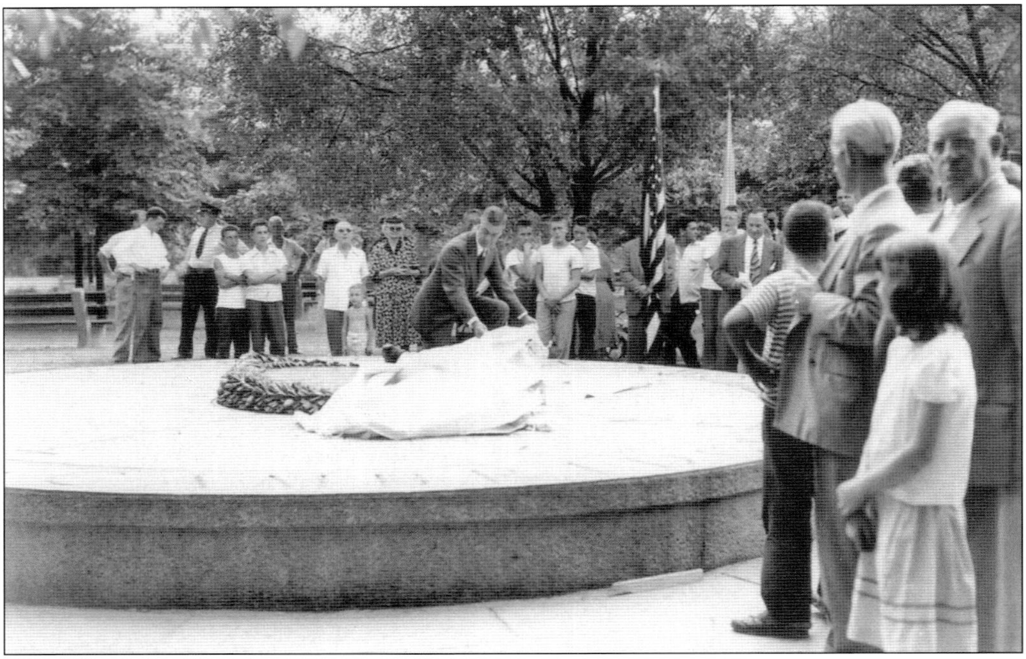

James Jackson Storrow III, the only child of James and Helen Storrow, unveils the bronze memorial to his late parents as members of his family, his friends as well as officials of the Commonwealth of Massachusetts and the public look on. Joseph Lee of Community Boating was the nephew of the Storrows as well as Henry Lee Higginson and Paul Cabot. (Courtesy of the BPL.)

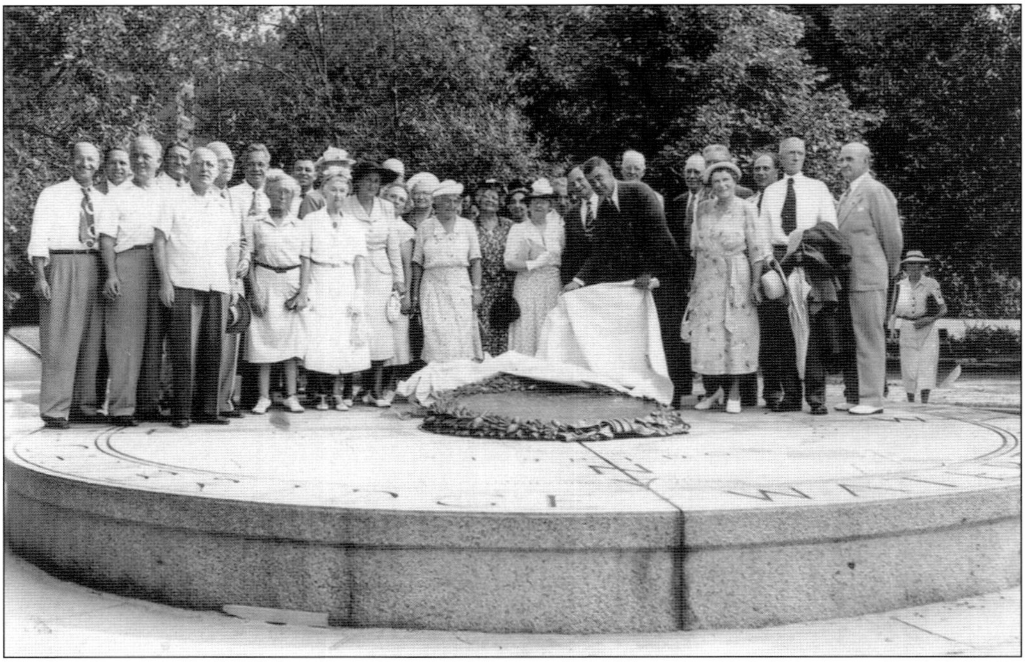

Members of the Storrow, Lee, Saltonstall, Shattuck, and Cabot families, all interrelated in the age-old Boston manner, along with Bostonians of all walks of life, surround James J. Storrow III as he unveils the bronze memorial to his parents. The vision of the Storrows ensured that their generosity would benefit generations of Bostonians for generations to come. (Courtesy of the BPL.)

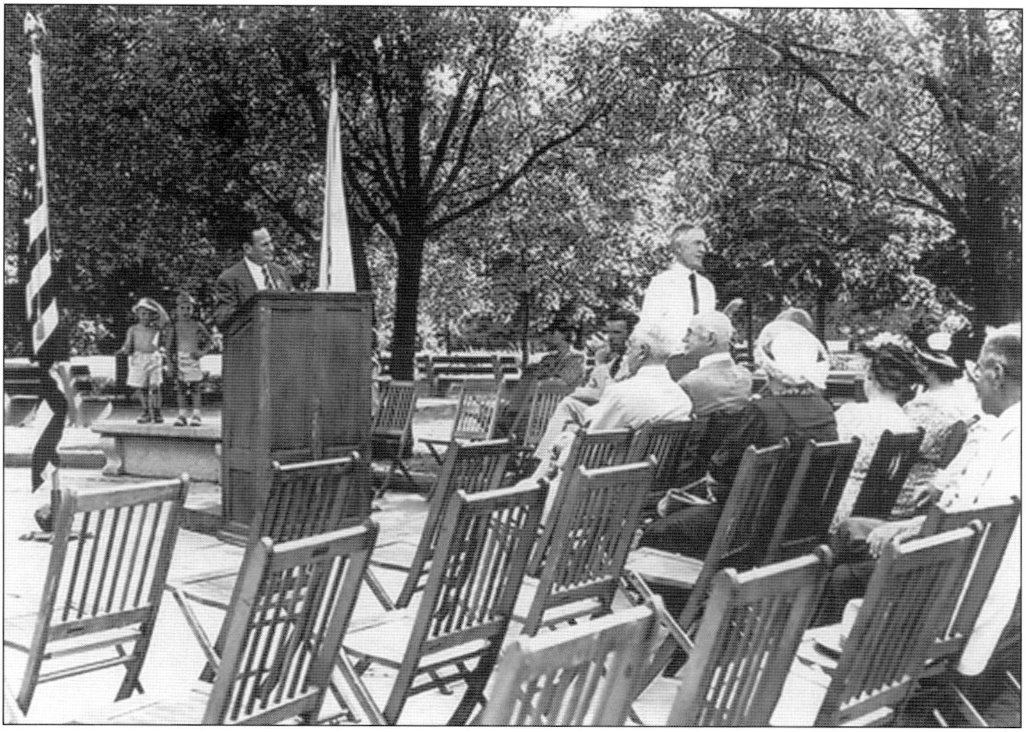

The dedication of the Storrow Memorial was held under the shade of mature trees along the Charles River. Flags of the United States and the Commonwealth of Massachusetts flank Gov. Robert Fiske Bradford, who was not just the governor but also a friend of the Storrows and a stalwart supporter of Community Boating. Other speakers included Fanny Goldstein of the West End Library, Rev. Palfrey Perkins of Kings Chapel, Jacob M. Burnes of West End House, and Judge Robert Walcott. (Courtesy of the BPL)

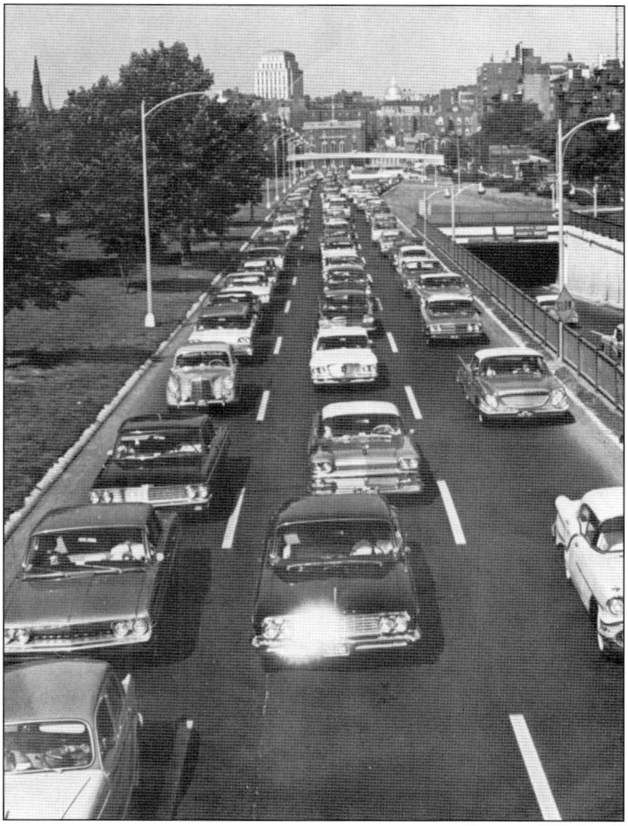

Storrow Drive, seen looking east from the walkway crossing over from Clarendon Street to the embankment in the 1960s, has become a major access road into and leaving the city. Following the Charles River from Leverett Circle to Soldiers Field Road, it is one of the more picturesque and continually busy roads in the city.

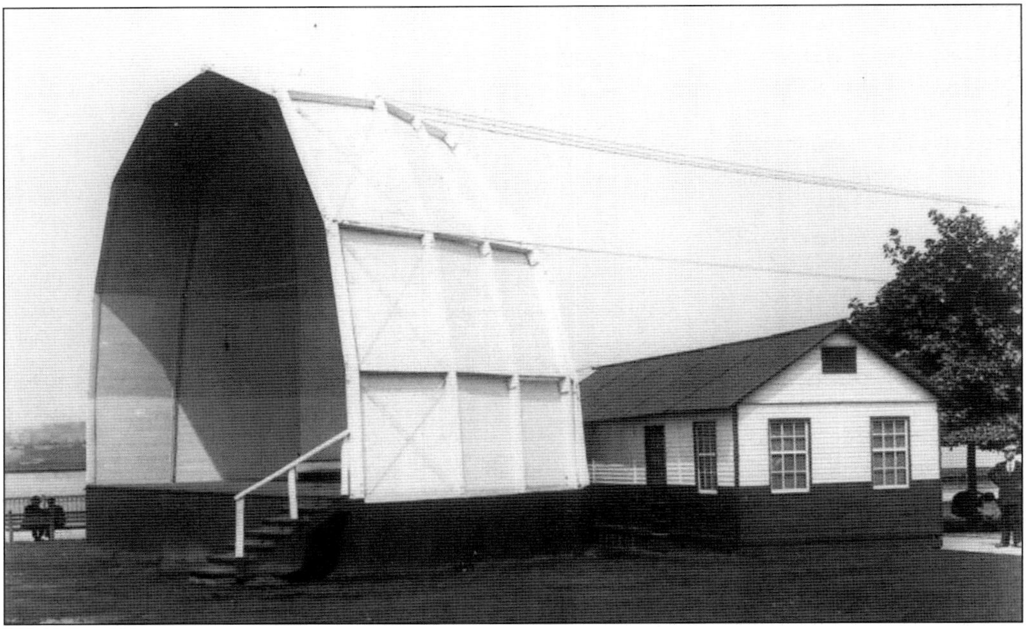

The original shell on the Esplanade was a wood-framed open stage and an octagonal gambrel roofed enclosure that was simple in its design and probably not very acoustical for music, but was where a long tradition of open air concerts that have been offered free of charge to Bostonians began. When the Hatch Shell was officially dedicated, Arthur Fiedler said that it was "a long-cherished dream come true."

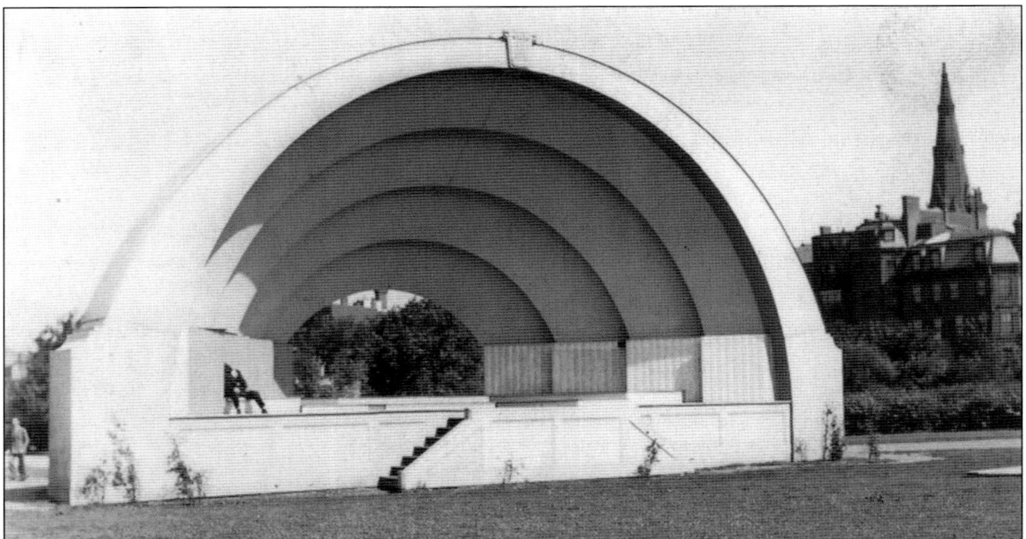

The Hatch Shell was a gift to the city of Boston in 1926 through the estate of Maria E. Hatch as a memorial to her brother Edward Hatch. Designed by Richard Shaw, it was built of concrete and polished granite with seven concentric rings under the inner ceiling creating a more acoustical projection of the music, thanks to Dr. William Barss, who taught in the MIT Acoustical Laboratory, along with recessed lighting. Dedicated on July 2, 1940, it has become a prominent feature of the Esplanade for almost eight decades. On the far right is the spire of the Church of the Advent at Brimmer and Mount Vernon Streets.

Arthur Fiedler (1894–1979) was the popular and longtime conductor of the Boston Pops Orchestra, a symphony orchestra that specializes in popular and light classical music that began in 1929 and was supported by those interested in the open-air performances. He had a dramatic and flamboyant style coupled with immense good looks; he enchanted Bostonians with popular music that was an adaptation of a more classical repertoire, keeping the performances more informal than in a concert hall, thereby attracting a wider and more inclusive audience.

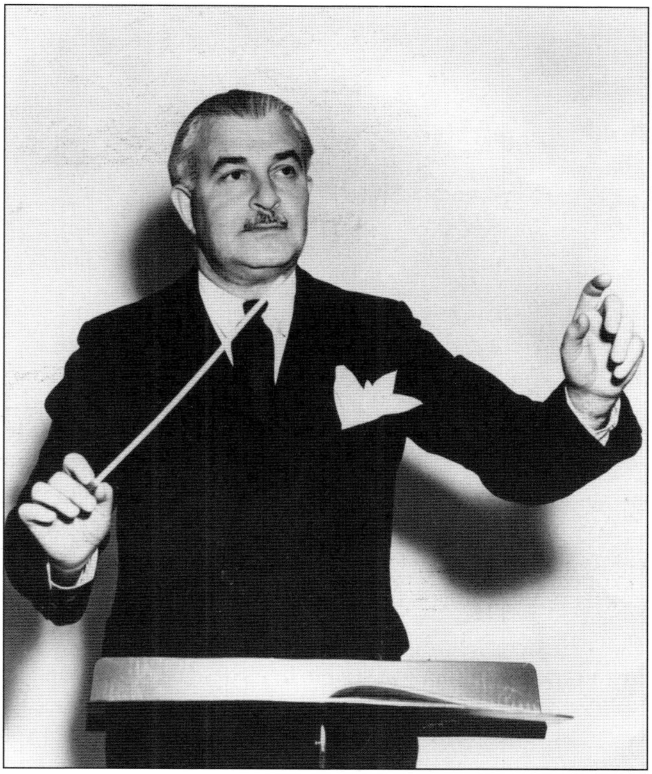

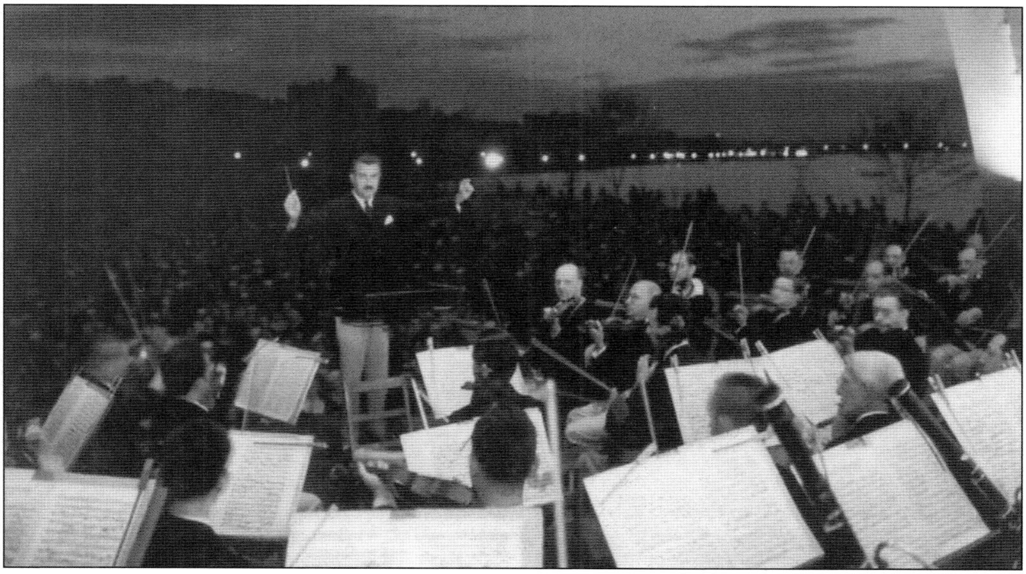

Seen on July 4, 1945, Arthur Fiedler conducts the Boston Pops at the Hatch Shell. Fiedler had been a member of the Boston Symphony Orchestra under Karl Muck as a violinist, and in 1930, he was appointed the 18th conductor of the Boston Pops Orchestra. With Fiedler's direction, the Boston Pops reportedly made more recordings than any other orchestra in the world, and the Pops brought music to the masses both in person as well as on the radio and, later, television. The rendition of the "1812 Overture" capped by a huge fireworks finale over the Charles River was the annual climax of a national holiday.

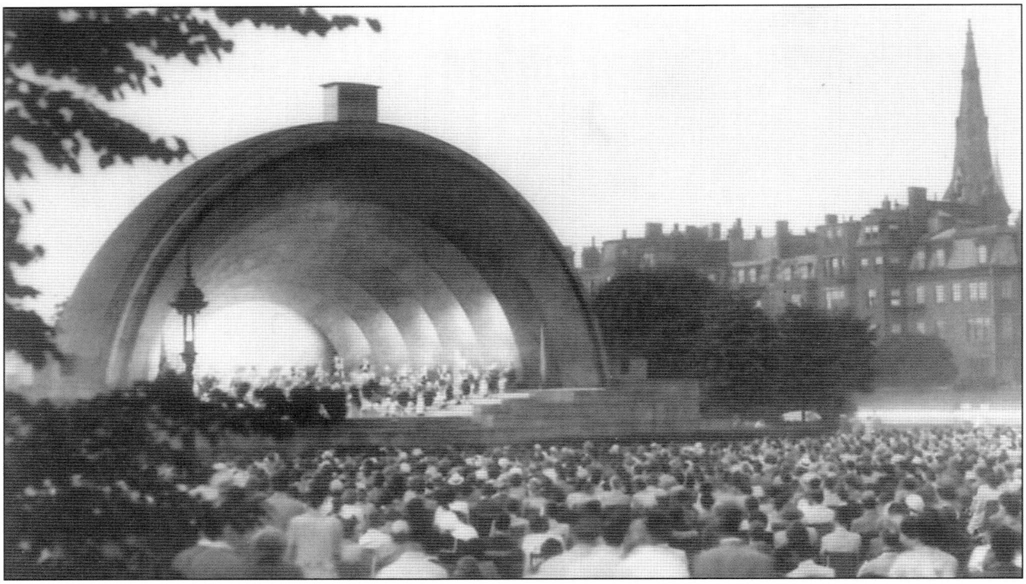

The open-air concerts at the Hatch Shell attracted thousands of Bostonians who, if they were fortunate to arrive early, could secure a wooden chair that was set up on the lawn facing the shell, otherwise lounging on blankets or the grass lawn. The concert repertoires ran the gamut from selections by the Boston Pops to classical and contemporary music concerts, all to the immense delight of those attending.

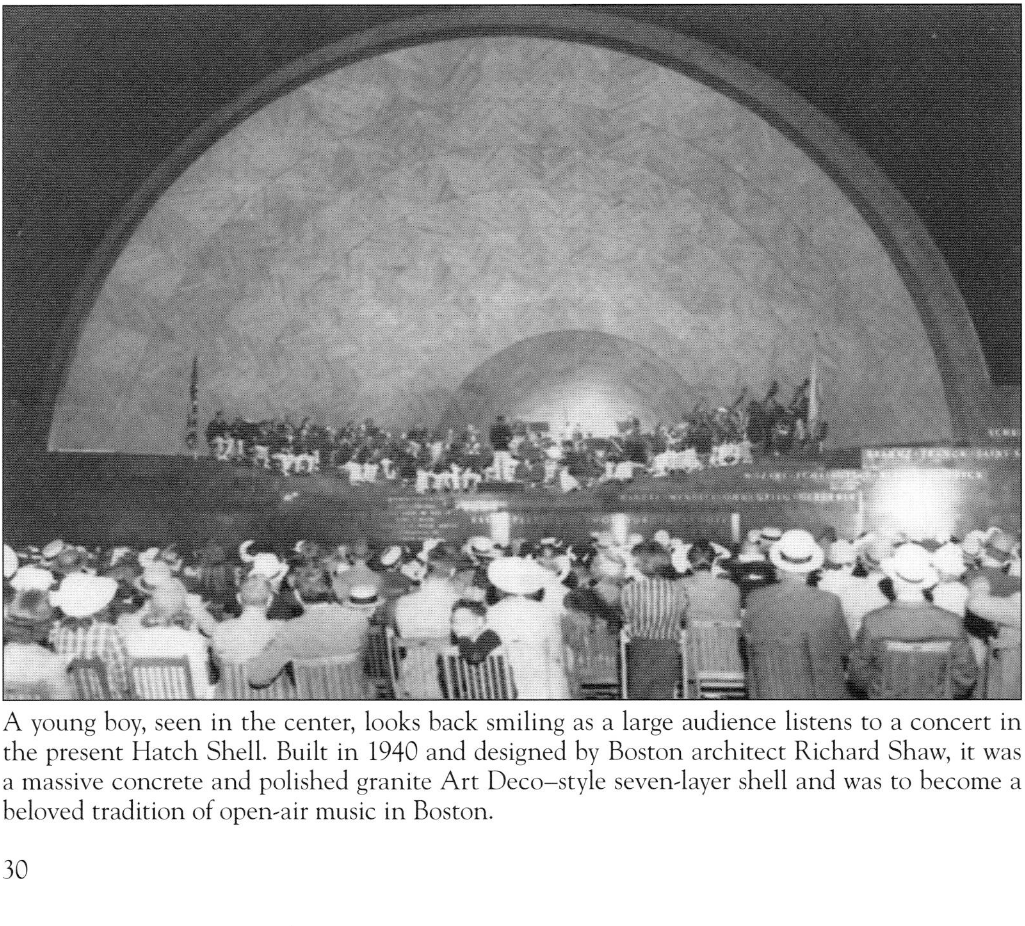

A young boy, seen in the center, looks back smiling as a large audience listens to a concert in the present Hatch Shell. Built in 1940 and designed by Boston architect Richard Shaw, it was a massive concrete and polished granite Art Deco–style seven-layer shell and was to become a beloved tradition of open-air music in Boston.

Three

Community Boat Club Early Years

My father believed people should learn to sail.

—Douglas Lee

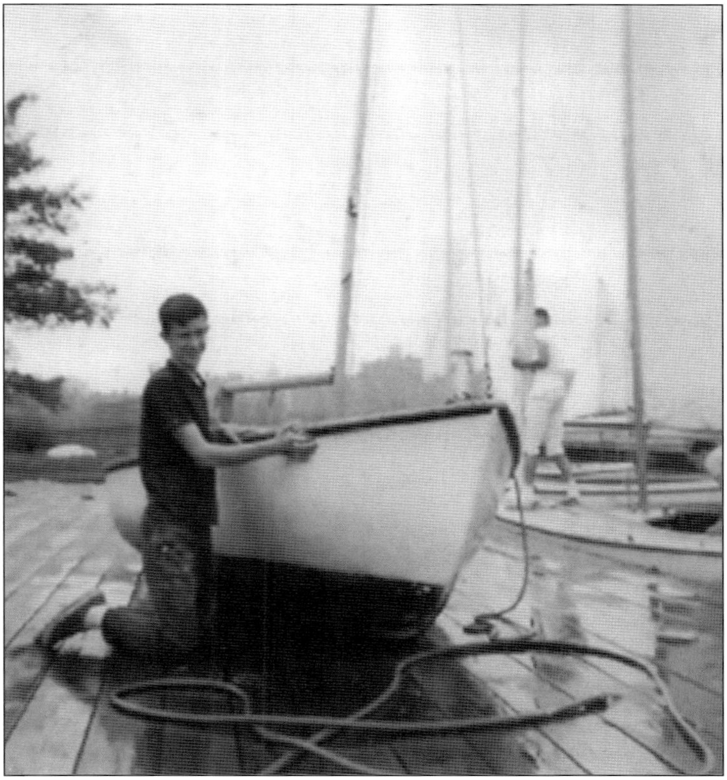

Founded by Joseph Lee, the new Community Boat Club welcomed members in 1937. Their excitement of learning to sail on the Charles River Basin must have been tremendous, especially as the boats were handcrafted on the rooftop of an apartment building in the West End. The premise of the club was "Sailing for All," and seen here is Billy Buckley shown washing one of the boats on the dock. (Courtesy of the Dan and Marilyn Farren collection.)

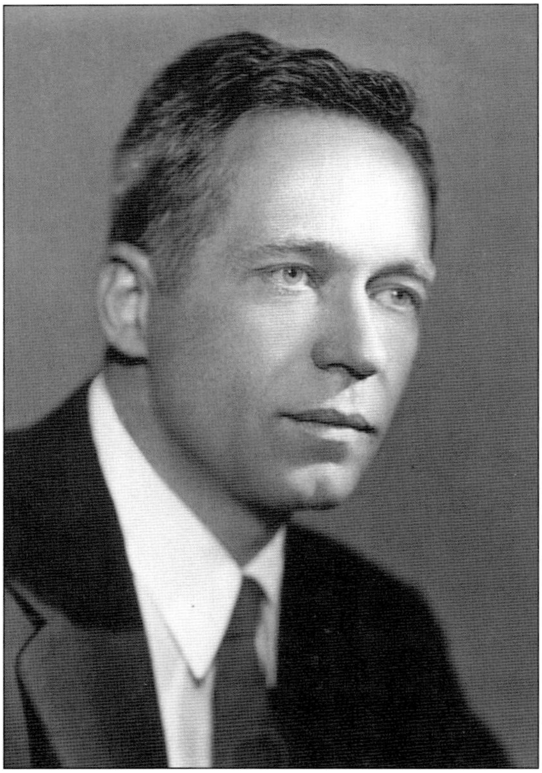

Joseph Lee Jr. (1901–1991) was the son of Joseph and Margaret Copley Cabot Lee and was raised at 96 Mount Vernon Street on Beacon Hill, an elegant row house designed by Jesse Shaw in the 1830s. His father was a graduate of both Harvard and the Harvard Law School and was to become a philanthropic Bostonian who devoted his life to the well-being of Bostonians while teaching his son the importance of community service. (Courtesy of Douglas Lee.)

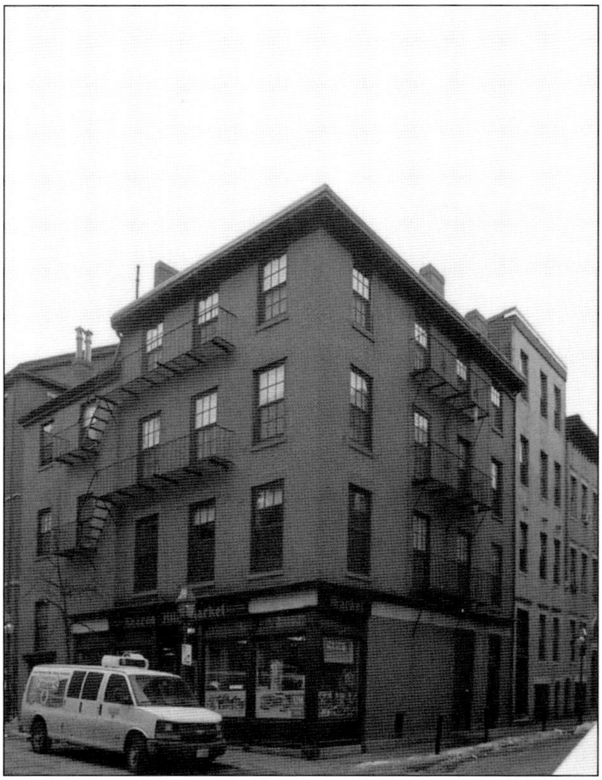

Joseph Lee lived on the top floor of this house at the corner of Anderson and Myrtle Streets on Beacon Hill in the 1930s. It was on the roof of this building that he and his nephews Kenny and Donny Robertson crafted the first prototype of his final design for a sailboat that was launched on the Charles River Basin in 1936. Today, the ground floor of the building is the Beacon Hill Market. Lee later lived at 43 South Russell Street on Beacon Hill, thought to be one of the earliest houses on Beacon Hill, built in 1797.

Joseph Lee, seen seated in his sailboat with a cigarette dangling from his lips and windswept hair, was the epitome of the Boston Brahmin. Rather than sailing off one of the fashionable summer resort towns north or south of Boston, he proudly sailed on the Charles River Basin and taught the youth of Boston's West End how to sail, much to their delight. (Courtesy of Douglas Lee.)

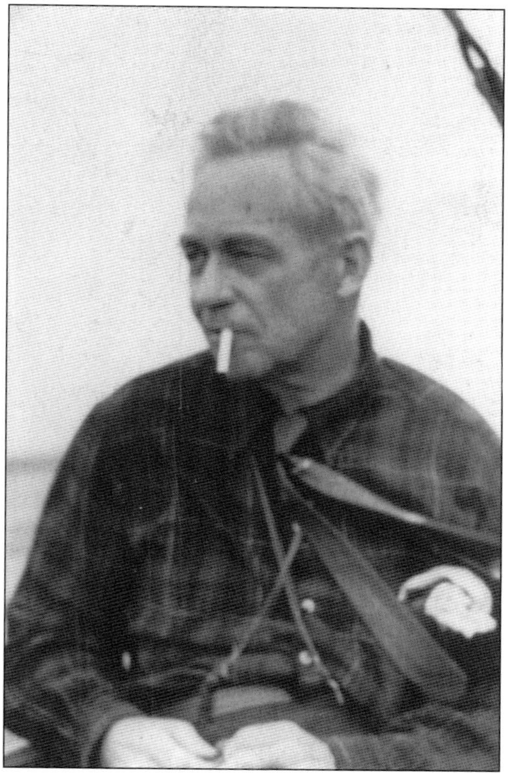

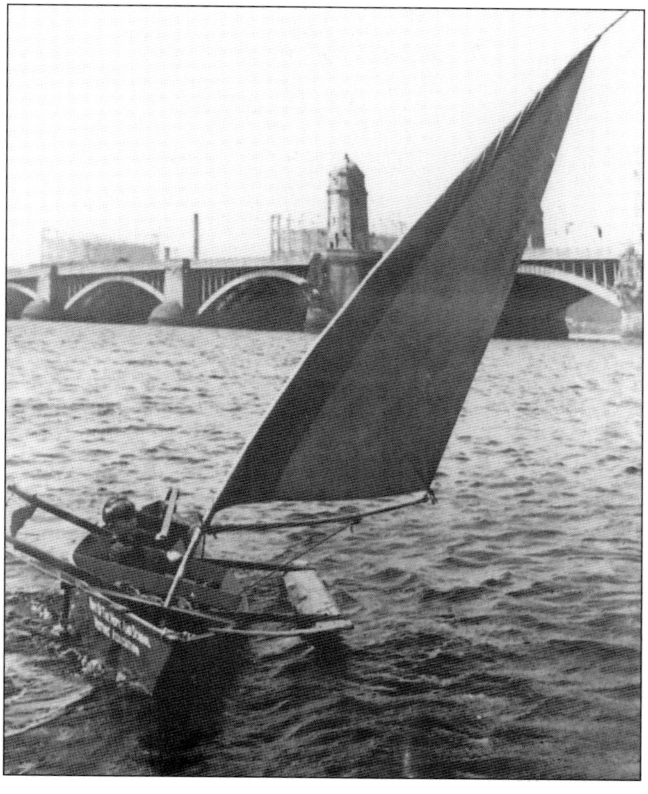

Joseph Lee III, the son of Joseph and Kathleen Nolan Lee, sails an early handcrafted sailboat on the Charles River Basin; Joseph Lee designed a simple, inexpensive watercraft that was easy enough for any child to sail. In the distance, the "pepper pot" towers of the Longfellow Bridge that connects Cambridge can be seen on the left, and the foot of Beacon Hill is on the far right.

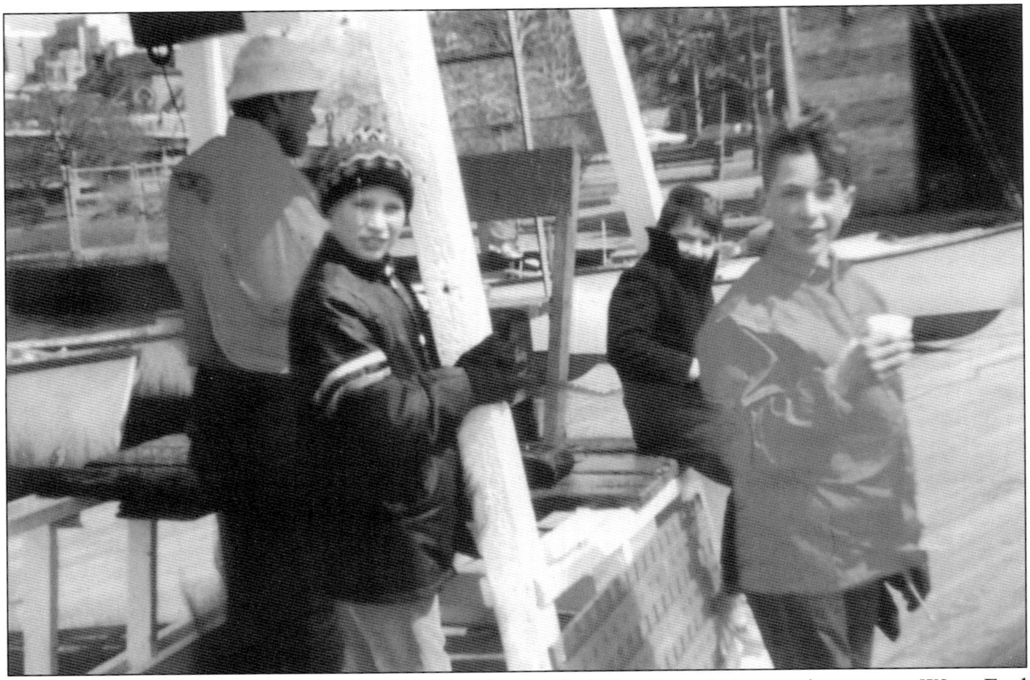

As Mari Snow said in her article "Sailing for All," "The first club members were West End neighborhood kids from the tenements, the sons (and occasional daughter) of first-generation immigrants" who thrived on the excitement of building and sailing the wood boats. Seen here is Greg Redd on the far left, with three junior members in 1970 on the dock. (Courtesy of the Dan and Marilyn Farren collection.)

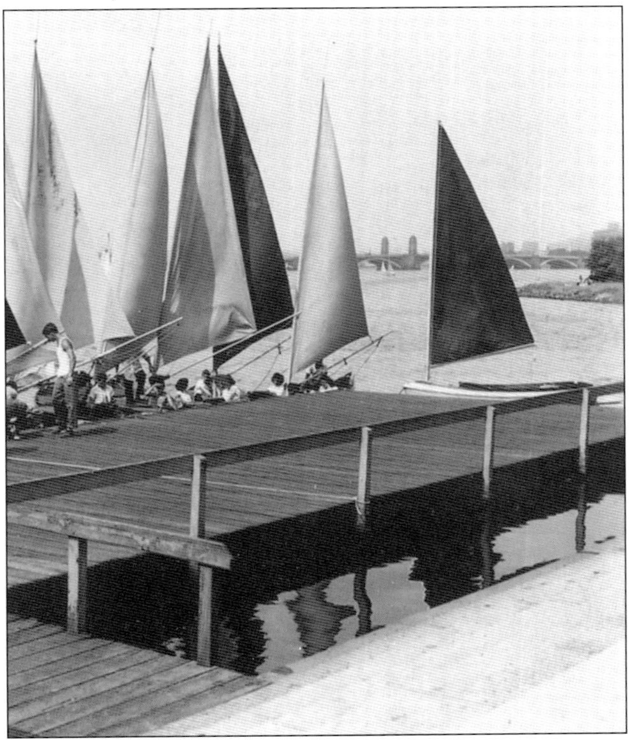

The young sailing club members from the West End get ready to sail their handcrafted boats, with the sails as tall as their pride on dedication day. It was said that with 12 hours of labor a simple 16-foot, fixed-keel boat derived from a kayak could be built and sailed. The materials and costs involved in the early years were supplied by Helen Storrow, Henry Lee Shattuck, Charles Cummings, Frances Curtis, and Susan Lee, almost all of whom were related to Joseph Lee.

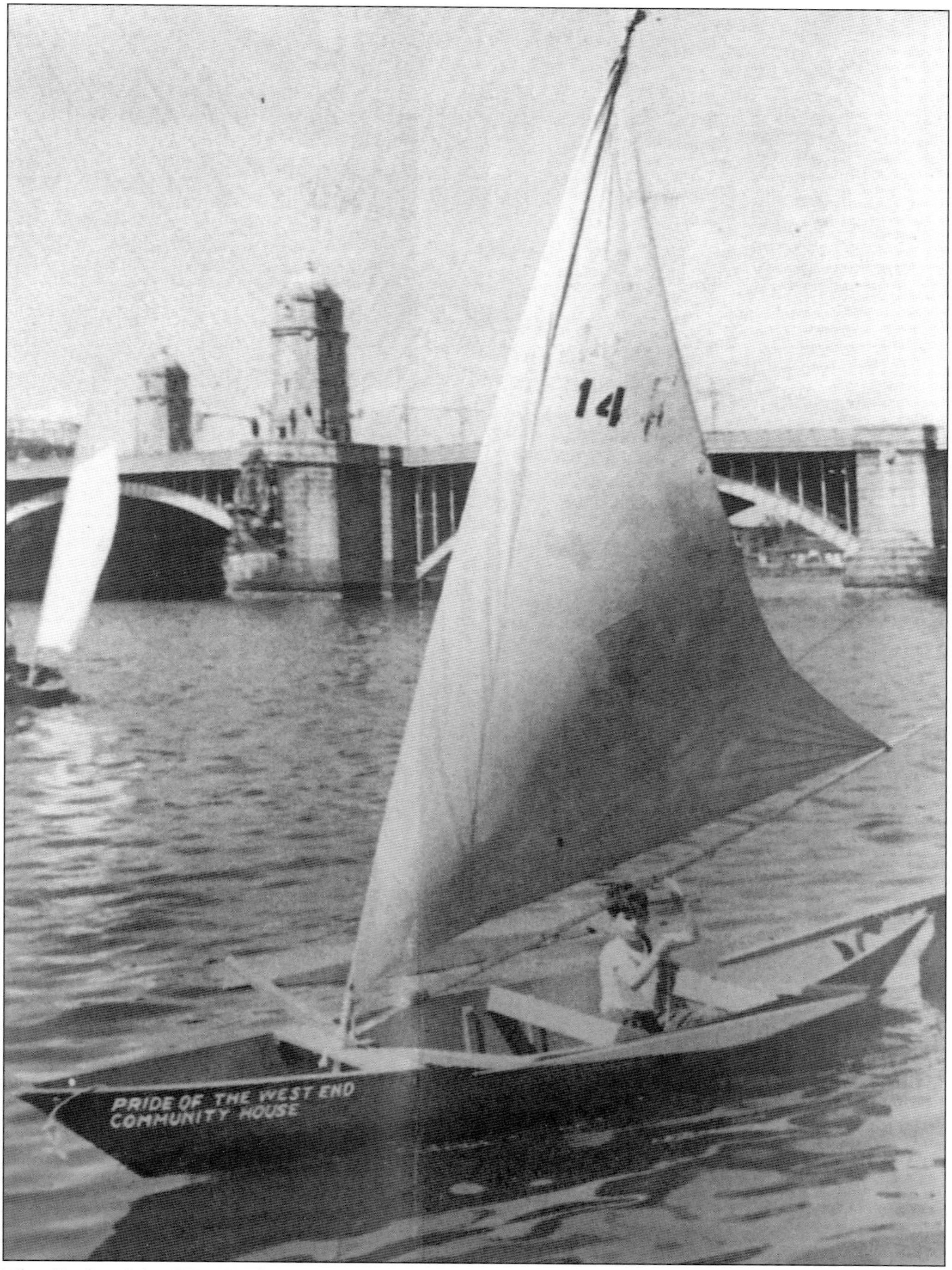

The *Pride of the West End Community House* was one of the early Joseph Lee sailboats. It was named for the settlement house in Boston's West End established to encourage, build and foster a strong sense of urban community and hopefully improve the quality of life for residents of all ages. These boats had a sturdy frame that was hewn from 24-foot-long pine boards. Joseph Lee III holds the rope as the sail allows the boat to glide along the water.

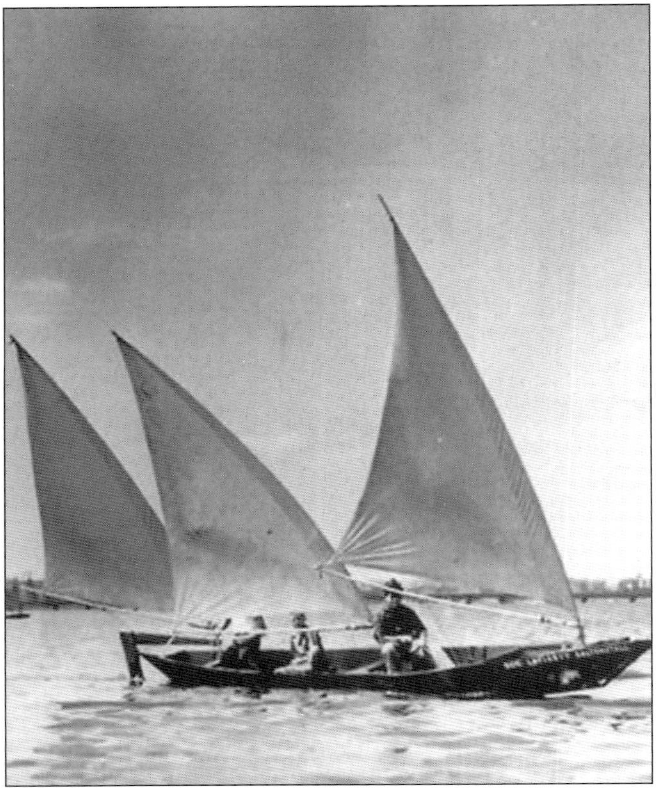

These three young sailors sail the *Gov. Leverett Saltonstall*, which was named for the 55th governor of the Commonwealth of Massachusetts from 1939 to 1945 and a cousin of Joseph Lee Jr., who founded the Community Boat Club in 1937. From left to right, Bradford Kurciviez, Everett Blais, and Patricia Cooke sail a three-sailed schooner on the Charles River Basin in the early 1940s, which often required four to six crew members. (Courtesy of the DCR.)

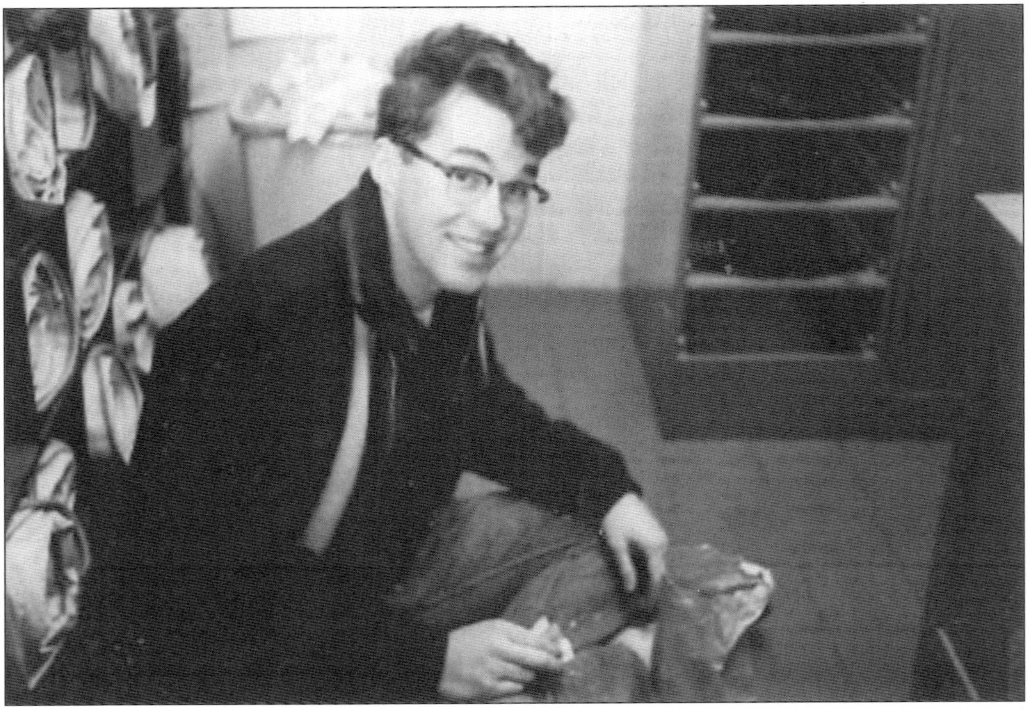

A smiling John Morey, who was head dockmaster in 1966, is seen stowing a spinnaker in a sail bag on the office floor. (Courtesy of the Dan and Marilyn Farren collection.)

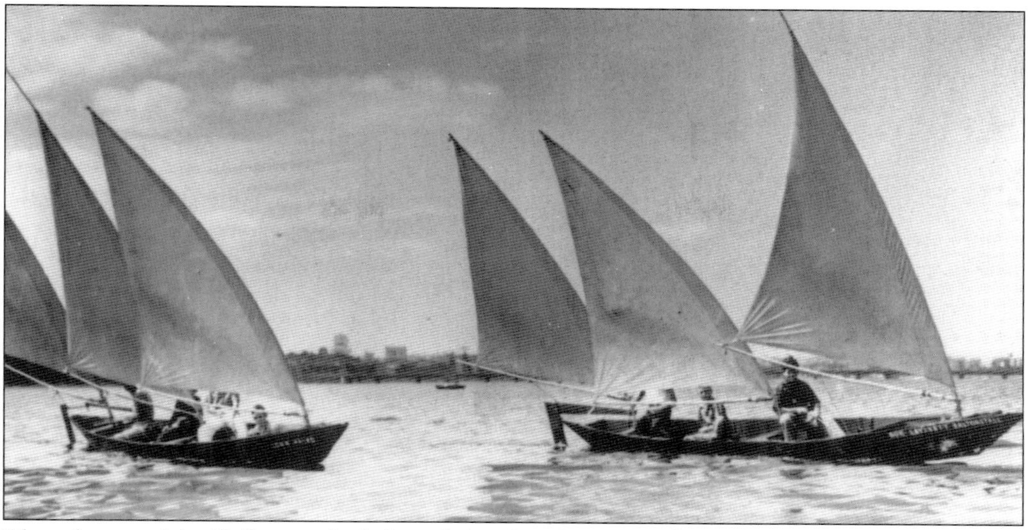

The schooner *John Halko*, on the left, and the *Gov. Leverett Saltonstall*, on the right, are seen in 1937 under full sail as they vie for preeminence on the Charles River Basin. John Halko was a friend of Joseph Lee and the director of the West End Community House for many years, and it was he who opened the community house basement in 1937 for Lee and "his boys" to construct additional boats during the winter months. The four three-masted schooners were the *John Halko*, *Leverett Saltonstall*, *Charles F. Hurley*, and *Eugene C. Hultman*. (Courtesy of the DCR.)

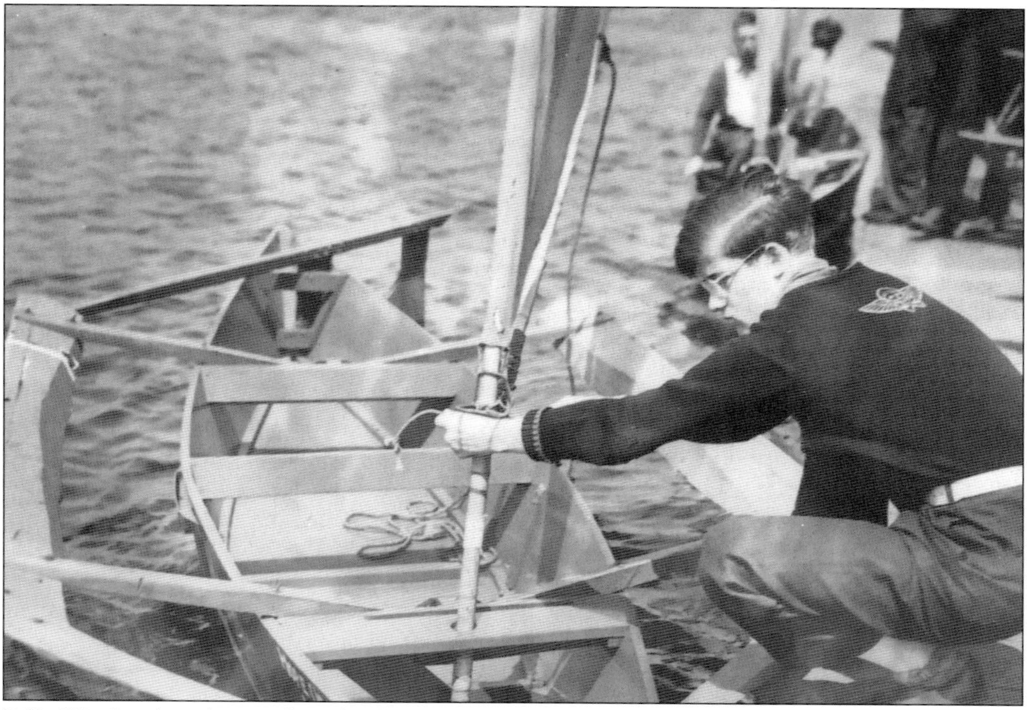

Billy Ward, referred to as the "chief petty officer," ties the rope securing the sail to the sail pole, which, according to George Manfredi, were bamboo masts and booms, before he sets out for an afternoon sail. These sails were sewn from heavy-duty hospital sheets. Repairs, when needed, were done by a local tailor. By 1938, there were 400 members and 14 sailboats. (Courtesy of the DCR.)

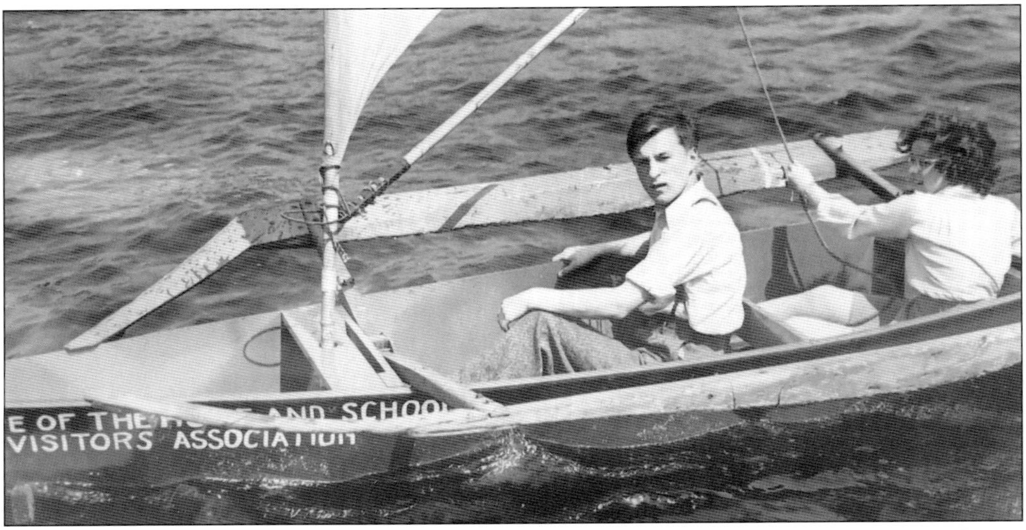

John Rudick and Jane Morgan sail the *Hope of the Home and School Visitors Association*. It was obvious that Joseph Lee's introduction to sailing for all was to include young girls as well as the boys of Boston's West End, as it was said in 1939 that "Girls are taken in [as members of the Community Boat Club] as well as boys; adults, as well as children." By 1939, there were 1,000 members of Community Boat Club. (Courtesy of the DCR.)

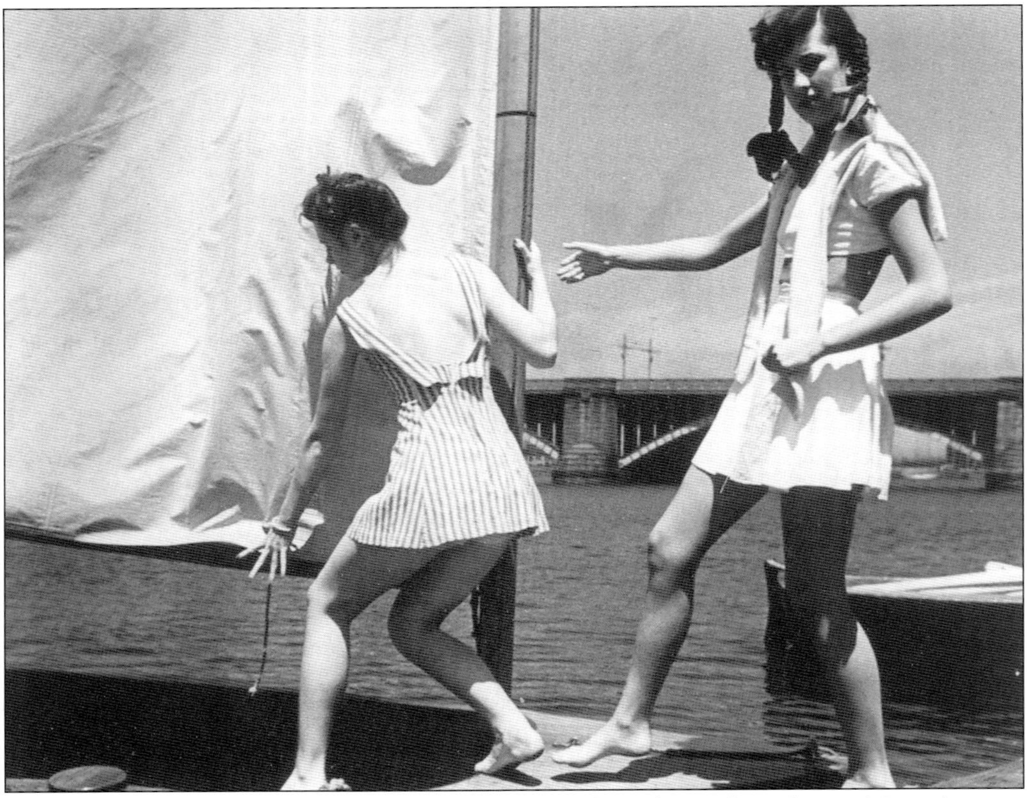

Mary Lou Lydon, seen on the left, and Marie Carey, both residents of Dorchester, Massachusetts, are two seemingly fearless young girls who boldly step barefoot onto a sailboat in 1939, dressed for a sunny afternoon of sailing on the Charles River Basin.

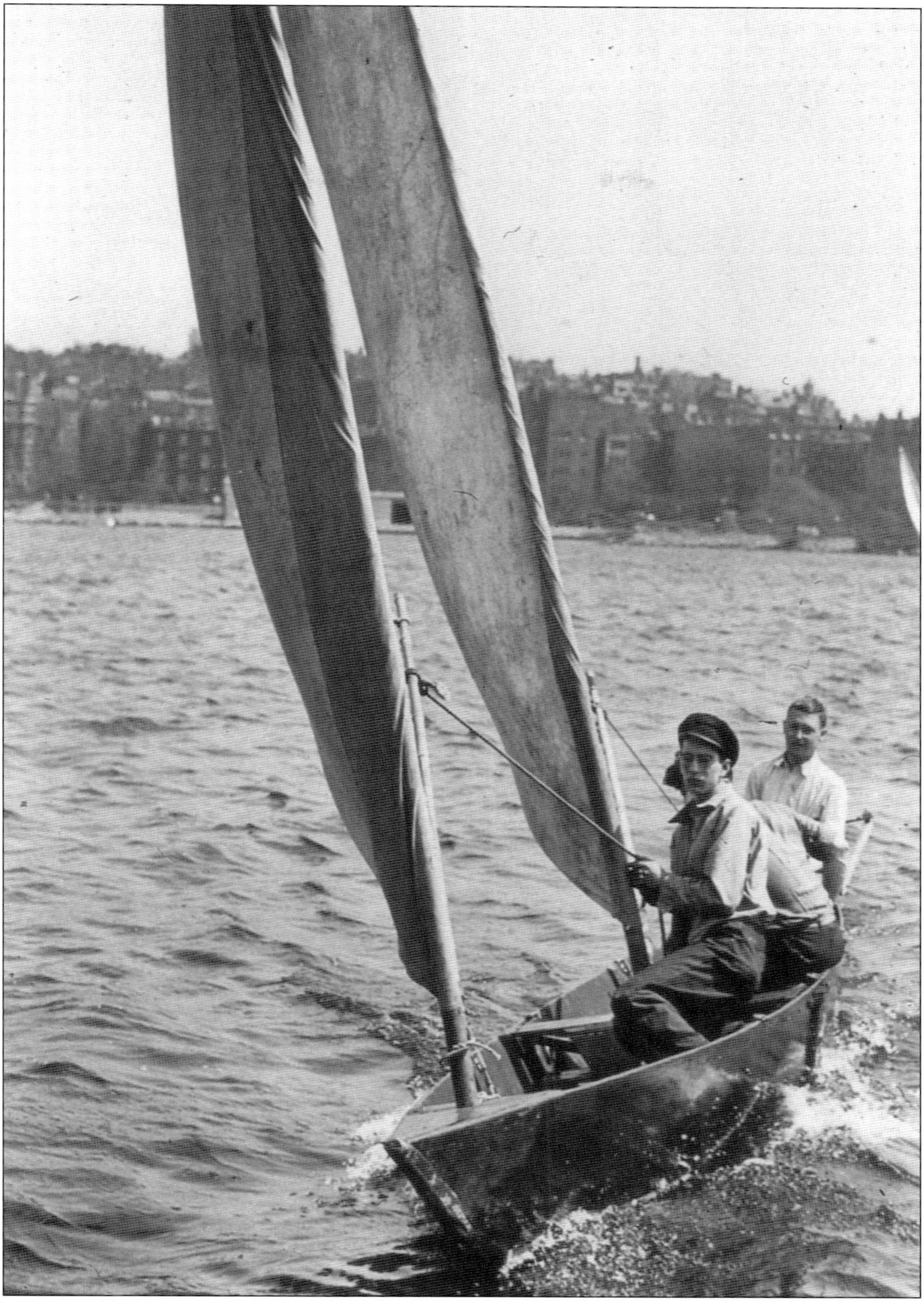

Billy Ward (in front, with glasses and hat) and two friends sail a boat along the Charles River Basin with the fashionable houses of the Flat of Beacon Hill seen in the distance. The embankment stretched along the riverfront and created panoramic views, but none of the city were as glorious as those seen from a boat on the water. (Courtesy of the DCR.)

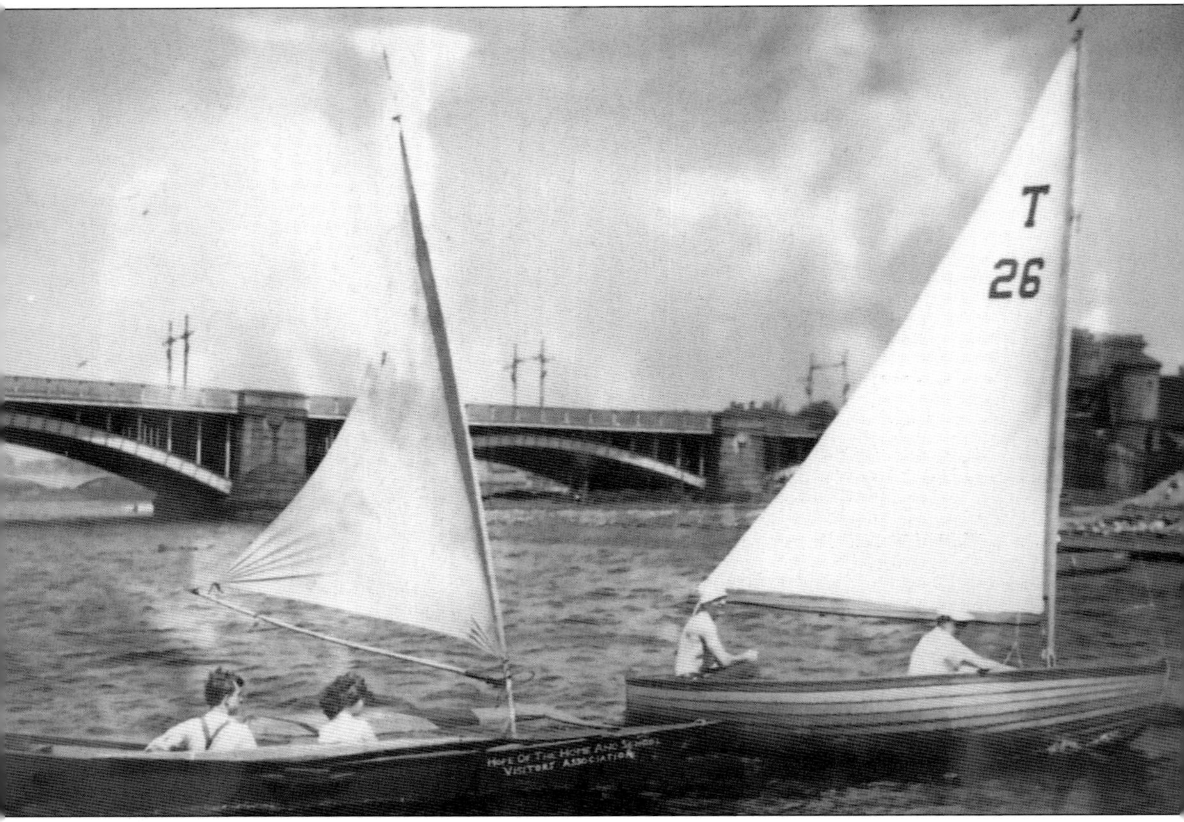

Dueling sailboats cross paths with their young sailors enjoying an afternoon on the water, with the Longfellow Bridge in the distance. The *Hope of the Home and School Visitors Association* (pictured on the left) was a popular boat and created great publicity for the public schools of Boston, of which Joseph Lee was a staunch supporter and would later serve on the Boston School Committee, many of those years as chairman. The dockmasters at that time were Arthur Robinson and "Spike" Harry Lee, who also ran the daily operation of the Community Boat Club and helped nurture young members of Community Boating. (Courtesy of the DCR.)

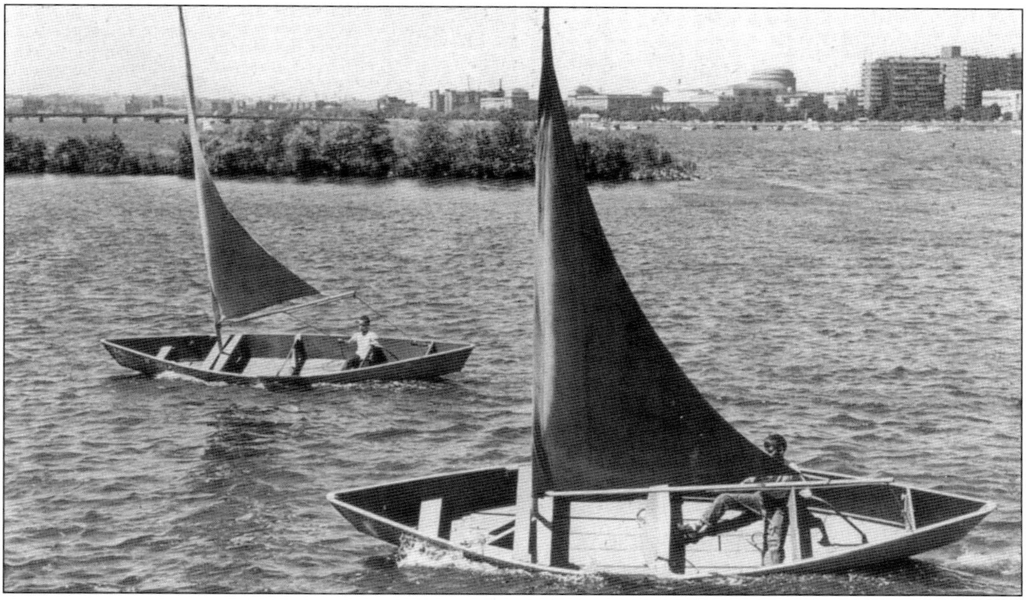

Two sailboats tip in the winds off the basin, yet both sailors hold tight the ropes of the sail. In the distance, the dome of the Massachusetts Institute of Technology of Cambridge can be seen, and on the right are the Eastgate Apartments at 100 Memorial Drive, designed by the architectural firm of Brown, de Mars, Kennedy, Koch & Rapson. These upscale apartments faced the Charles River and were a major part of the development of the Cambridge shore in the 1950s. (Courtesy of the DCR.)

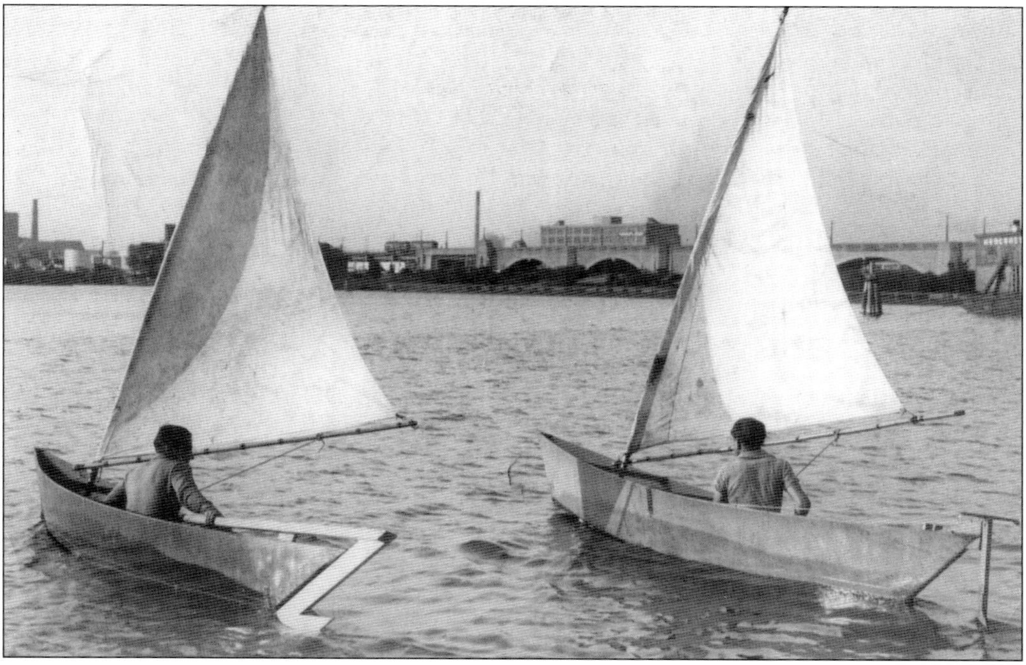

This beautiful photograph of two sailboats sailing out into the Charles River Basin show each of these young sailors demonstrating the sailing lessons learned well but also coming close together to share words of encouragement. The Cambridge waterfront can be seen in the distance. (Courtesy of the DCR.)

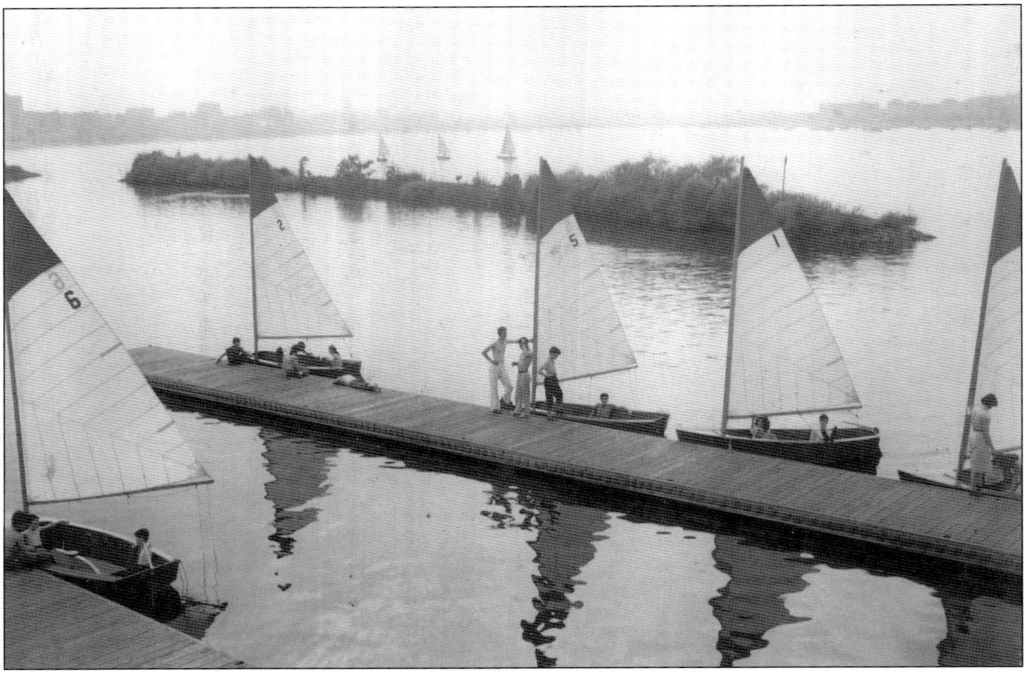

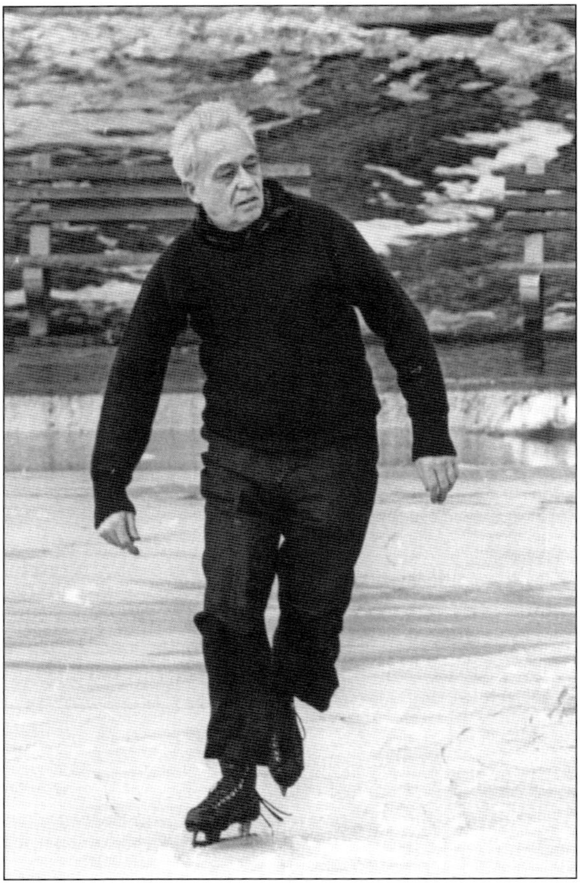

Young men and women relax in both the sailboats as well as along the wood boat slips that were adjacent to the boathouse. In the distance are a naturalistic barrier with shrubs and greens as well as sailboats on the basin in the distance. (Courtesy of the DCR.)

Joseph Lee Jr. was a major proponent for physical exercise, be it sailing on the Charles River Basin or ice skating on the Boston Frog Pond. His father had been referred to as the "Father of the American Playground Movement," and he continued his father's vision and legacy with a commitment to a lifetime of public service for Bostonians. (Courtesy of Douglas Lee)

Four

The Quest of Joseph Lee

Joe Lee, a social worker and educator, was convinced that disadvantaged children living throughout the tenements of Boston could benefit from learning how to sail.

—The Boston Globe

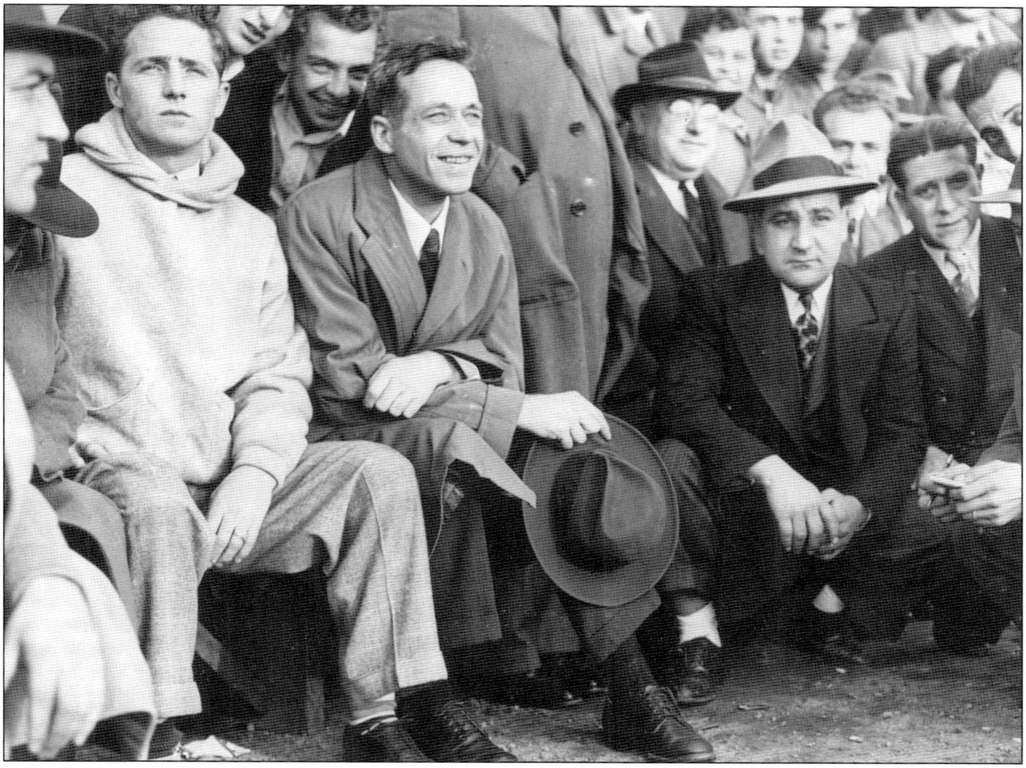

Joseph Lee Jr., seen in the center with hat in hand, dedicated his life to public service. Born to wealth and with all the public responsibilities that it entailed, he mounted a campaign for mayor of Boston in 1941, losing to Maurice Tobin, as did James Michael Curley, the incumbent mayor. Seen here in November 1941 just prior to the election, he enjoys a football game at Noyes Park in East Boston between the East Boston Merchants and the South Boston Chippewas, all the while campaigning for mayor to the end. (Author's collection.)

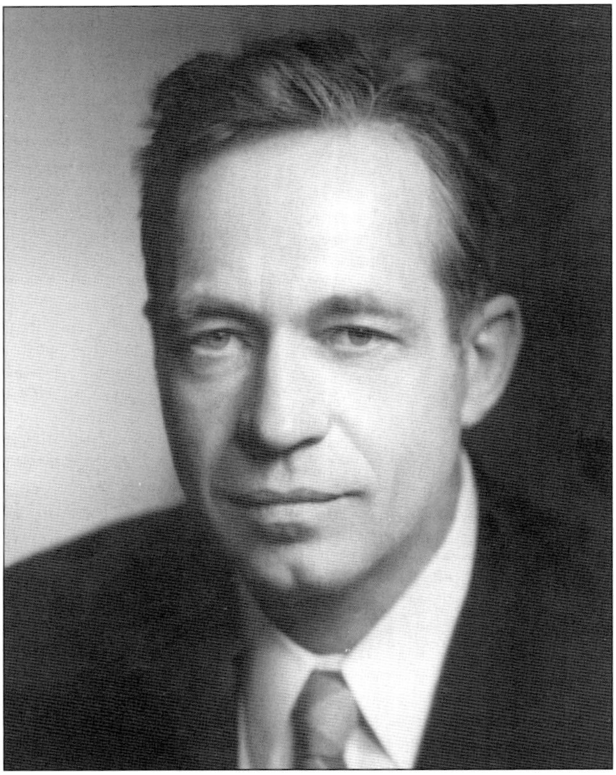

Joseph Lee Jr. was a visionary whose idea of community sailing in Boston was commendable but fraught with difficulty as he built sailboats with an eagle eye of precision but sailing then was even more difficult. He challenged the Metropolitan District Commission and its stalwart chairman, Eugene C. Hultman, to have a boathouse built for the burgeoning fleet of sailboats. Hultman repeatedly thwarted Lee in his determined quest for the boat club, but his family connections ultimately secured the site and the new boathouse. (Courtesy of Douglas Lee.)

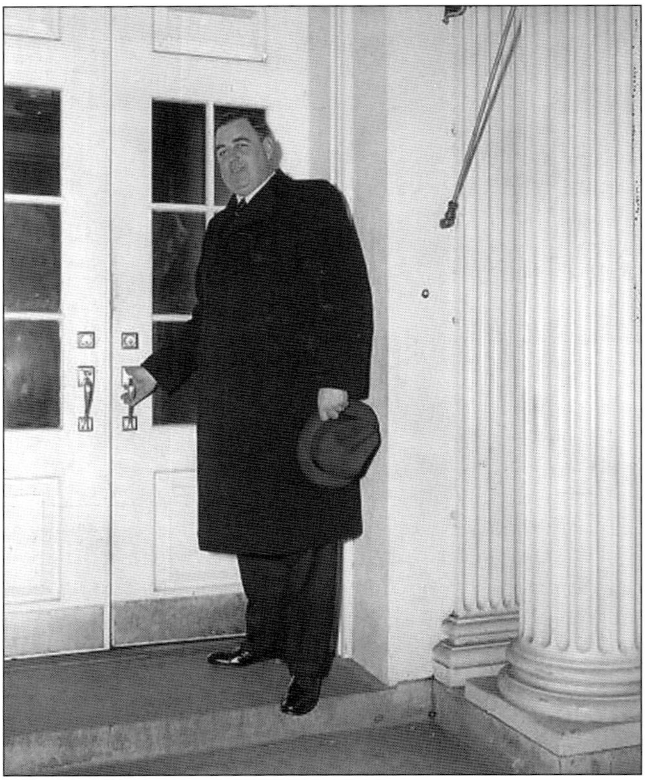

Governor Hurley (1893–1946) was elected governor of the Commonwealth of Massachusetts in 1937 and vowed to clean up the civil service, regulate labor practices, and focus on individual rights. He was a great supporter of Joseph Lee and Community Boating on the Charles River Basin. When Lee's boys marched on the Massachusetts State House in 1937 with homemade banners and signed petitions demanding the club be allowed access to the Basin, they dragged the boat *Eugene C. Hultman*, which they docked at the Hall of Flags at the Massachusetts State House; it was a bold and politically decisive move not unnoticed by the governor.

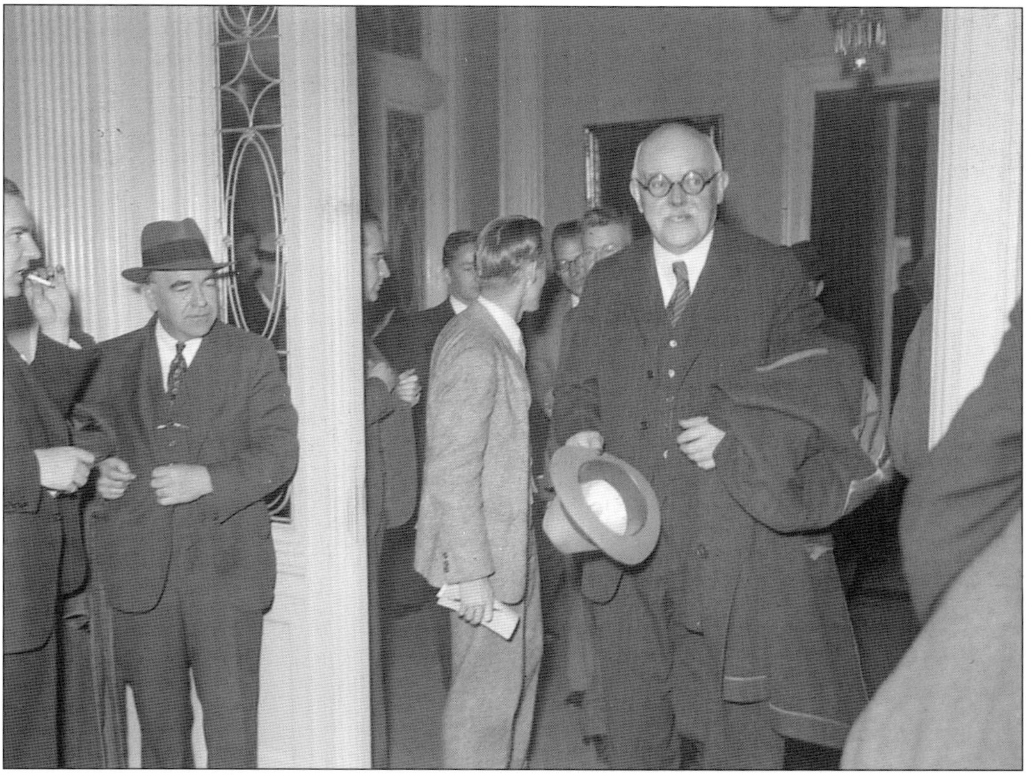

Eugene C. Hultman (1875–1945) served in both state and local government in Massachusetts as commissioner of the Boston Police, Fire, and Building Departments, as well as serving as a member of the Massachusetts General Court. In 1934, he was appointed chairman of the Metropolitan District Commission (MDC) and became an opponent of Joseph Lee and Community Boating. Hultman did anything that he possibly could to thwart their efforts to sail on the Charles River Basin. Though Governor Tobin tried to replace him, Hultman continued as chair of the MDC until his death.

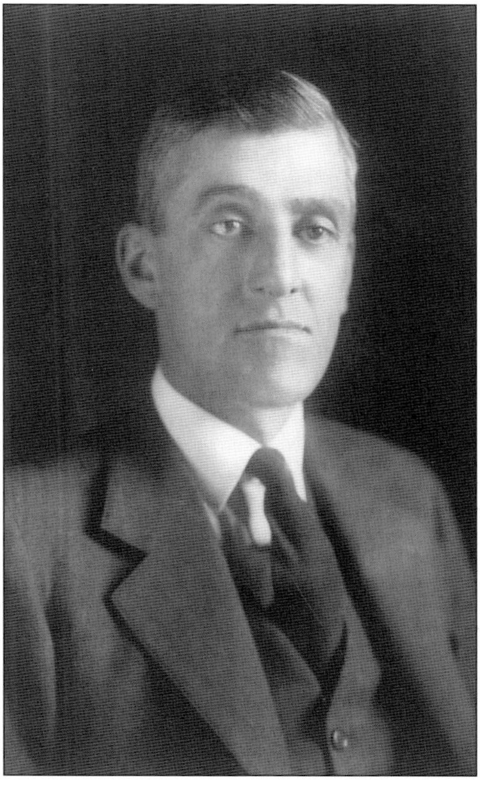

Leverett Saltonstall (1892–1971) served as the 55th governor of the Commonwealth of Massachusetts, serving from 1939 to 1945. He was a first cousin of Joseph Lee Jr., who founded the Community Boat Club in 1937, and served as president of the National Governors Association from 1943 to 1944. In 1944, he also served as the fifth president of the Council of State Governments. He was a great supporter of Community Boating and often walked down Beacon Hill to watch the sailboats.

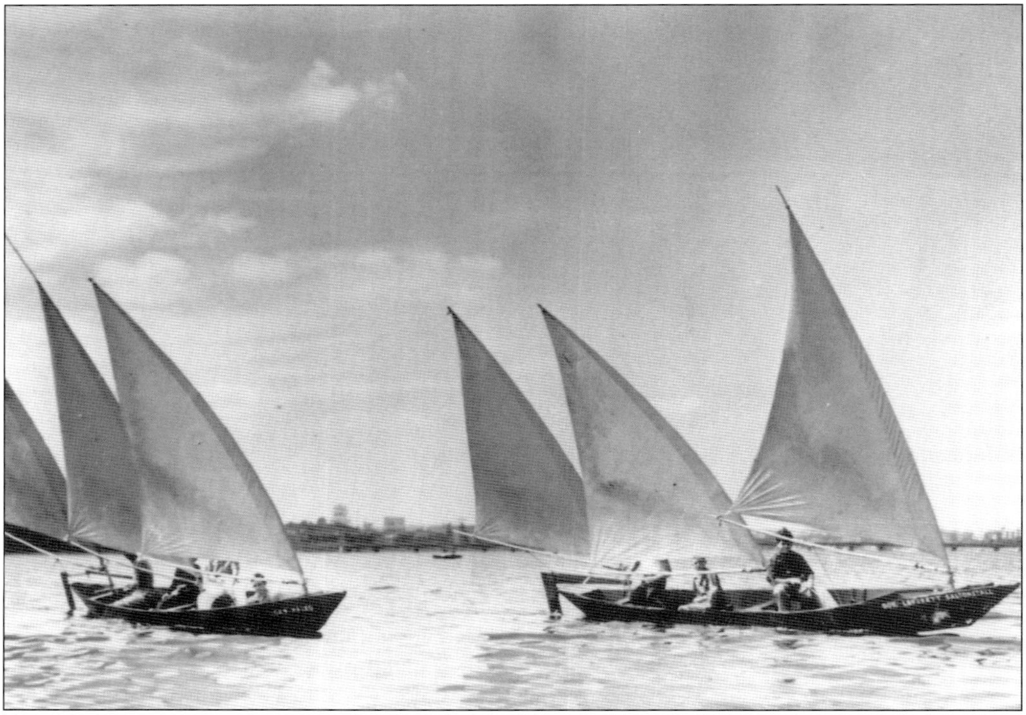

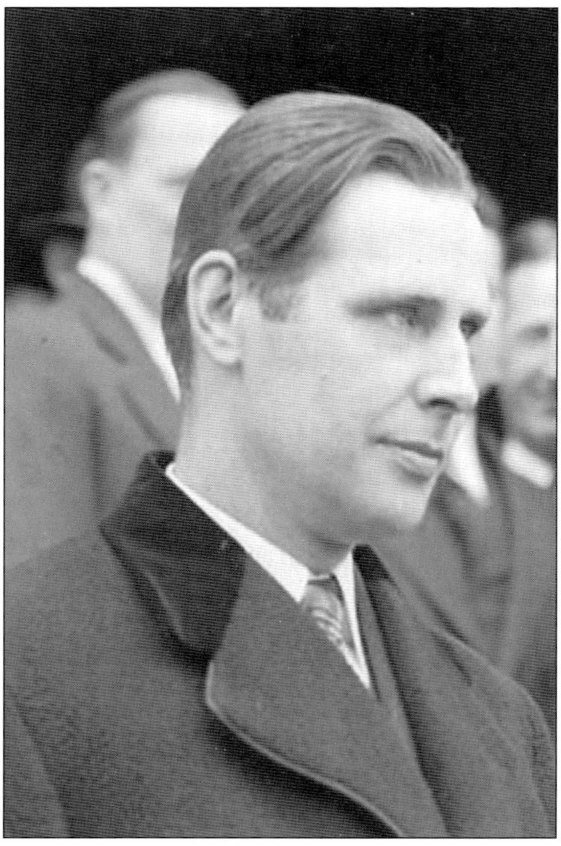

The *Governor Leverett Saltonstall*, a three-mast schooner on the right, was named for the governor of the Commonwealth of Massachusetts. It was fortuitous for Lee that during a difficult period for Community Boating, he would rally his young sailors to carry a sailboat to the Massachusetts State House, where it was deposited to the delight of the public. Governor Saltonstall would christen "his boat" with a bottle of champagne as the public cheered. The *John Halko* is on the left. (Courtesy of the DCR.)

Maurice Tobin (1901–1953) served on the Boston School Committee from 1931 to 1937 before defeating incumbent mayor James M. Curley in the 1937 mayoral race as well as Joseph Lee Jr. in 1941. A friend of Lee, Tobin was to become a stalwart supporter of Community Boating and a powerful political ally of those who sailed on the Charles River Basin. In 1944, Tobin was elected governor of Massachusetts; he later served as the US secretary of labor under Pres. Franklin D. Roosevelt.

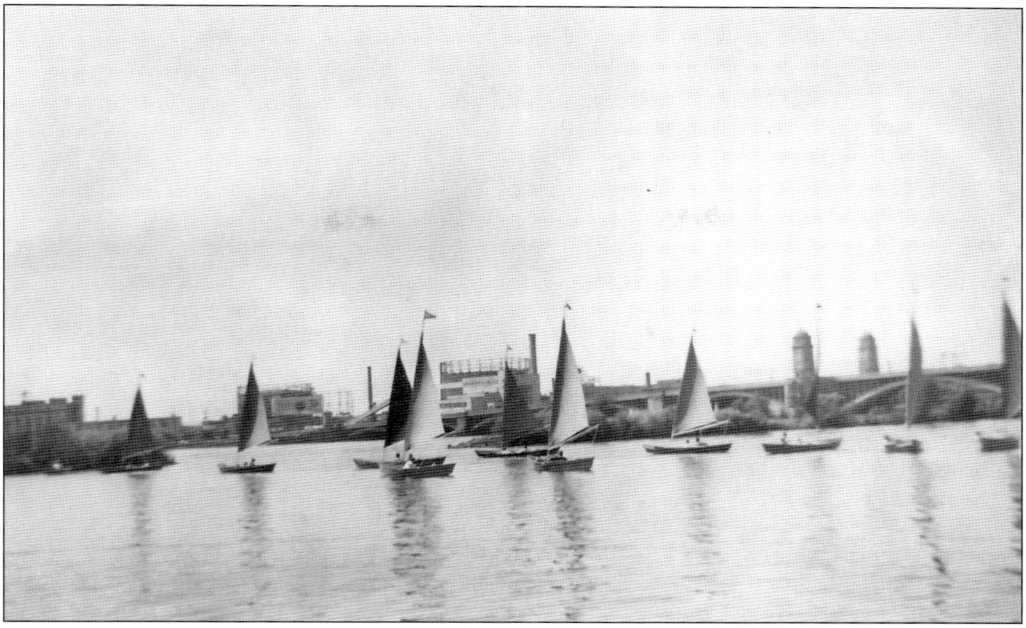

A bucolic summer scene by the early 1940s included the rapidly increasing fleet of sailboats that were handcrafted by Lee and the boys of the West End. It was said that these boats were to cost an average of $20 to build and that the sails were sewn by hand by a Mr. Binder, a stitcher from the local shoe factory, from heavy-duty hospital sheets acquired from the Massachusetts General Hospital.

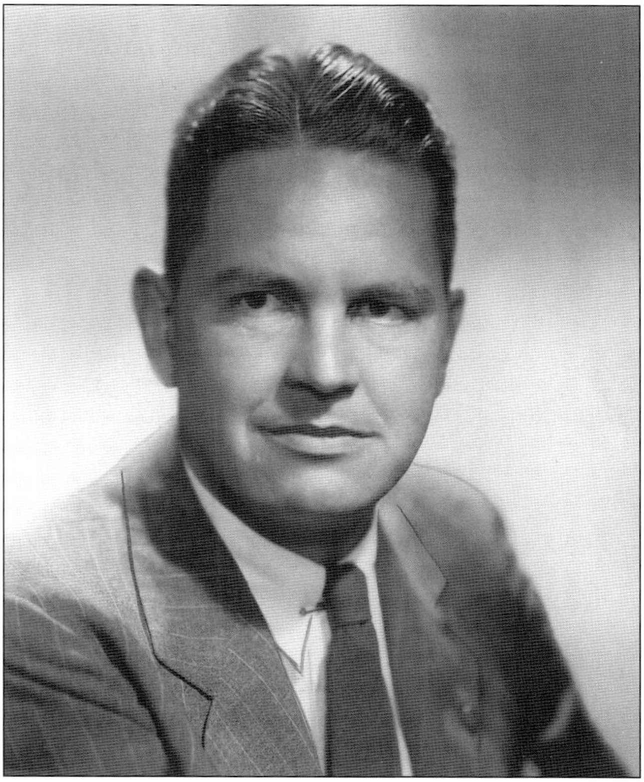

Gov. Robert Fiske Bradford (1902–1983) served as the governor of Massachusetts, from 1947 to 1949. A graduate of both Harvard and the Harvard Law School, he was a noted attorney in Boston. Bradford was a friend of Lee, and he supported the efforts of the club as a trustee of the Community Recreation Service. Composer Leroy Anderson wrote a piece he called the "Governor Bradford March" that premiered on July 6, 1948, at a concert by the Boston Pops Orchestra under the direction of Arthur Fiedler.

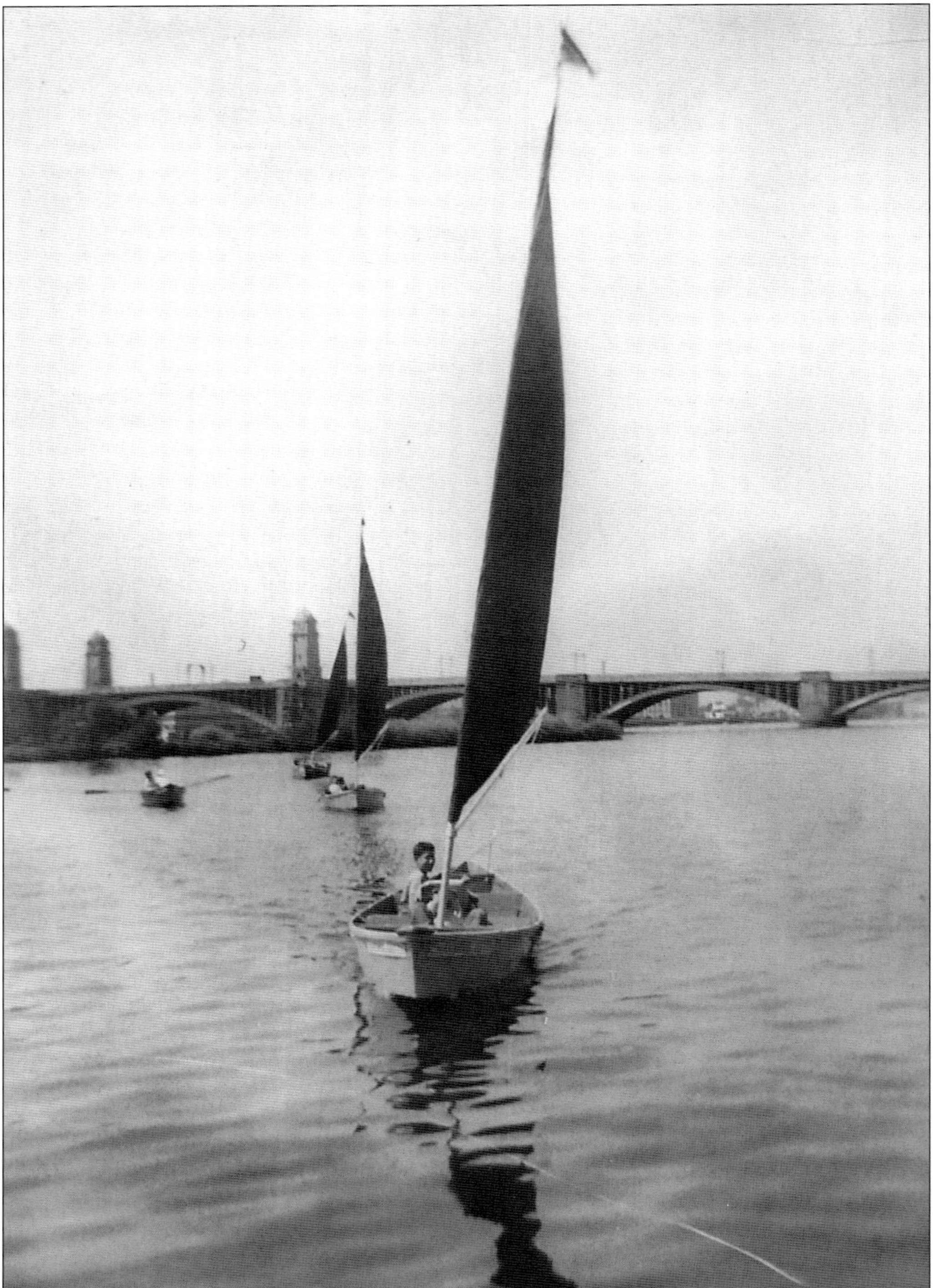

A line of sailboats head toward the dock returning from a late afternoon sail as their gentle movement causes a ripple in the waters of the Charles River Basin, creating a bucolic photograph. By 1940, the club was under the direction of the Community Recreation Service, and in 1946, it would officially become Community Boating, Inc. (Courtesy of the DCR.)

Helen Osborn Storrow (1864–1944) was a prominent American philanthropist, Girl Scout leader and chair of the World Committee of the World Association of Girl Guides and Girl Scouts. She and her husband, James J. Storrow, were long interested in the settlement movement and charity work, helping to build playgrounds in poor immigrant neighborhoods, sponsoring night schools, vocational schools, and evening centers such as the Saturday Evening Girls, and was instrumental in establishing the West End House. Helen took a keen interest in her nephew Joseph Lee's Community Boating and eventually committed funding for its boathouse.

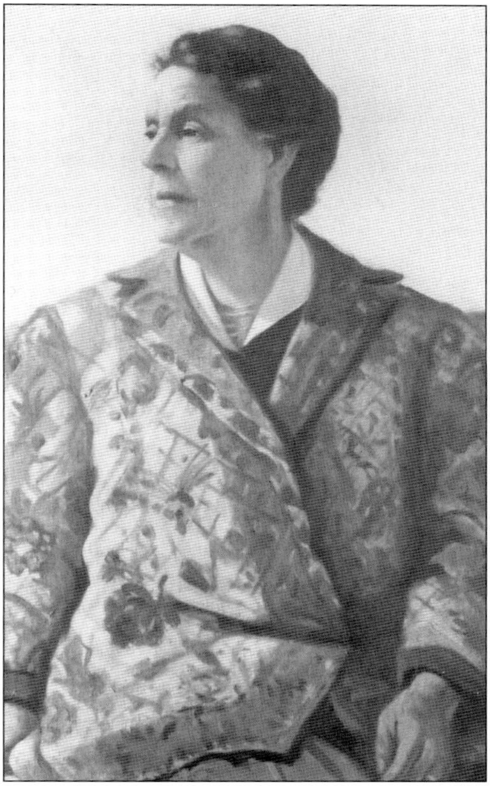

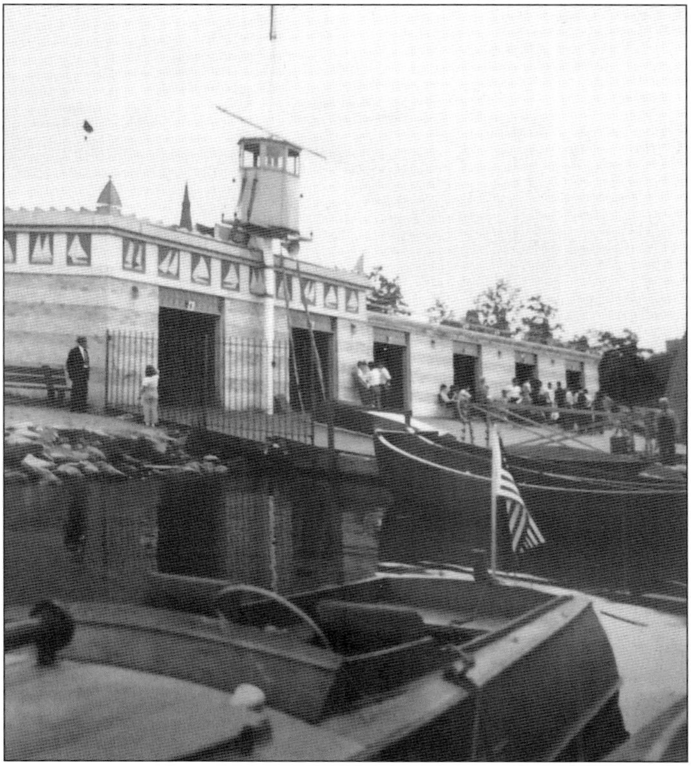

The boathouse was a longed for and much-needed place for not just the storage of the boats but also as a clubhouse for the ever-growing membership of "100 members and a seven-boat, boy-built fleet," where they could put down roots and learn sailing techniques on the wood boat slips, as well as have a place they could call their own. By 1939, there were 20 sailboats and 4 three-mast schooners. (Courtesy of the DCR.)

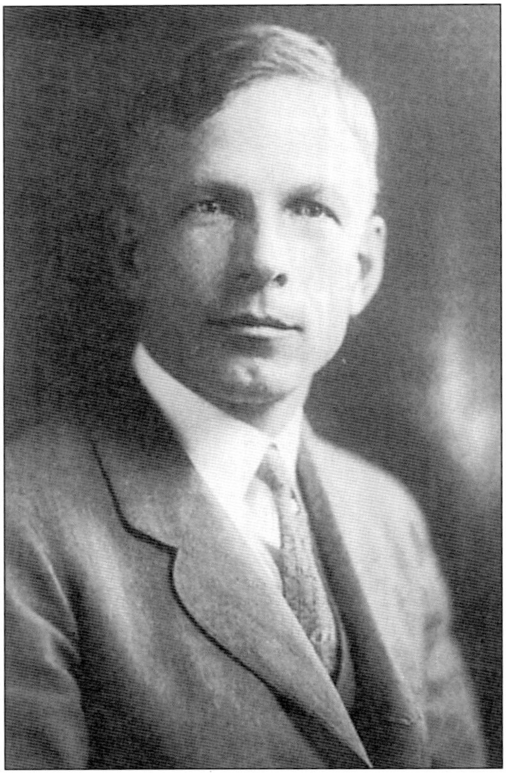

William Roger Greeley, an architect and principal with the prominent Boston architectural firm of Kilham, Hopkins and Greeley, designed the new Community Boat Club boathouse of gray brick trimmed with rough granite at a cost of $55,000. The boathouse was formally dedicated on June 28, 1941, by the Commonwealth of Massachusetts to the joys of sailing, with a $1 per year rent paid to the MDC.

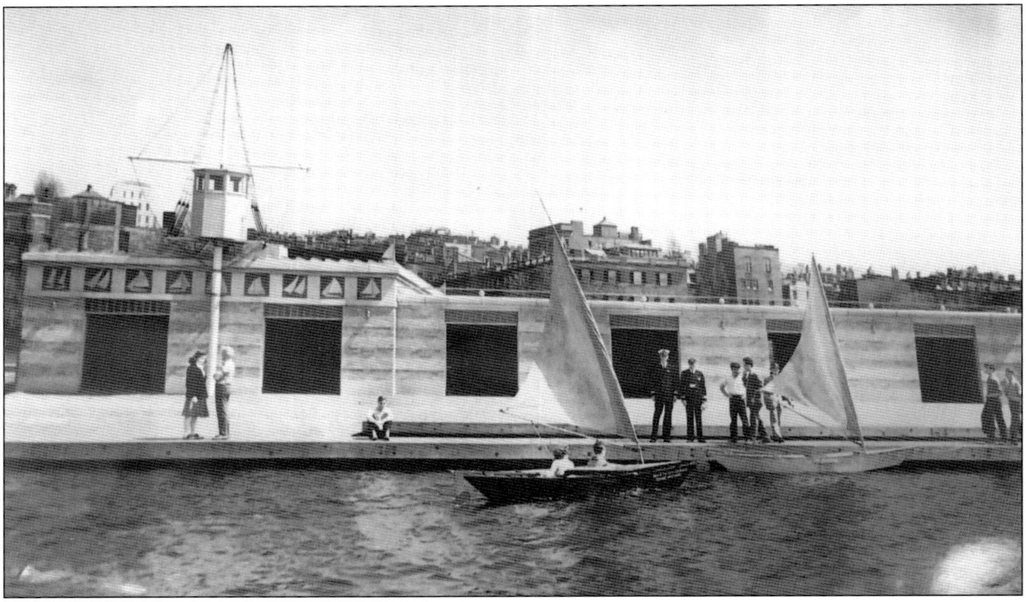

The Community Boat Club boathouse made a dramatic statement when it was built along the edge of the Charles River Basin. Its one-story roughhewn granite structure was embellished with a frieze of sailboats along the cornice as well as a floating boat dock that projected along the facade facing the basin, with racks for 100 sailboats as well. A crow's nest with a flagpole was prominently sited on the dock in front of the boathouse, which afforded a view of the sailboats and any needed assistance. (Courtesy of the DCR.)

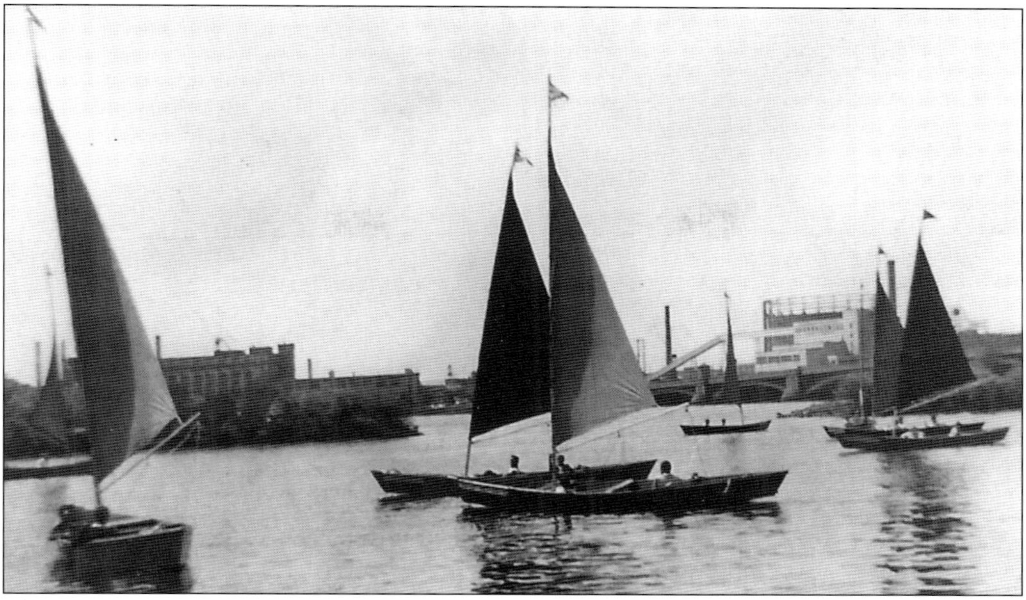

These were some of the original sailboats designed and built by Joseph Lee in the 1937 and 1938 period and were often called "Joe Lee Boats." They had bamboo masts and booms, and according to George Manfredi, these boats were to be the inspiration for the 110-class built in 1939. Many were still in use as late as 1953. (Courtesy of the Leo and Audrey Manfredi collection.)

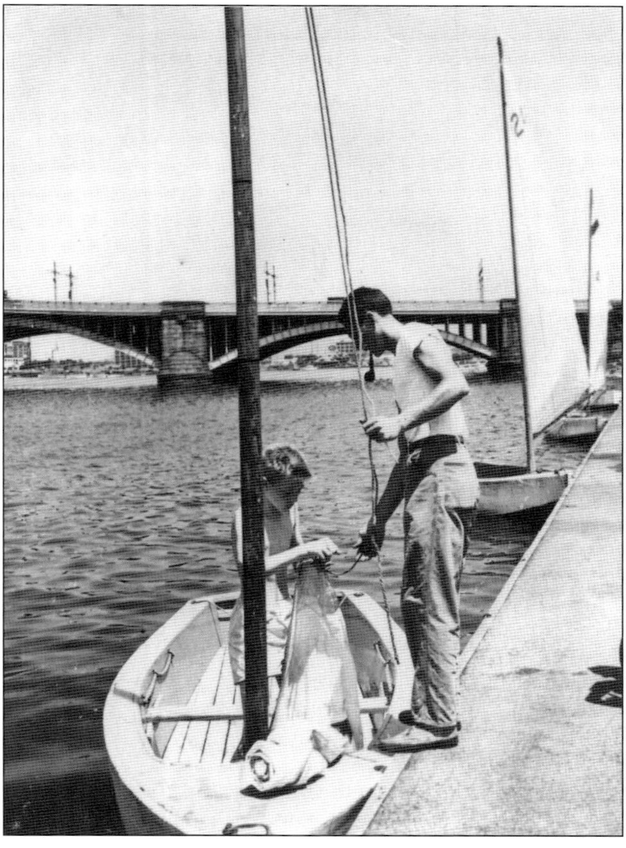

Seen in the 1940s, a young sailor with a pipe smoking instructor prepare the canvas sail to be hoisted before heading out onto the Charles River Basin. Note the asphalt dock on the right, with the original Joe Lee Boats lining the dock. (Courtesy of the Leo and Audrey Manfredi collection.)

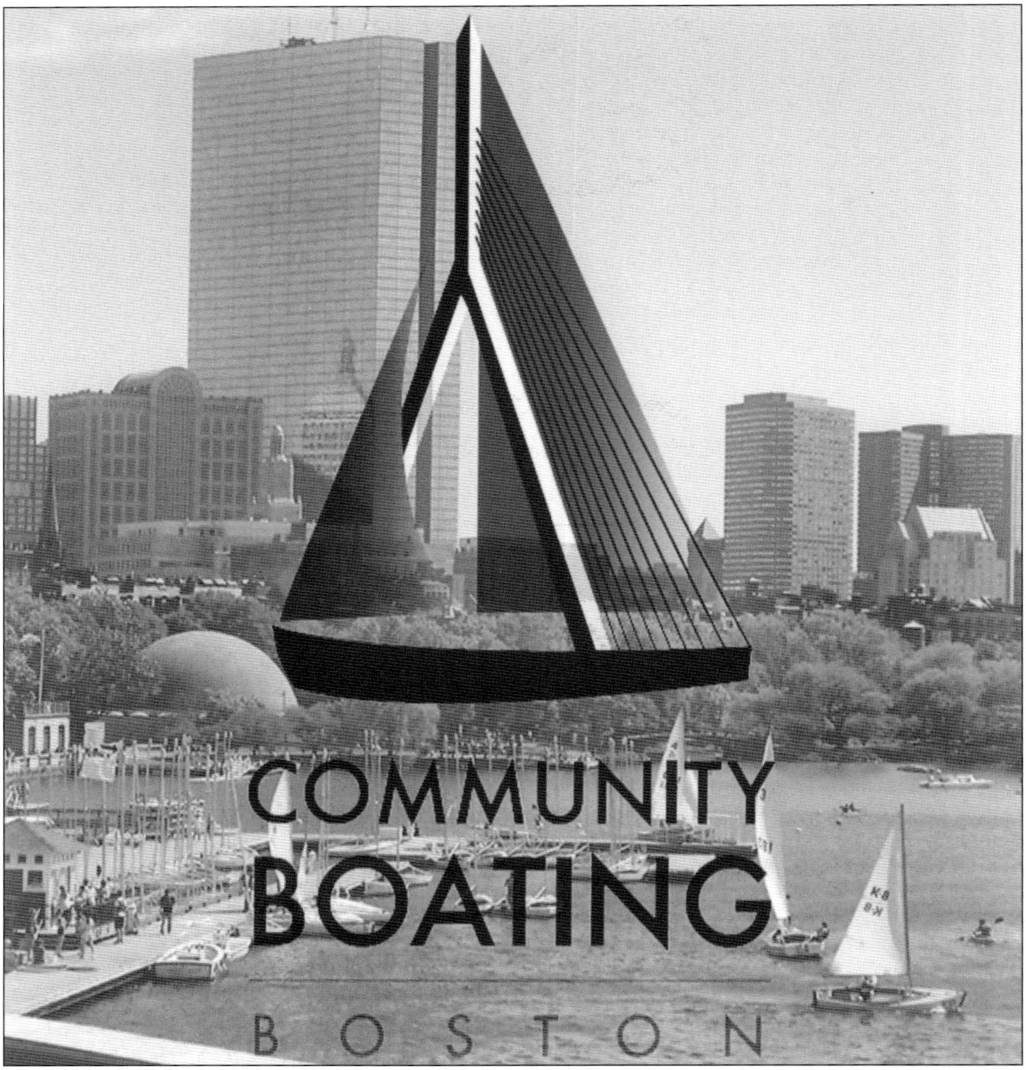

The Community Boating of Boston has long been a prominent part of the city, and its presence on the Charles River Basin is not just popular but also a major anchor. Here, one of the sailboats is superimposed on a contemporary photograph of the clubhouse, docks, and high-rises of the Back Bay of Boston.

Five

Sailing Here for All!

The mission of Community Boating is to enable "Sailing for All." We offer sailing and other water sports to people of all ages, abilities, and means in the greater Boston area.

—Community Boating

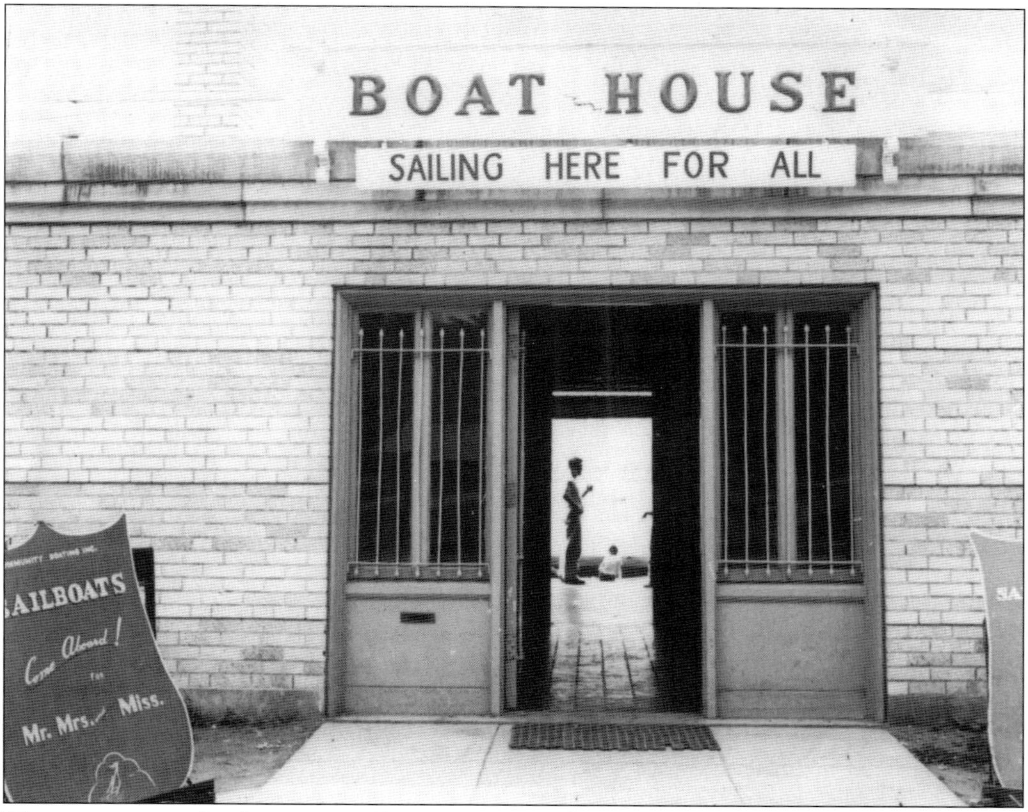

The entrance to the Community Boating Inc. Boathouse had a sign above the entrance that welcomed everyone and said, "Sailing Here for All." The shield-shaped sign on the left said, "Sailboats, Come Aboard! For Mr. Mrs. and Miss," inclusive in and of itself. Seen through the open doorway are three young sailors who were part of the large group of people that participated in the many activities of Community Boating. Passing through this doorway opened not just the horizon of many young people to the joys of sailing but also offered a whole new activity in life. (Courtesy of the Leo and Audrey Manfredi collection.)

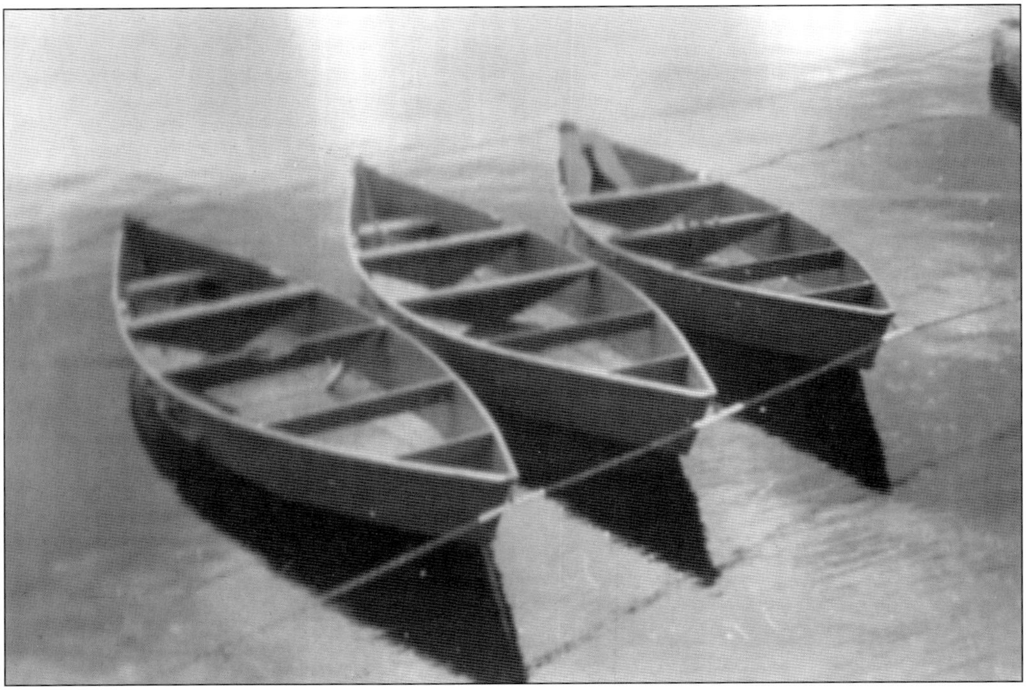

Three of the original "Joe Lee Boats" can be seen after having been stored overnight. The bamboo masts and the sails were removed every night and stored in lockers on the dock. (Courtesy of the Leo and Audrey Manfredi collection.)

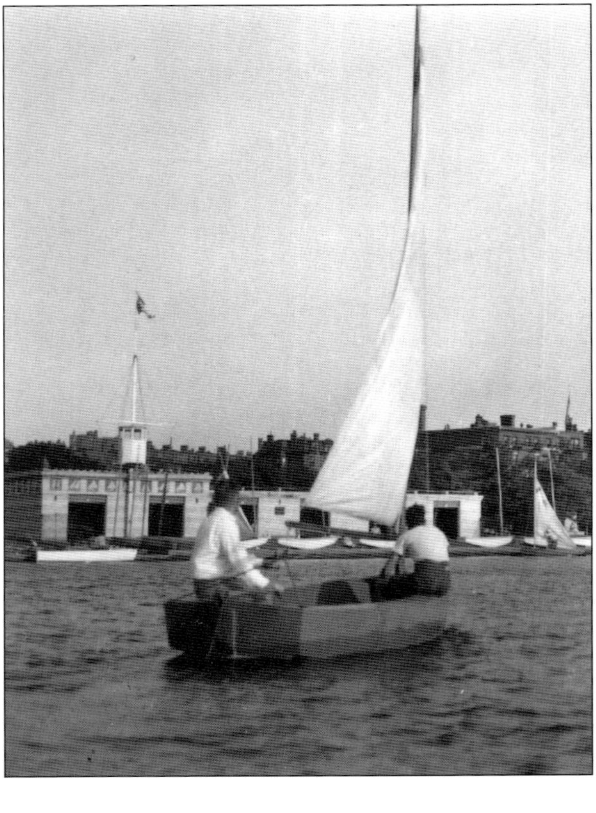

The boathouse was to become a prominent part of the Charles River Embankment, and with its own crow's nest flying the United States flag, it was not only the departure and arrival point of every Community Boating sailor but also a vantage point to gauge one's distance from the dock. By 1940, Community Recreation Service oversaw the operation of the club, with George Owen, Douglas Lawson, and Walter Wood as advisers. All persons previously associated with the club were excluded, unfortunately. (Courtesy of the DCR.)

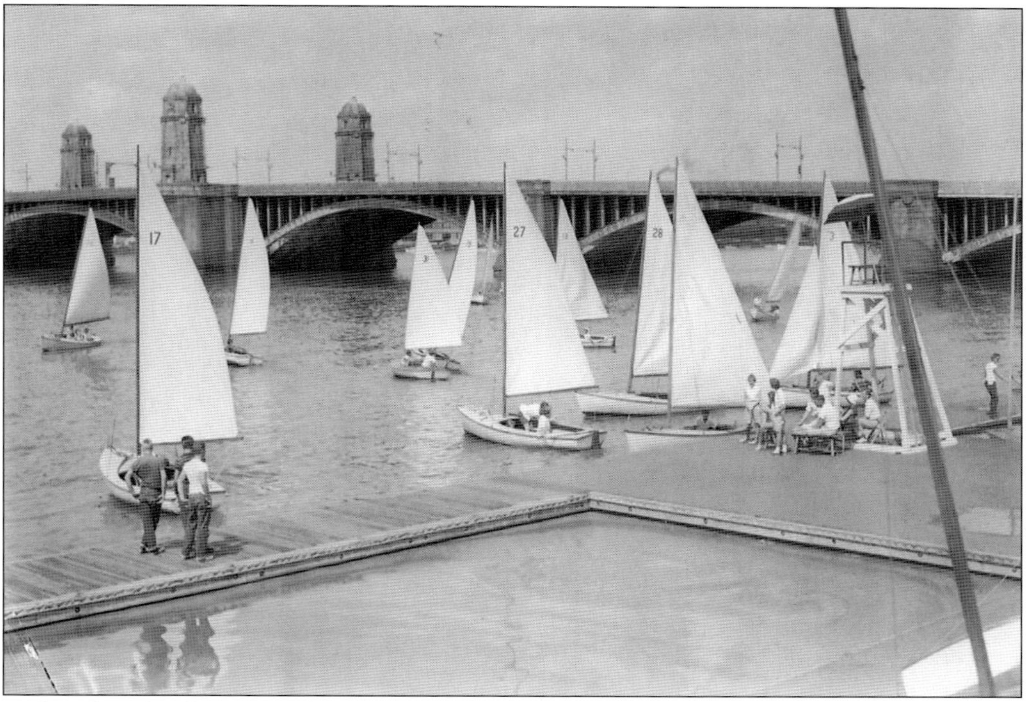

Multitudes of stiff canvas sails seemingly float on the Charles River Basin and thereby create a dramatic effect as people watch from the dock. A group stands by the lifeguard chair on the right as they start toward a sailboat pulled up against the dock.

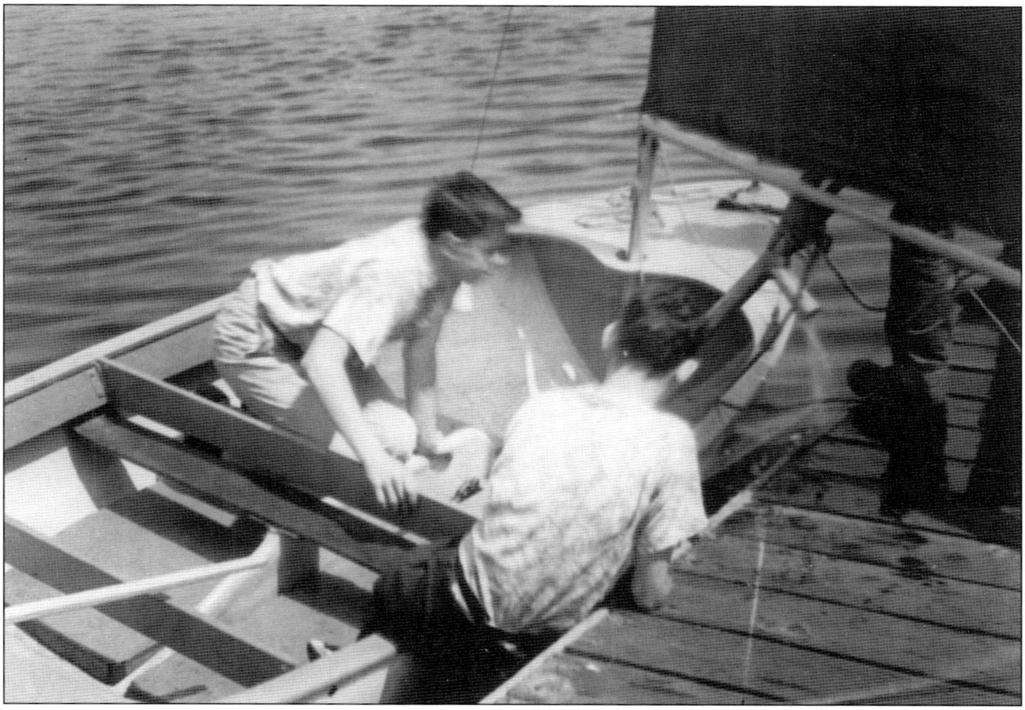

These two young men enjoyed an afternoon sail and are getting ready to jump on the dock. (Courtesy of the Leo and Audrey Manfredi collection.)

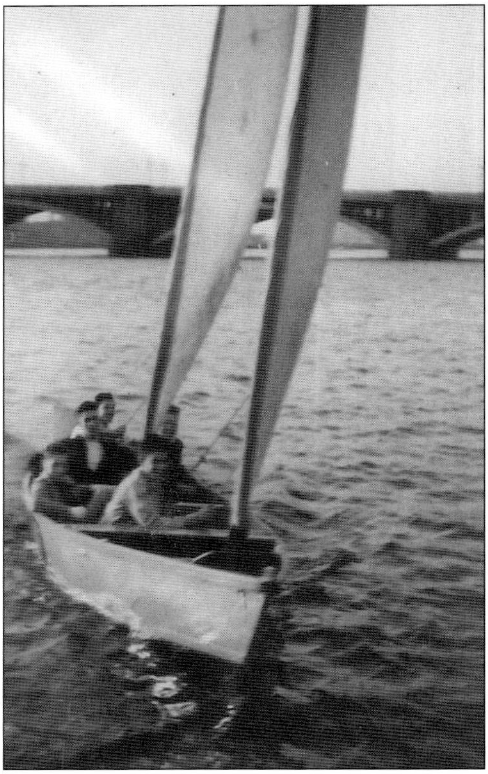

This sailboat has five young friends manning a two-masted sailboat in 1948. This was one of the original boats built by Joseph Lee, which in its decade-plus of service survived remarkably well and was testimony as to how well built and well designed these sailboats really were. (Courtesy of the Leo and Audrey Manfredi collection.)

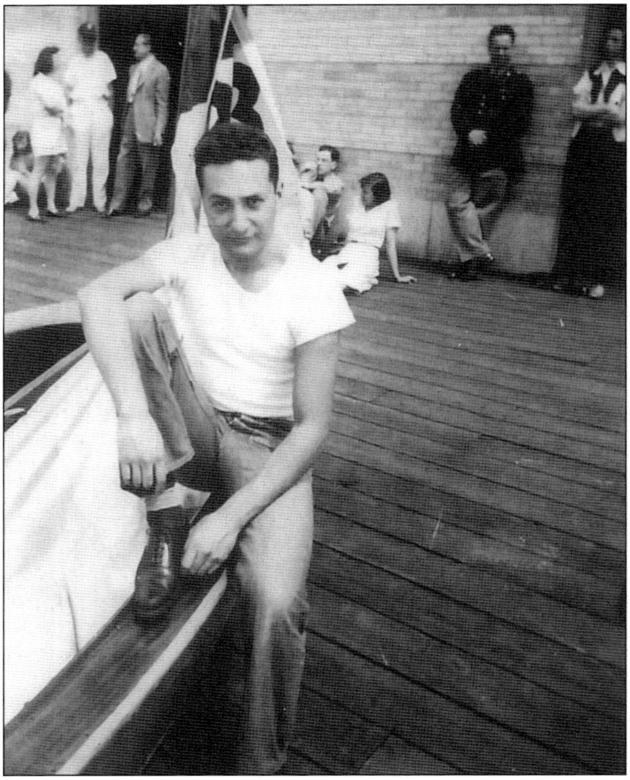

Leo Manfredi sits on the edge of one of the sailboats on the dock in front of the boathouse in the 1940s. His presence at the boathouse, doing repairs and painting on the docks and virtually in every aspect of Community Boating, was not just welcoming but also ensured that his sense of dedication was known, appreciated, and widely respected by the many members of the club. Note the people standing and sitting on the dock, awaiting their turn to sail on the Charles River Basin. (Courtesy of the Leo and Audrey Manfredi collection.)

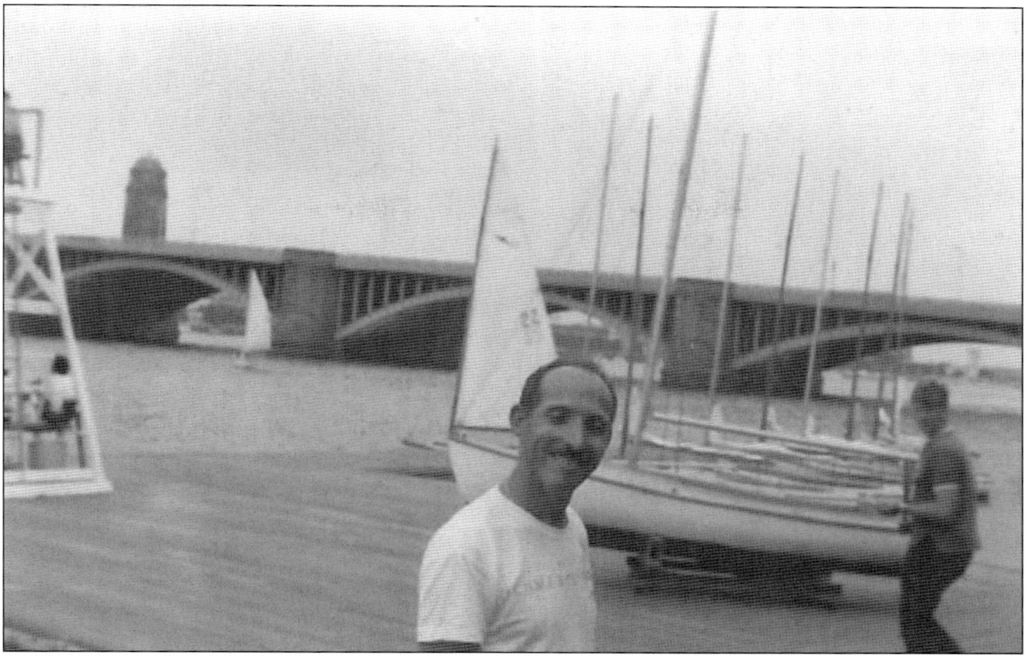

This wonderful view of the Charles River Basin and Longfellow Bridge includes a lineup of the sailboats that were to become an iconic image of Boston. Seen in 1966 on the dock are a smiling Manny Rosenfeld (center) and Dan Winkler (far right). (Courtesy of the Dan and Marilyn Farren collection.)

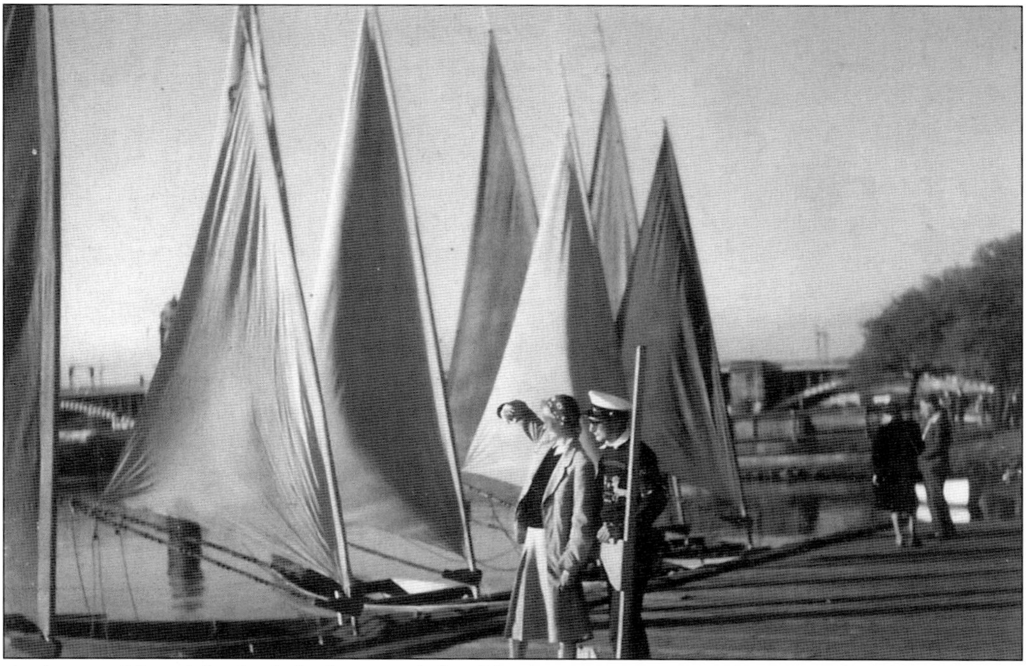

Audrey and Leo Manfredi look toward the Charles River Basin with a panoply of canvas sails acting as a striking backdrop to the wood boat dock. They were stalwart members of Community Boating for 25 years and encouraged and nurtured two generations of sailors, including their daughters. (Courtesy of the Leo and Audrey Manfredi collection.)

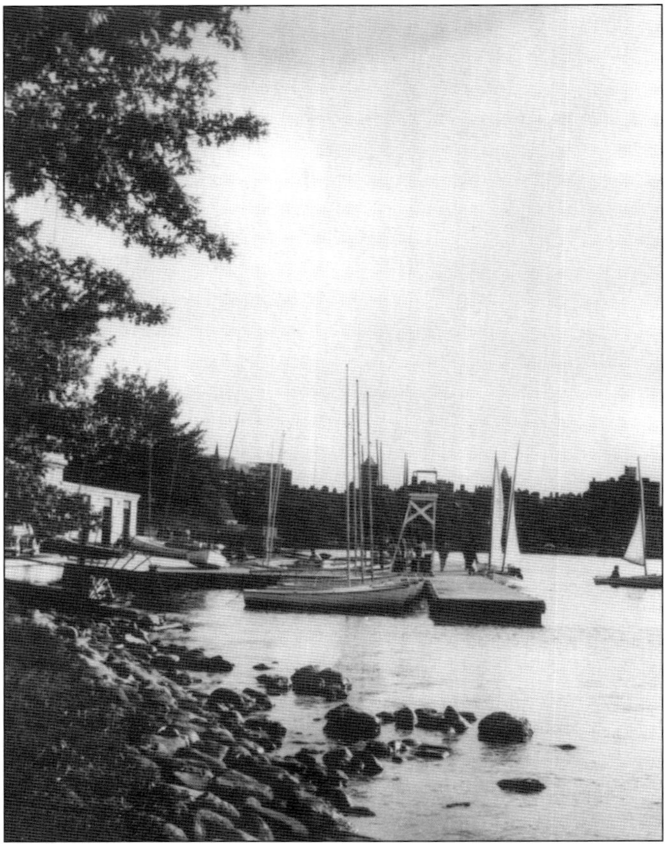

Looking south along the edge of the embankment, these rocks act as a barrier reef to the shoreline as the sailboats are lined up along the boat slip. Note the skyline of the Back Bay of Boston, long before the high-rises of the Prudential and Hancock were built. (Courtesy of the Leo and Audrey Manfredi collection.)

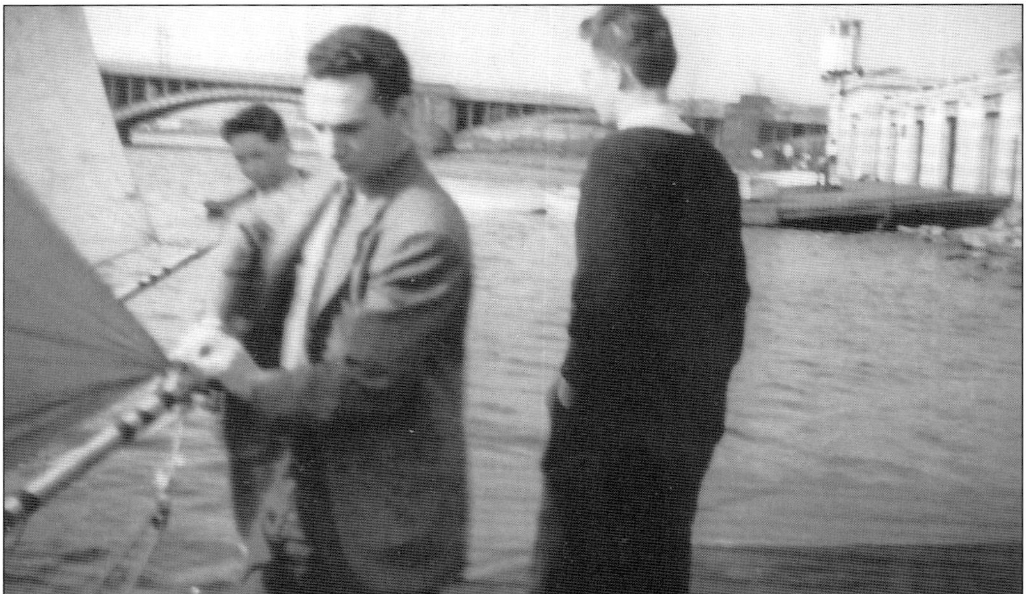

Leo Manfredi, in the center, adjusts the canvas sail and the boom on a sailboat. The sail would be held to its three-cornered shape at all times by a pole projecting from the mast and running along the under edge of the sail. (Courtesy of the Leo and Audrey Manfredi collection.)

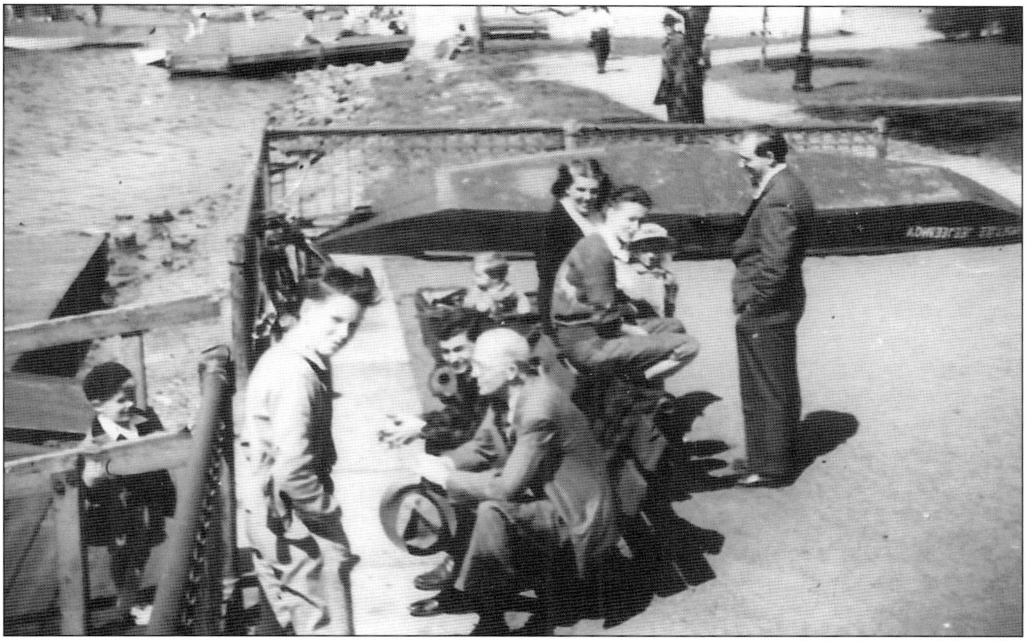

A group of friends and their children relax on a section of the Esplanade overlooking the river enjoying a sunny afternoon. An upturned sailboat can be seen laying along the fence, and the wood docks in front of the boathouse are visible in the distance. (Courtesy of the Leo and Audrey Manfredi collection.)

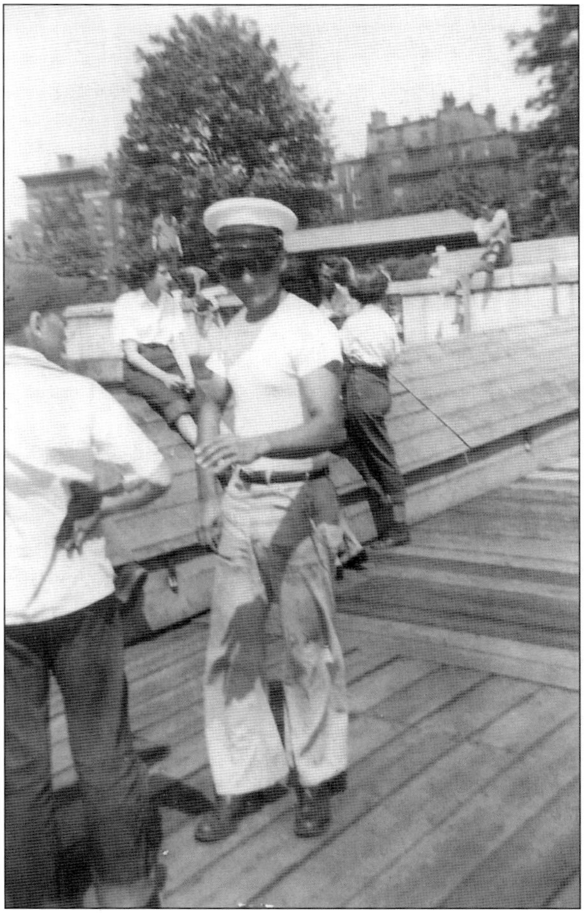

Leo Manfredi, sporting a dapper white nautical captain's hat and sunglasses, walks along the boat slip as people converse while sitting on the lockers on the boat dock and awaiting their turn to take the sailboats out in the afternoon. (Courtesy of the Leo and Audrey Manfredi collection.)

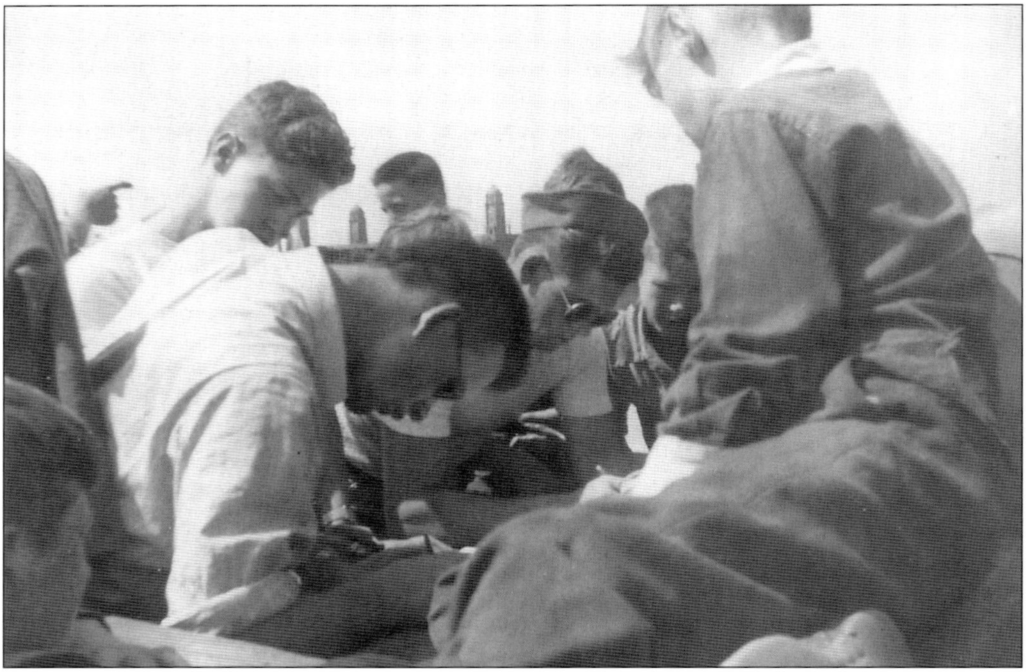

Encouraging people of all ages to join Community Boating was important, but often, there were sign-up sheets for those interested in joining Community Boating and learning the "art of sailing," as Joseph Lee referred to it. (Courtesy of the Leo and Audrey Manfredi collection.)

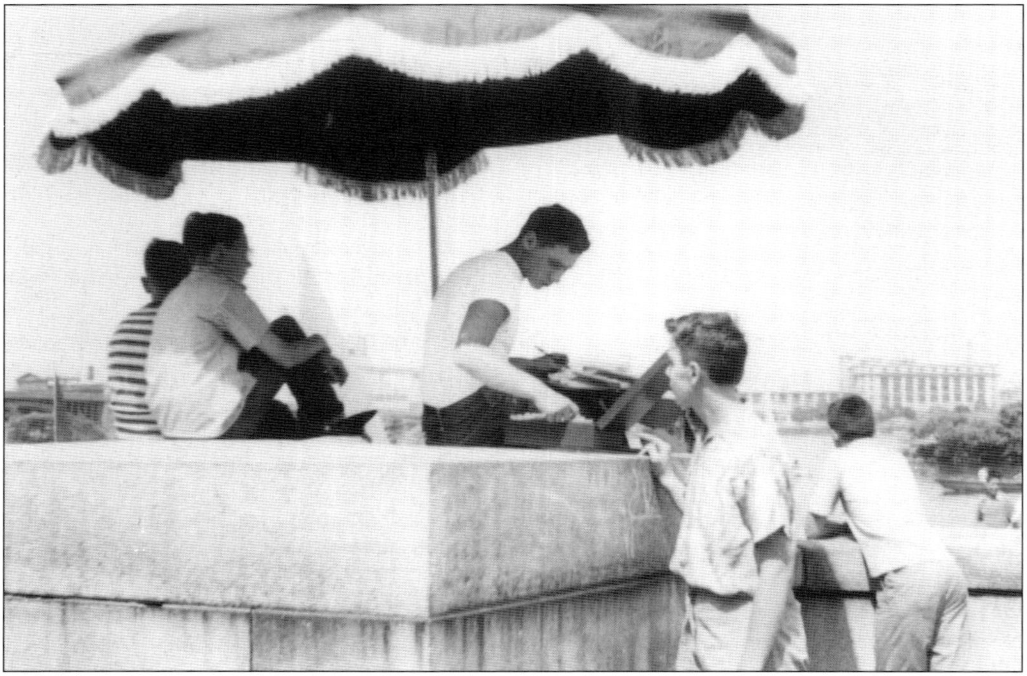

Perched on one of the solid granite walls that lined the Esplanade, a young volunteer, shaded by a huge umbrella, refers to an index card file of members and possible new members, many who had never known anything of sailing before—and even some who had never even seen a sailboat. (Courtesy of the Leo and Audrey Manfredi collection.)

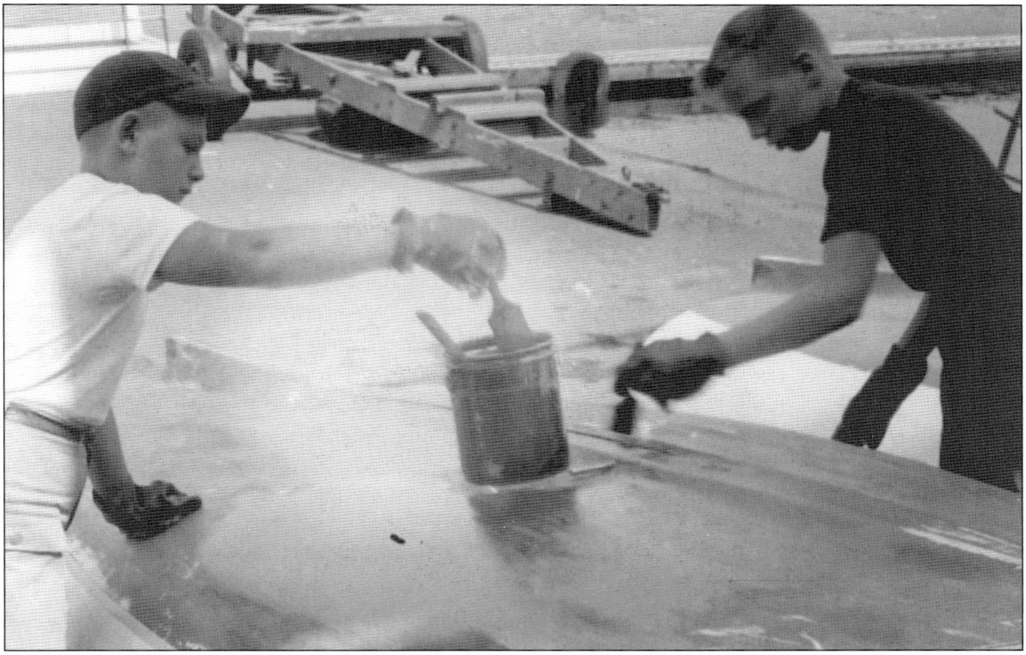

Young and old alike came together, especially on weekend mornings, to maintain the sailboats at Community Boating. After having been stored for the winter months, these two boys had caulked, sanded, and now paint the underside of the sailboat, preparing it for another season of sailing. (Courtesy of the Leo and Audrey Manfredi collection.)

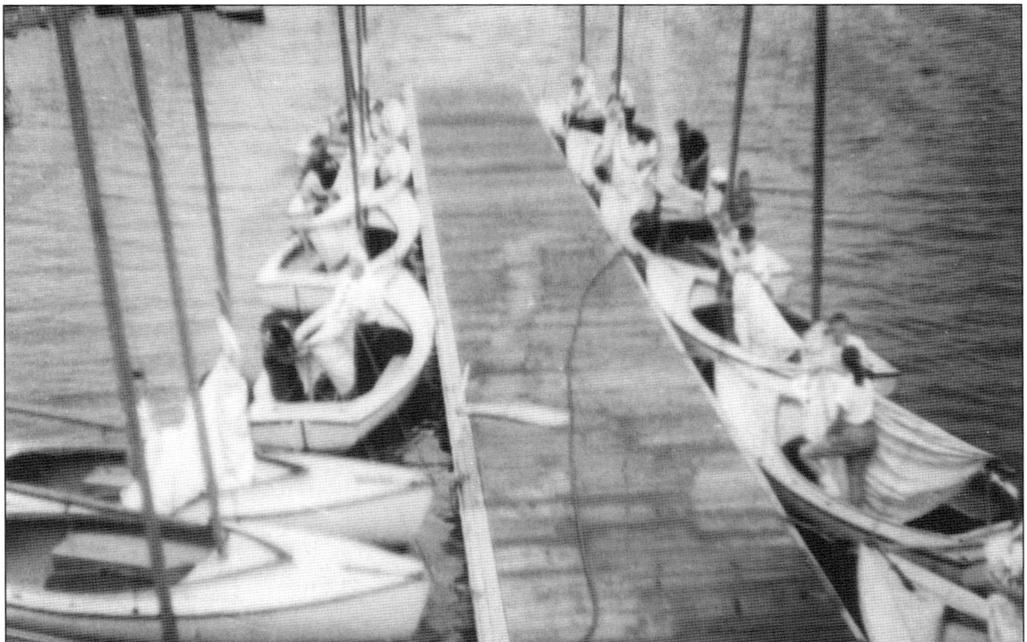

Flanking a long wood dock are the sailboats of Community Boating, with the sailors just beginning to hoist their canvas sails before they set out for a sail. (Courtesy of the Leo and Audrey Manfredi collection.)

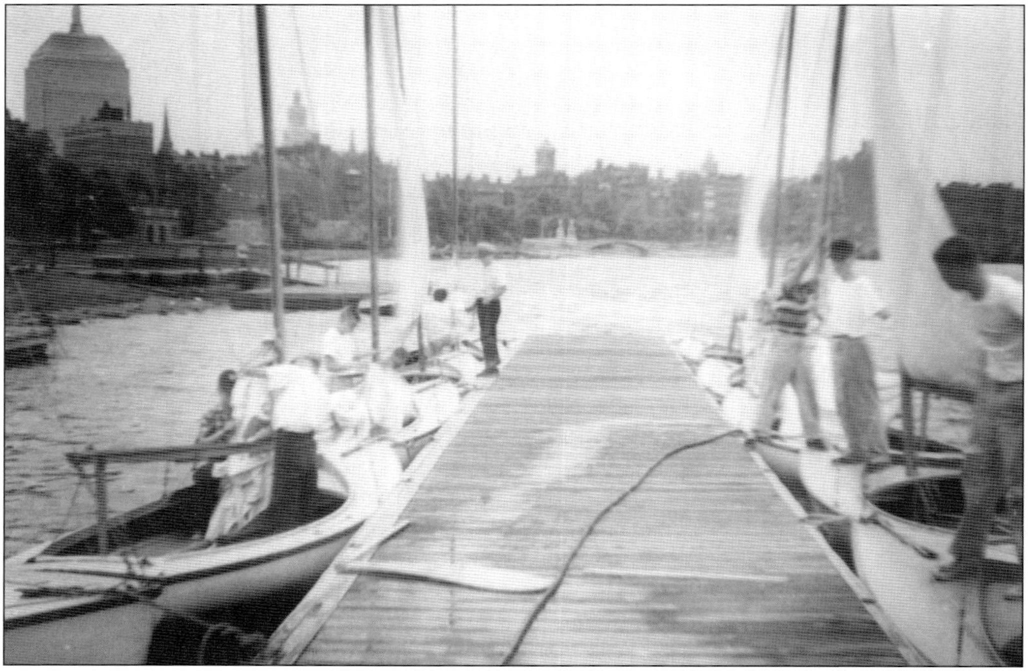

These sailors are hoisting their canvas sails before they set out on a sail. Before they left the dock, Lee advised them to "learn to look at the wind and see what it is doing," as the wind was said to be their engine—every course one took or every turn one made, the sail is reckoned on it. (Courtesy of the Leo and Audrey Manfredi collection.)

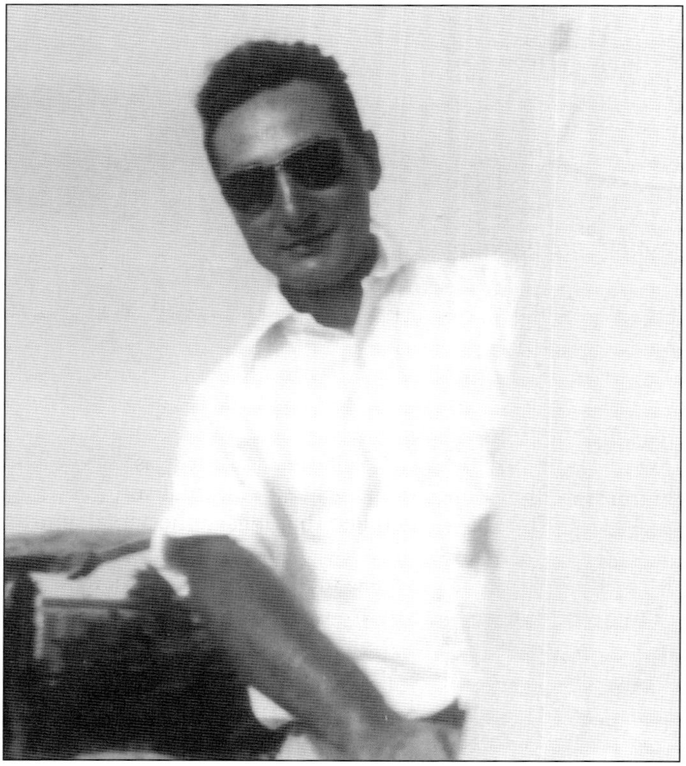

Leo Manfredi, deeply tanned from a summer of sailing, pulls the canvas sail on the right. These sails were often sewn by hand and were of a heavy dense grain of cloth from hospital sheets. (Courtesy of the Leo and Audrey Manfredi collection.)

Leo Manfredi would not only caulk, sand, and paint the sailboats but would also oversee many dockmasters and maintenance crew who would maintain the sailboats throughout the year—especially in the spring just before they were made ready for a season of sailing. (Courtesy of the Leo and Audrey Manfredi collection.)

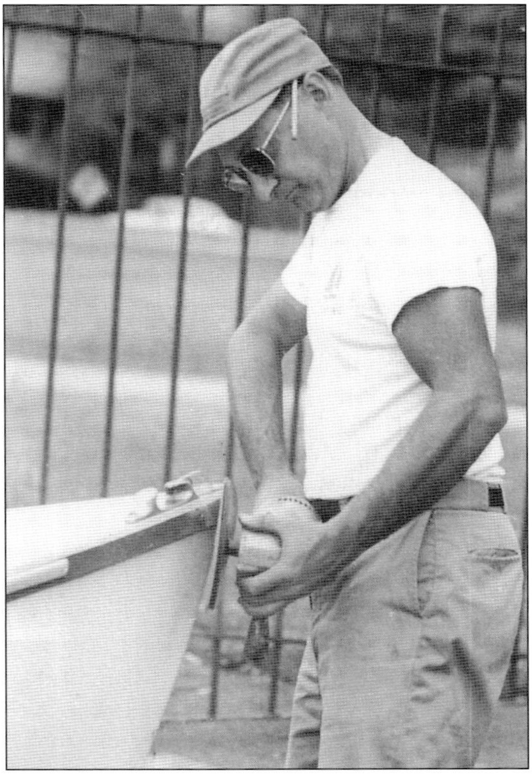

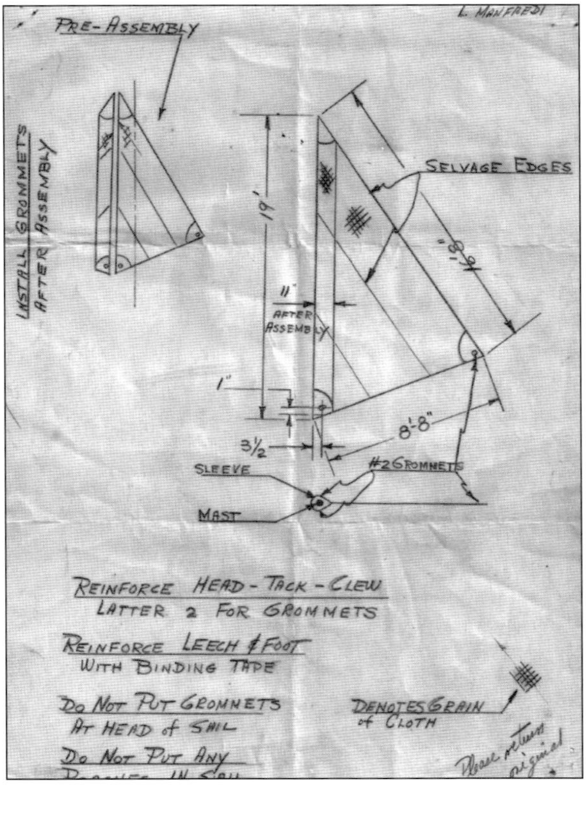

A "Sail Making Plan" was hand drawn by Leo Manfredi and was so detailed that it gave the actual grain of the cloth for the sails. From the preassembly to the installation of the grommets after assembly, the plan was an extremely well-detailed drawing and allowed everyone the ability to make their own sail if they followed it. (Courtesy of the Leo and Audrey Manfredi collection.)

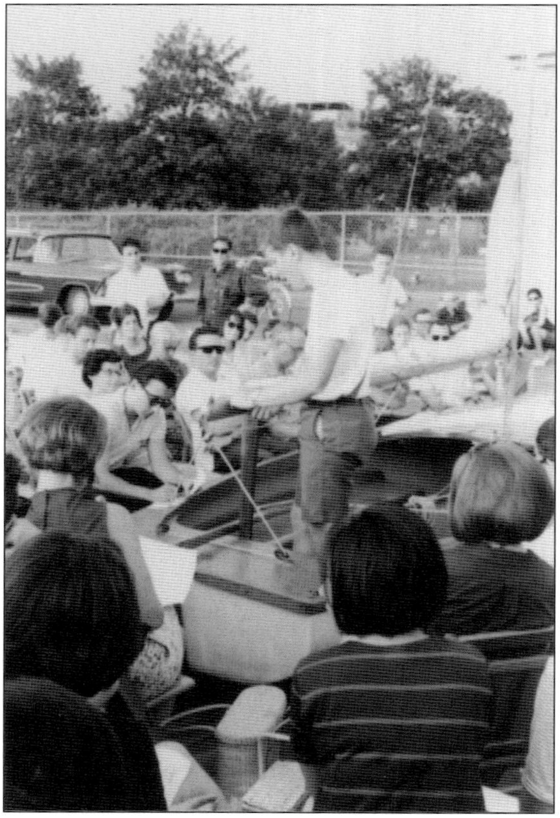

Shore School was a very popular sailing class that allowed prospective sailors at Community Boating to tour the Boathouse, inspect the sailboats, and then join in a question-and-answer period on the boat slip. Brendan O'Brien is pictured in the center demonstrating how to operate the sail for those attending the class. What is remarkable is that there are people of all walks of life and ages attending Shore School. (Courtesy of the Dan and Marilyn Farren collection.)

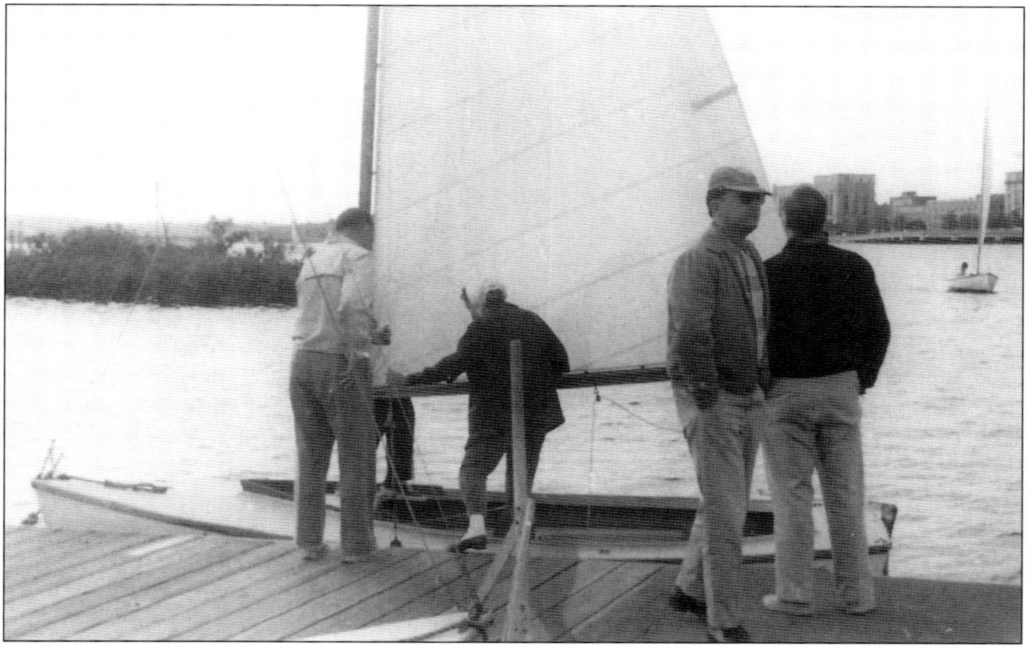

A woman, with her headscarf in place to protect her coiffure from the unrelenting wind, steps from the wood dock into the sailboat as the man on the left holds the painter, which secured the boat to the landing dock. (Courtesy of the Leo and Audrey Manfredi collection.)

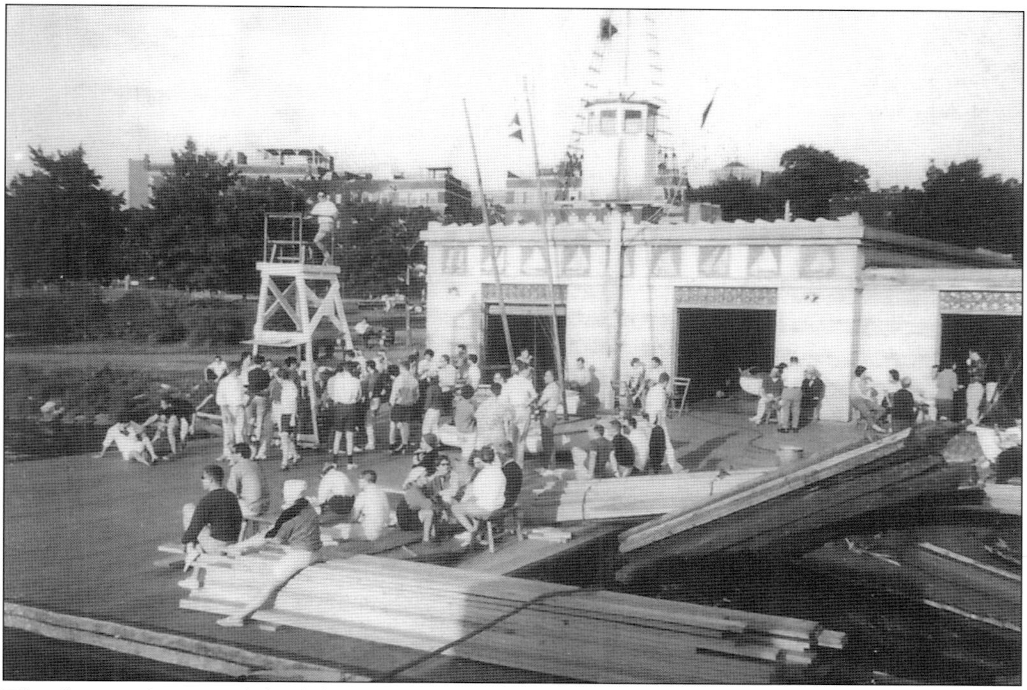

This festive photograph had dozens of people on the wood dock enjoying the sunny afternoon. The piles of wood boards were on the dock, as these would be used to build the new wood docks. (Courtesy of the Leo and Audrey Manfredi collection.)

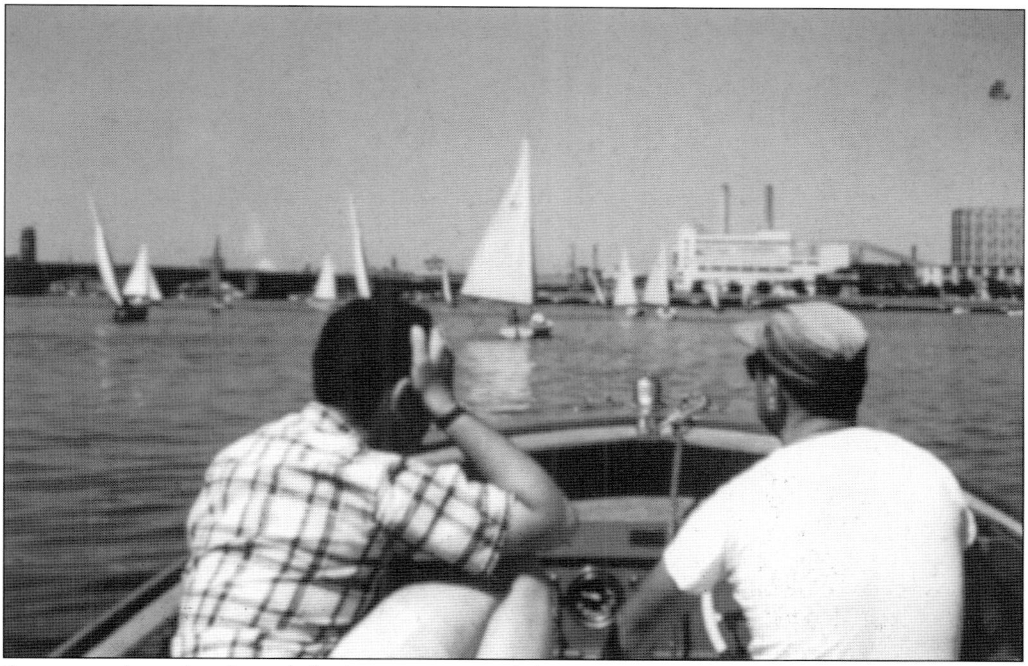

Sitting in the safety launch looking out toward the sailboats, these young men seem perfectly contented and relaxed awaiting the return of the sailboats and their turn at sailing. The dockmasters would always keep a close eye on the junior members who were out sailing, just in case of upset or accident. (Courtesy of the Leo and Audrey Manfredi collection.)

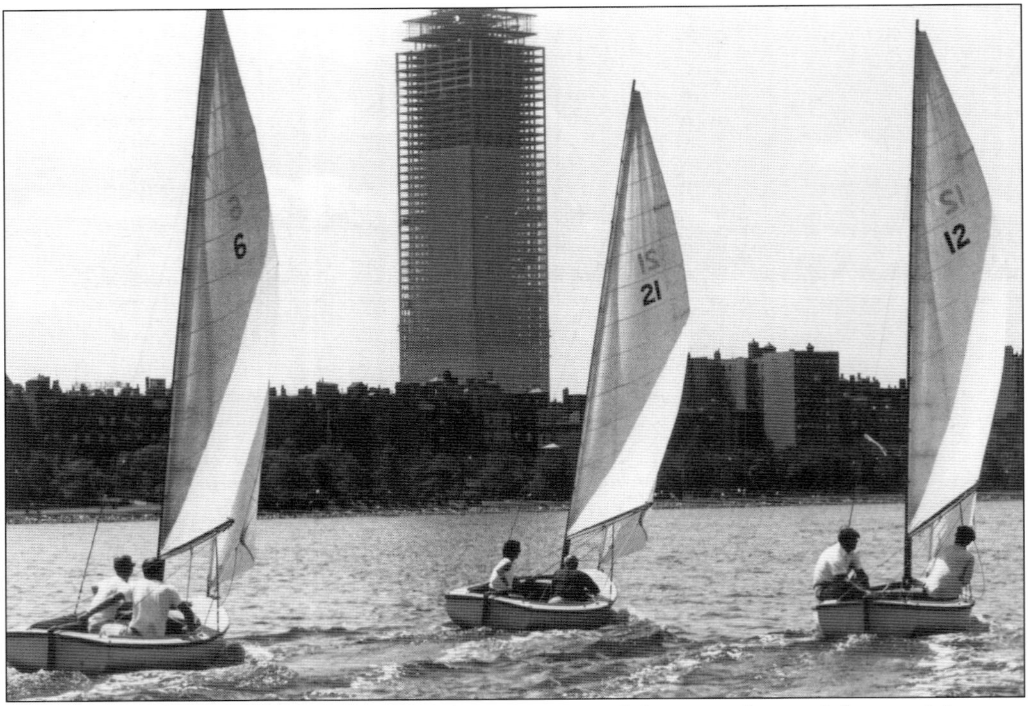

Three stiff canvas sails point upward and act as a virtual frame to the steel frame of the new high-rise of the Prudential Tower. Under construction from 1960 to 1964, this was the tallest building in the Back Bay for less than a decade until the John Hancock Tower was completed in 1975. (Courtesy of the Leo and Audrey Manfredi collection.)

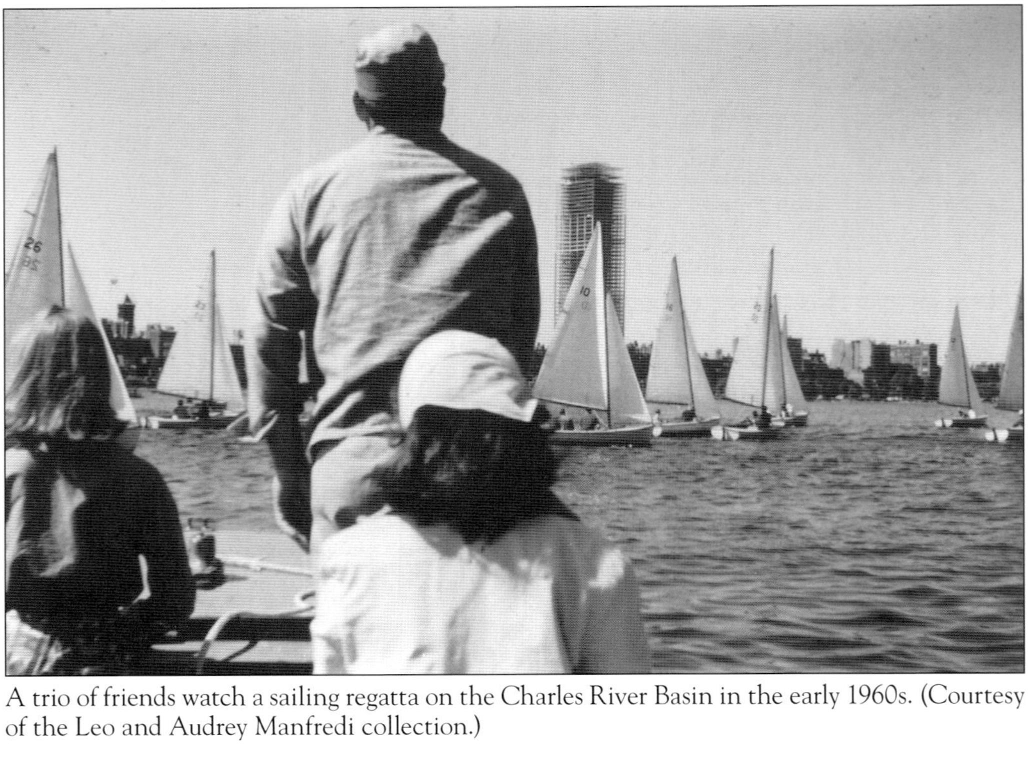

A trio of friends watch a sailing regatta on the Charles River Basin in the early 1960s. (Courtesy of the Leo and Audrey Manfredi collection.)

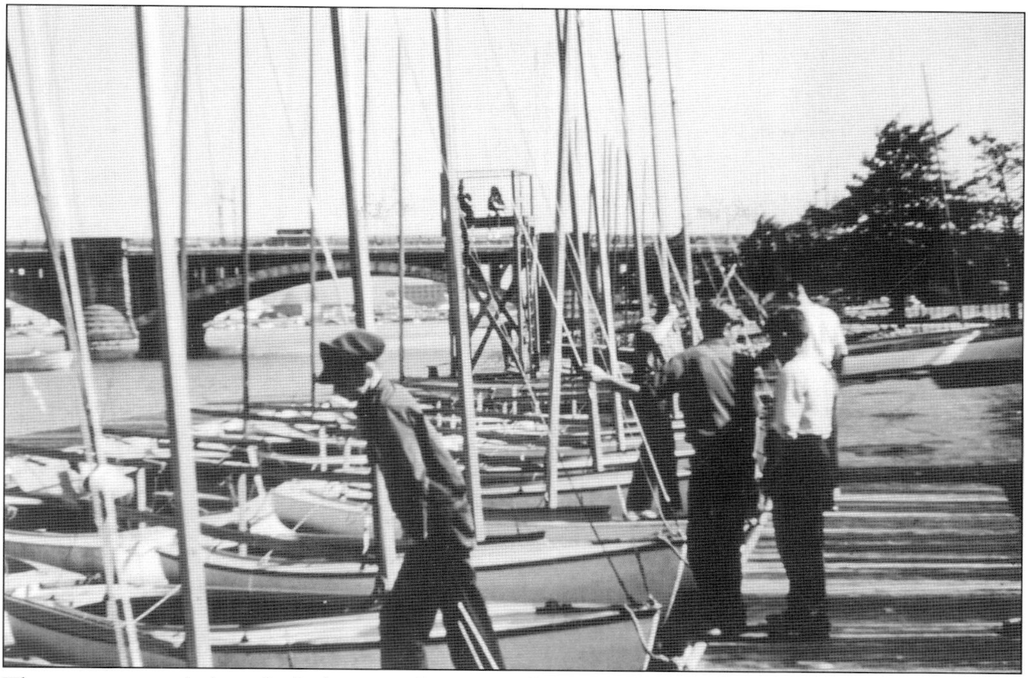

These young men help with the boats in the spring of 1963, just before the asphalt docks were removed and replaced with wood docks. (Courtesy of the Leo and Audrey Manfredi collection.)

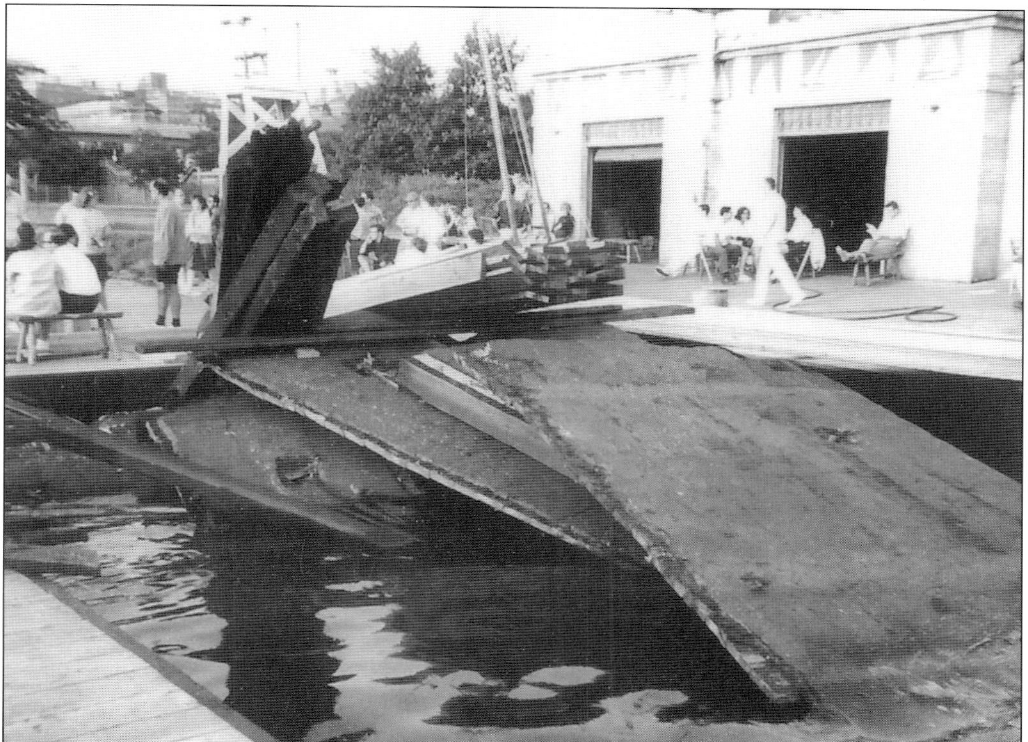

The asphalt docks were removed in 1963, and the slabs of hard asphalt are stacked adjacent to the boat docks on the left and right. (Courtesy of the Leo and Audrey Manfredi collection.)

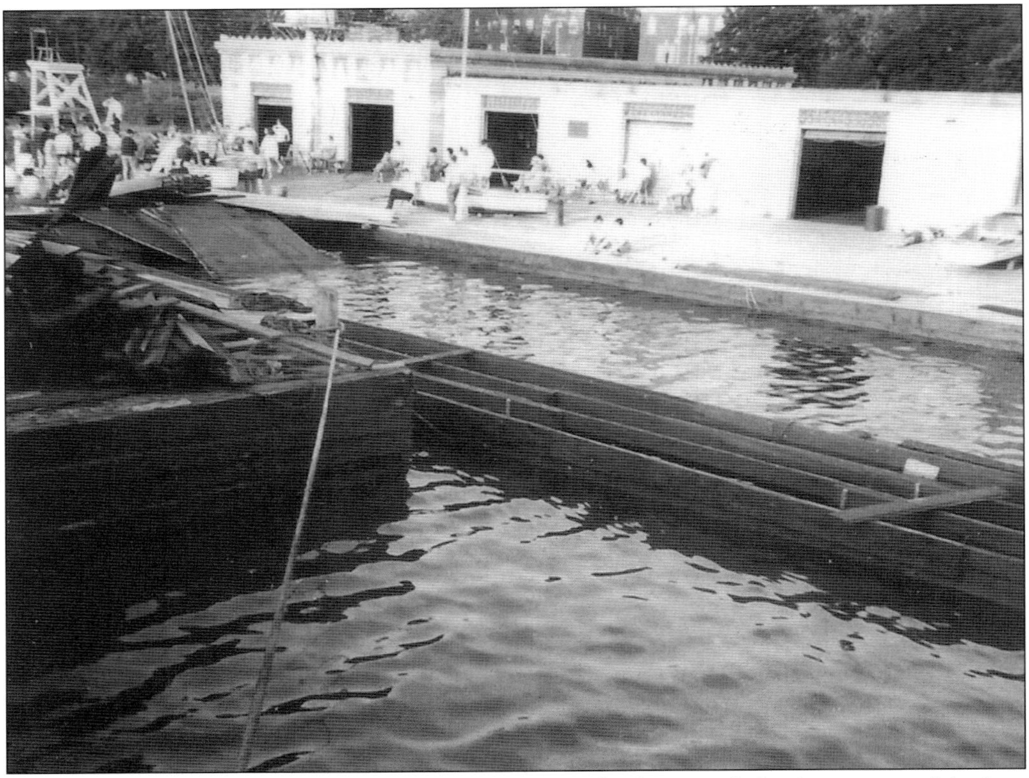

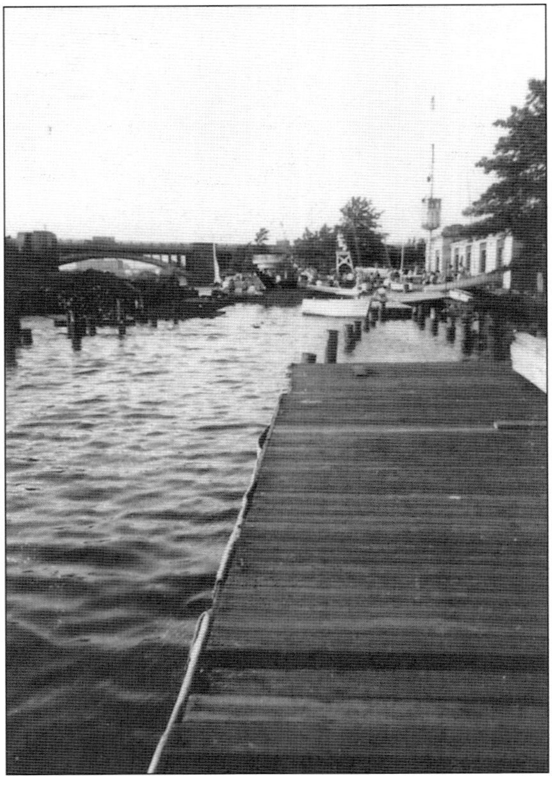

The framework for the new wood docks was being built as the asphalt docks can be seen on the left before their removal. This was a major undertaking for Community Boating. (Courtesy of the Leo and Audrey Manfredi collection.)

The partially completed wood dock, with the piers in the distance awaiting the dock, was much better and eco-friendlier than the now-removed asphalt docks. The boathouse, and its iconic crow's nest in the distance, await the completion of the wood docks, which, by 1964, transformed the space and greatly expanded areas to dock sailboats. (Courtesy of the Leo and Audrey Manfredi collection.)

Six

Sailing on the Charles River Basin

Boston's eight-mile-long Charles River Basin sits at the heart of one of the country's first regional waterfront park systems.

—Goody Clancy Associates

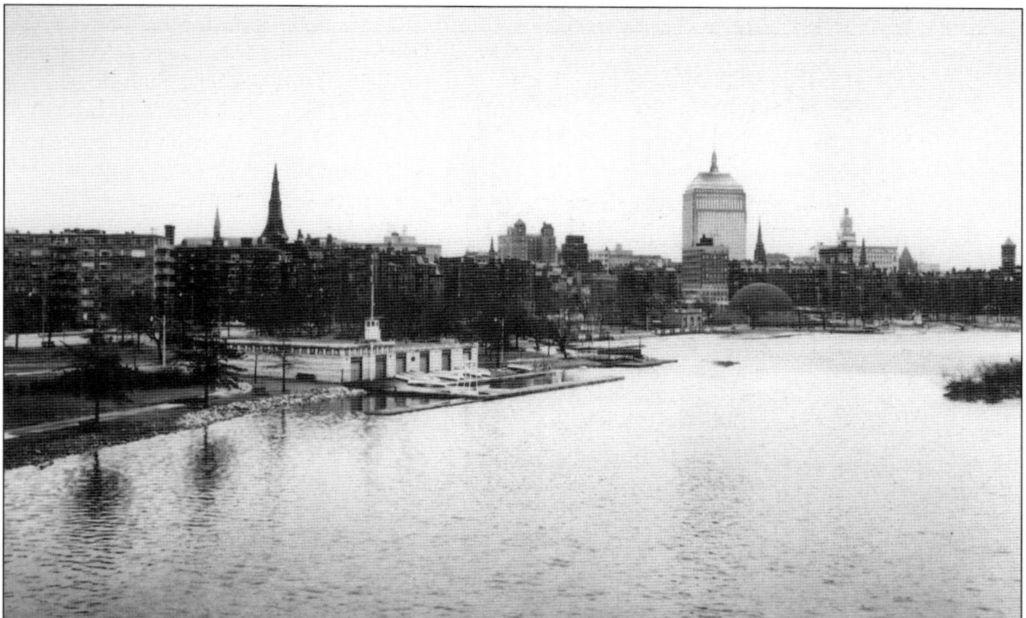

In the early 1960s, the Esplanade had truly come into its own with mature trees flanking the Charles River with Beacon Hill and the Back Bay as a backdrop. The Community Boating boathouse is seen in the center, with its prominent crow's nest flagpole. In the distance, from left to right, the spire of the Church of the Advent, the original John Hancock Tower, the cupola of the New England Mutual Life Insurance Company and the spire of the First Baptist Church in Boston can be seen. (Courtesy of the DCR.)

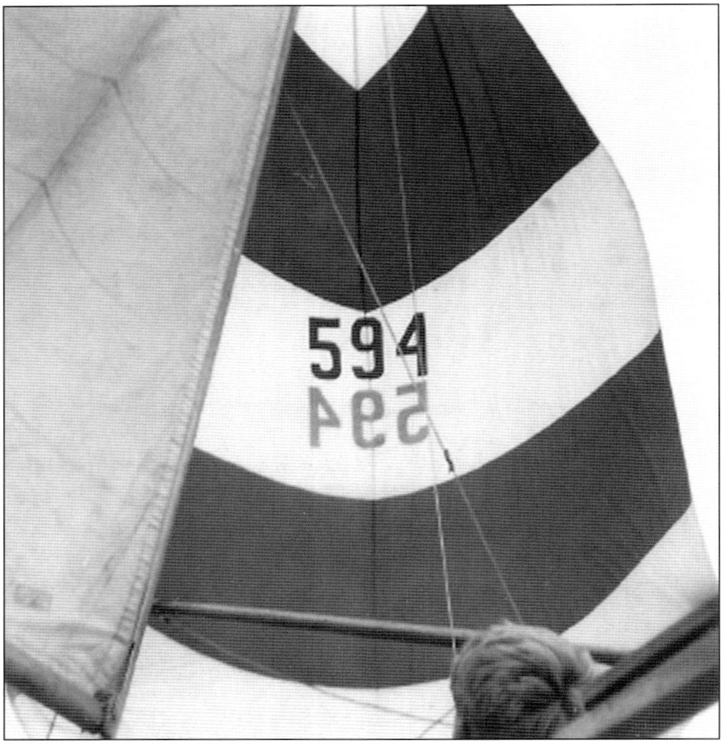

One of the most beautiful and exhilarating sights is a boat racing with the spinnaker sail flying. (Courtesy of the Dan and Marilyn Farren collection.)

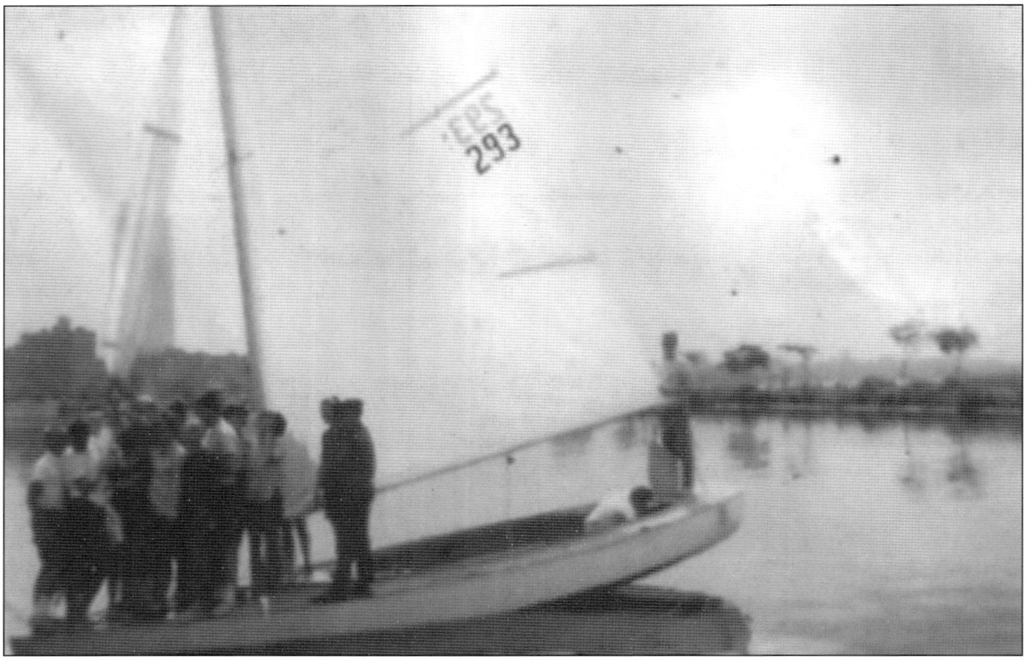

The original sailboats were handmade by Lee, his nephews, and an ever-increasing cadre of young boys from the West End. The boats were said to cost $20 per boat. Seen here are a group of volunteers who stand on the bow of *The Raven*. Their combined weight raised the stern out of the water to allow the dockmasters, seen on the right, to make repairs to the rudder. (Courtesy of the Dan and Marilyn Farren collection.)

George Owen (1877–1959) was a professor at the Massachusetts Institute of Technology and head of the Pratt School of Naval Design. Seen here at his drafting table, he is surrounded by boat models and photographs of boats and marine art. It was he who, in 1941, was hired by the Community Sailing Association to supervise and design a new fleet of sailing boats. Along with Douglas Lawson and Jack Wood, they represented the new advisory committee in conjunction with Eugene C. Hultman and the Metropolitan District Commission. (Courtesy of MIT.)

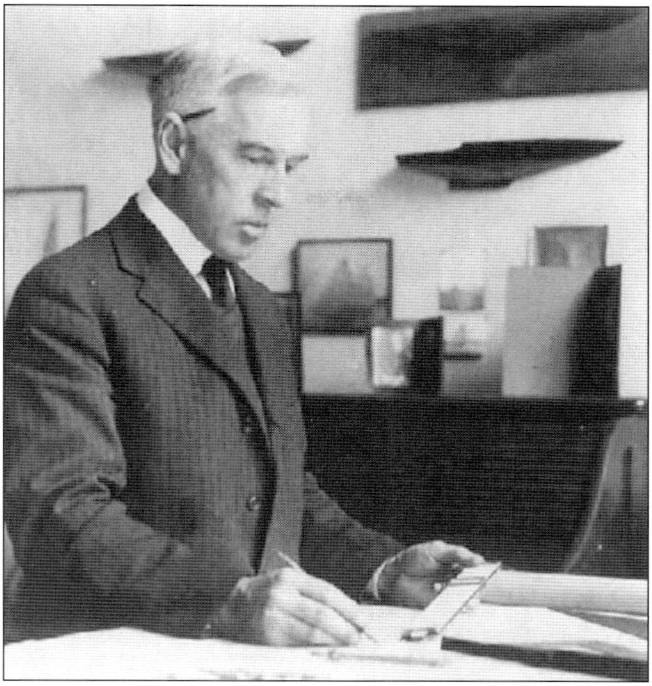

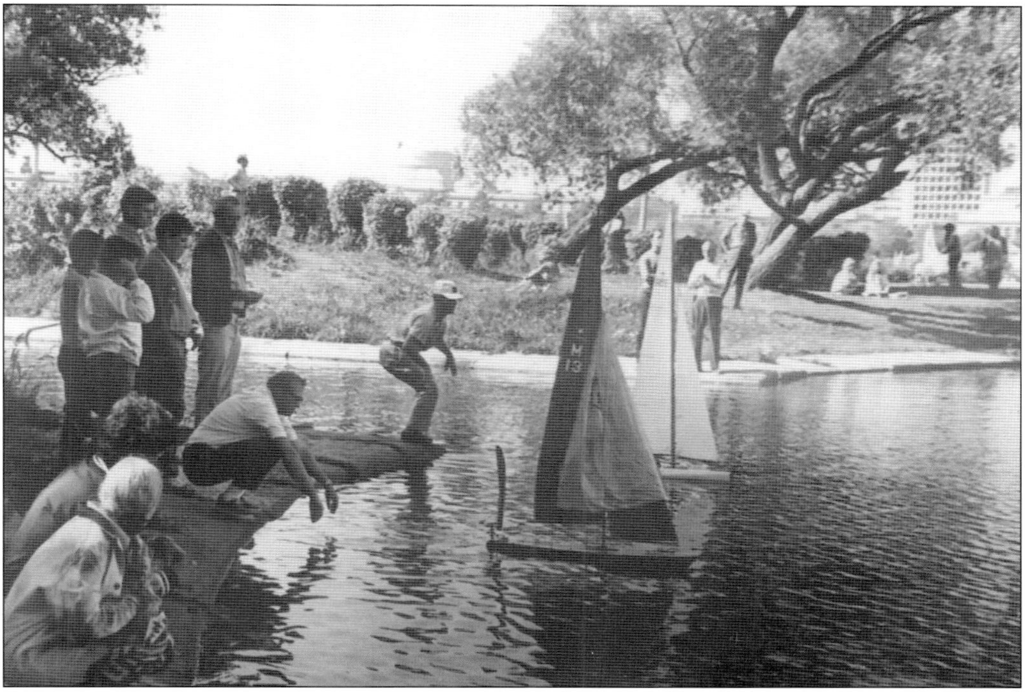

The models, designed and built by Prof. George Owen, were tested on the Charles River Basin in the early 1940s. The boat Professor Owen envisioned was a 13-foot-4-inch, chine-built centerboard vessel built on the Class B Frost-bite dinghy. Owen was an appropriate choice, as he produced more than 200 designs over more than five decades, though he was only a full-time yacht designer for seven years. The contract to build the boats was given to John C. Graves of Marblehead, Massachusetts, a close friend of Owens. (Courtesy of MIT.)

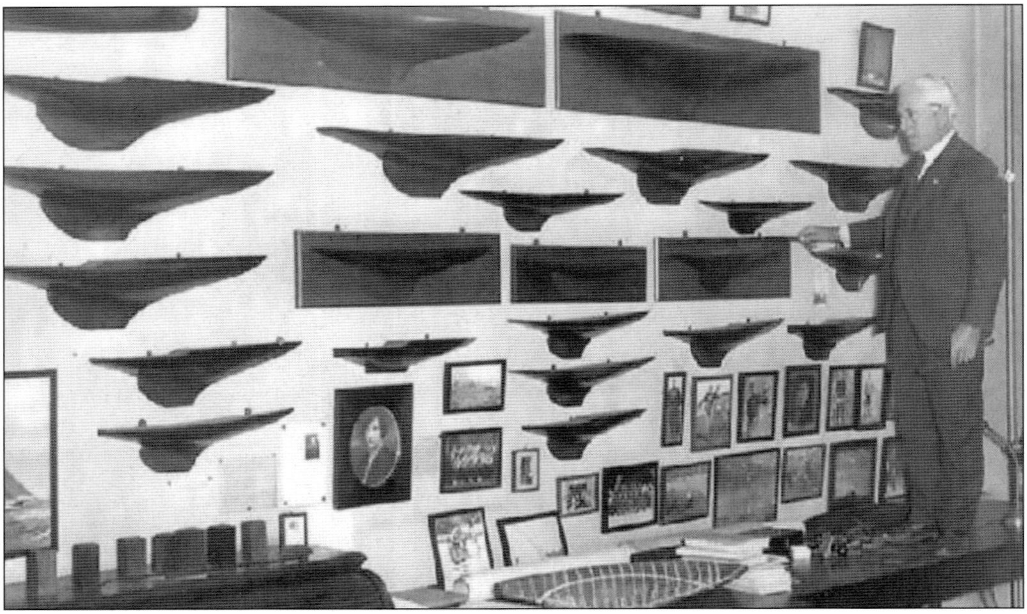

Professor Owen, a successful yacht designer and authority, is seen standing on a side table as he is surrounded by half-hull boat models at his office at MIT, from which he graduated in 1894. After his death, his daughter Florence Owen Preble donated the majority of his plans and remaining models to the Hart Nautical Museum, which later merged with the MIT Museum in 1982. (Courtesy of MIT.)

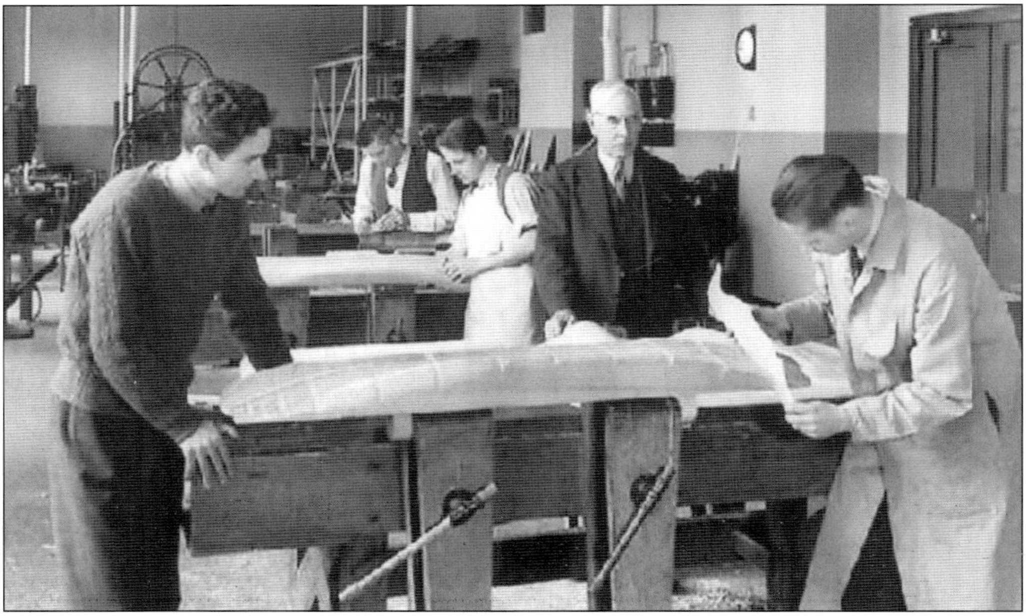

The hull of a boat model is being hand hewn in a shop at MIT as Professor Owen oversees the process. Unlike the earlier Lee-built boats that were made of marine plywood, these new boats were made of plywood manufactured by John Graves, and the expense had escalated to an excessive $435 for the hull, $60 for the mast, with additional cost for the two sails. When he heard of the new cost, "Joe Lee, ever a frugal Yankee, was apoplectic," according to a local newspaper. (Courtesy of MIT.)

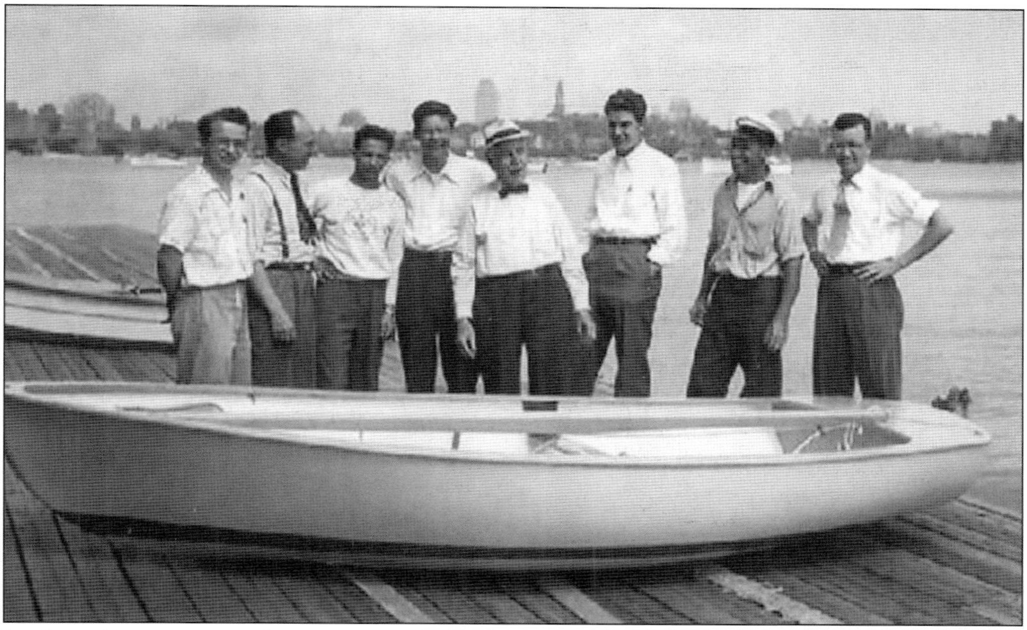

Professor Owen, seen in the center in a dapper bow tie and white Fedora, stands with his associates in front of one of the newly built boats for the Community Boating fleet. Because of the cost to fabricate them, only 30 boats were eventually built, which meant that the early Joseph Lee–designed boats had to be used to augment the fleet required to serve the ever-growing sailing members well into the early 1950s. (Courtesy of MIT.)

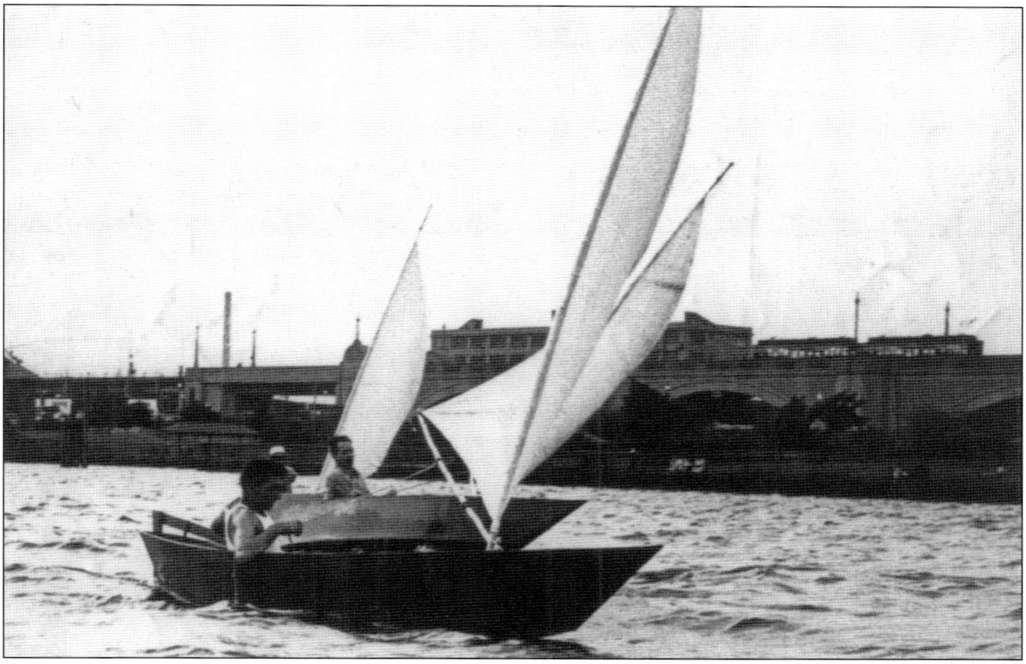

Whether with earlier boats designed by Joseph Lee or later boats designed by George Owen, sailing on the Charles River Basin was an exhilarating, peaceful, and self-fulfilling experience that each sailor undertook. These friends sail their boats toward the dock as the Longfellow Bridge acts as a backdrop, complete with the Red Line train and automobile traffic. (Courtesy of the DCR.)

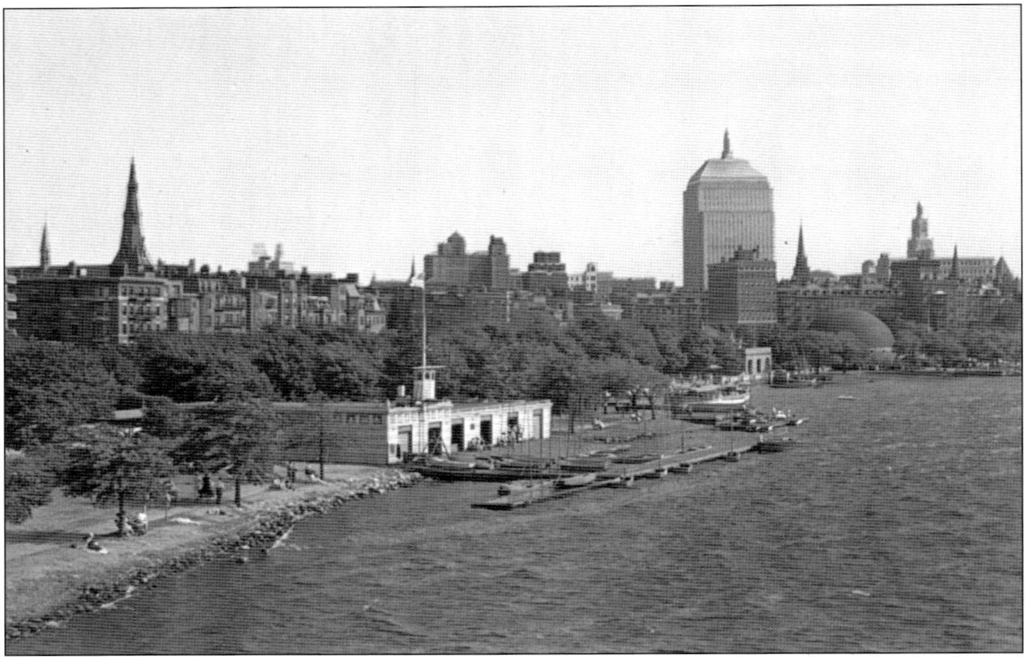

Seen in a commemorative postcard just after its dedication on June 28, 1941, the new boathouse of Community Boating is a proud addition to the James J. Storrow Memorial Embankment, as it was officially known, with wood docks projecting into the Charles River Basin.

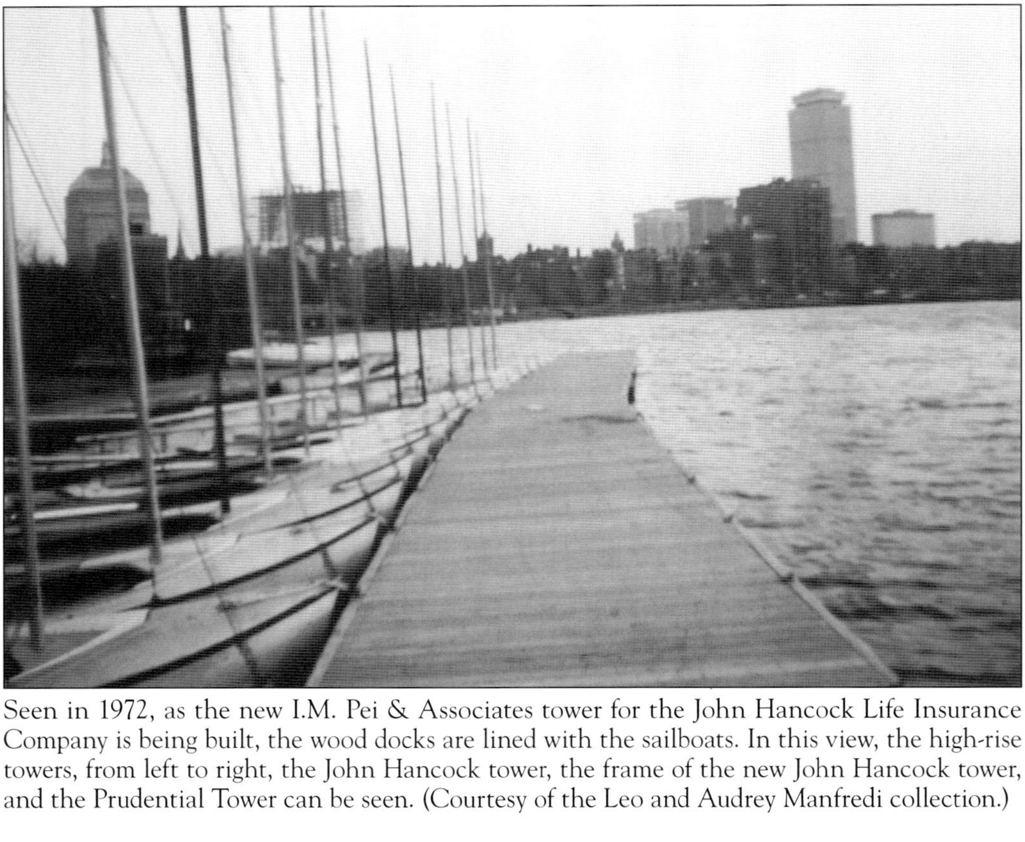

Seen in 1972, as the new I.M. Pei & Associates tower for the John Hancock Life Insurance Company is being built, the wood docks are lined with the sailboats. In this view, the high-rise towers, from left to right, the John Hancock tower, the frame of the new John Hancock tower, and the Prudential Tower can be seen. (Courtesy of the Leo and Audrey Manfredi collection.)

Seven

Shore School

Shore School has always been a popular six week class that demonstrated proper sailing techniques.

—Brendan O'Brien

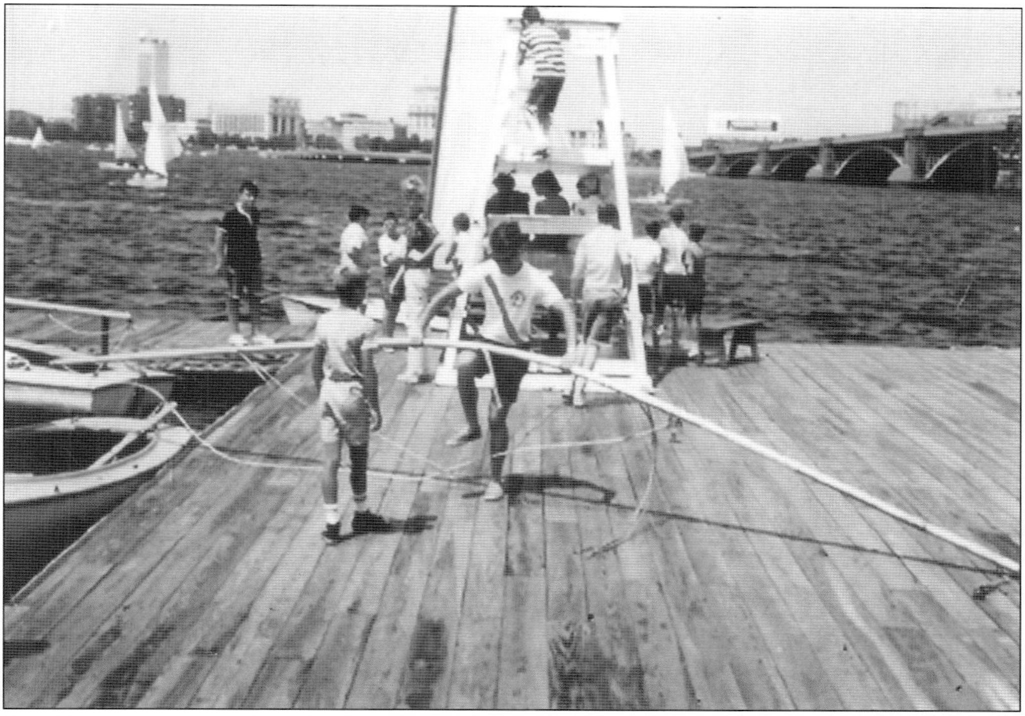

Dan Farren is seen in his Chicken Stripe T-shirt in the center working to straighten a mast while others keep an eye on the juniors sailing on the basin. (Courtesy of the Dan and Marilyn Farren collection.)

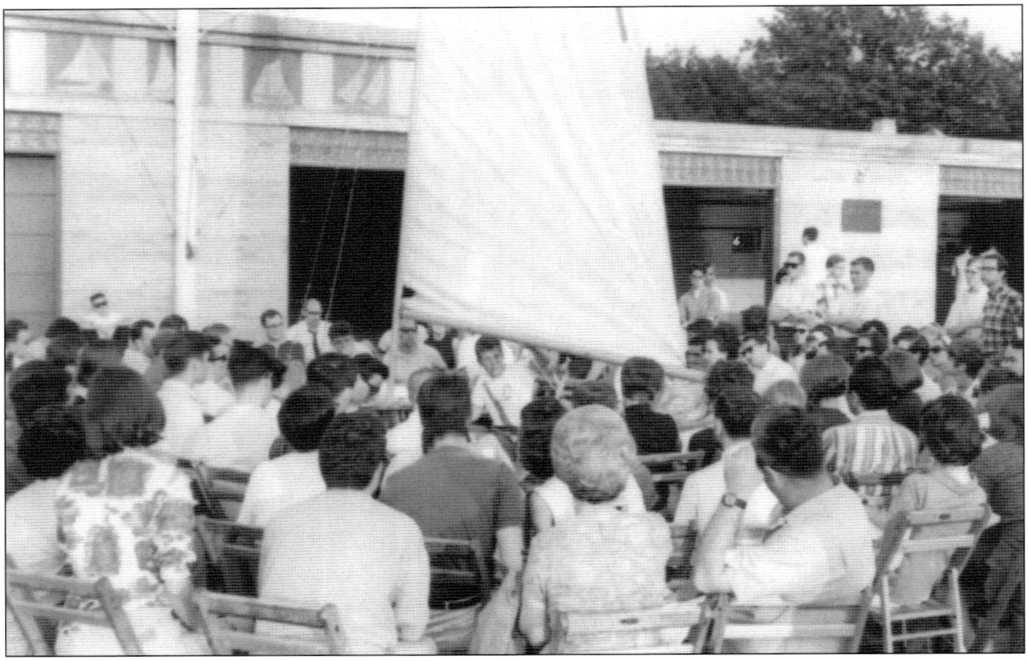

During the 1960s, the ever-popular Shore School was thronged with both potential as well as new members of Community Boating who attended these sessions to ensure that they gained much-needed skills. The courses would prepare new members to safely sail the sailboats. Seen conducting Shore School is Brendan O'Brien.

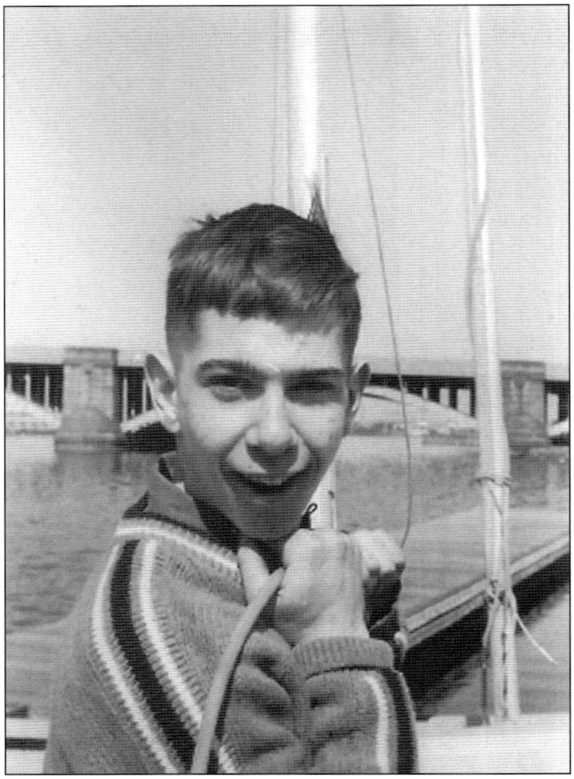

Often, Community Boating also offered refresher, tutored, or even custom instruction for individuals or even families to improve their sailing skills. Among those who were part of these classes was Kirk Siegfried, a junior member, seen in 1967 on the dock. (Courtesy of the Dan and Marilyn Farren collection.)

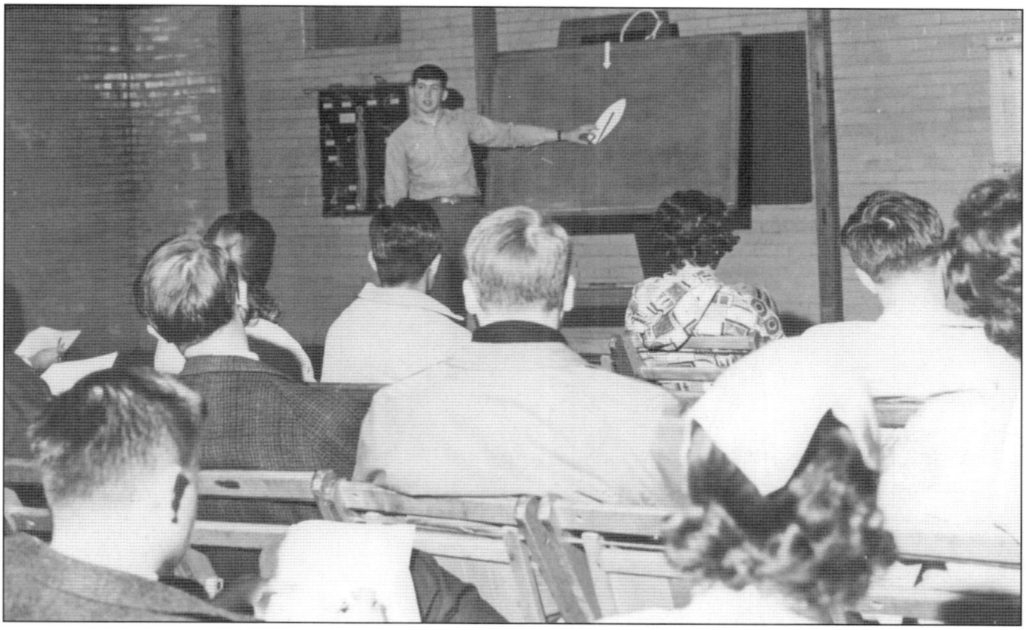

Steve Winkler was a popular teacher in the Shore School that Community Boating offered on a regular basis for sailors. Seen here in 1965, he was probably describing the aspects of boating on the Charles River Basin with a sailboat on the board. Whether it was learning to sail, orientation, rigging, Shore School, or one's first sail, it was stressed that safety was paramount. (Courtesy of the Leo and Audrey Manfredi collection.)

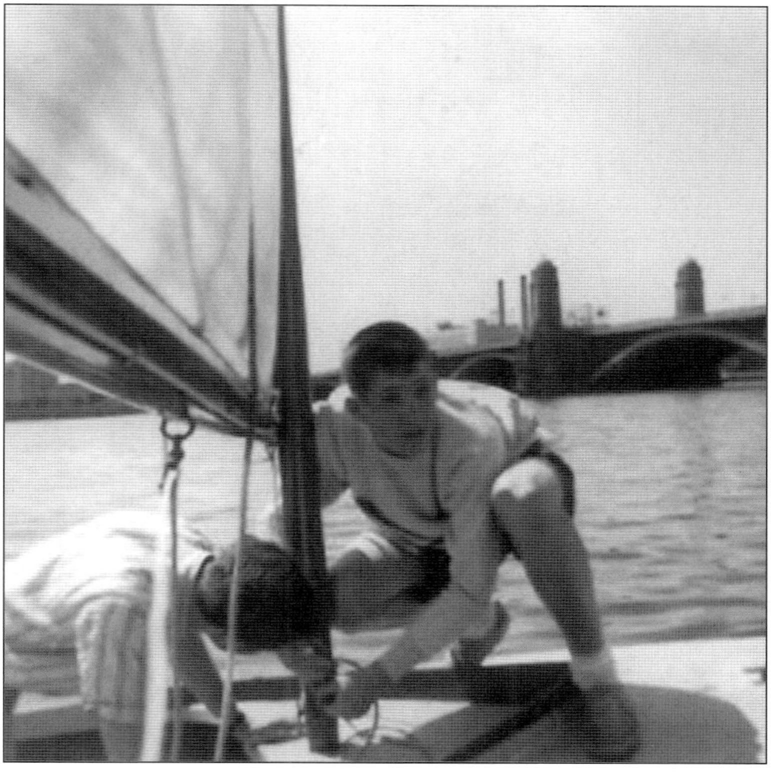

Steve Winkler, seen on the right, is teaching a junior member how to rig a sail in 1964. (Courtesy of the Dan and Marilyn Farren collection.)

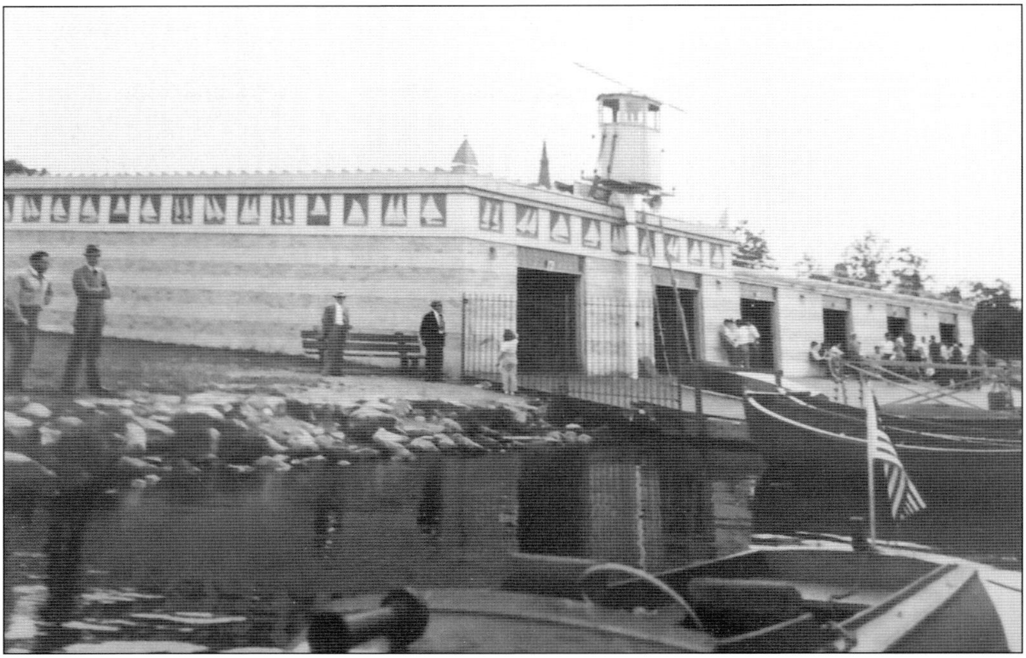

The Community Boating boathouse was a one-story building that had openings that led onto the wood docks. A decorative frieze of sailboats created an attractive decorative element just below the roof cornice that was a replica of mini-waves. Note the large rocks on the left, which were a river-edge breakaway. (Courtesy of the DCR.)

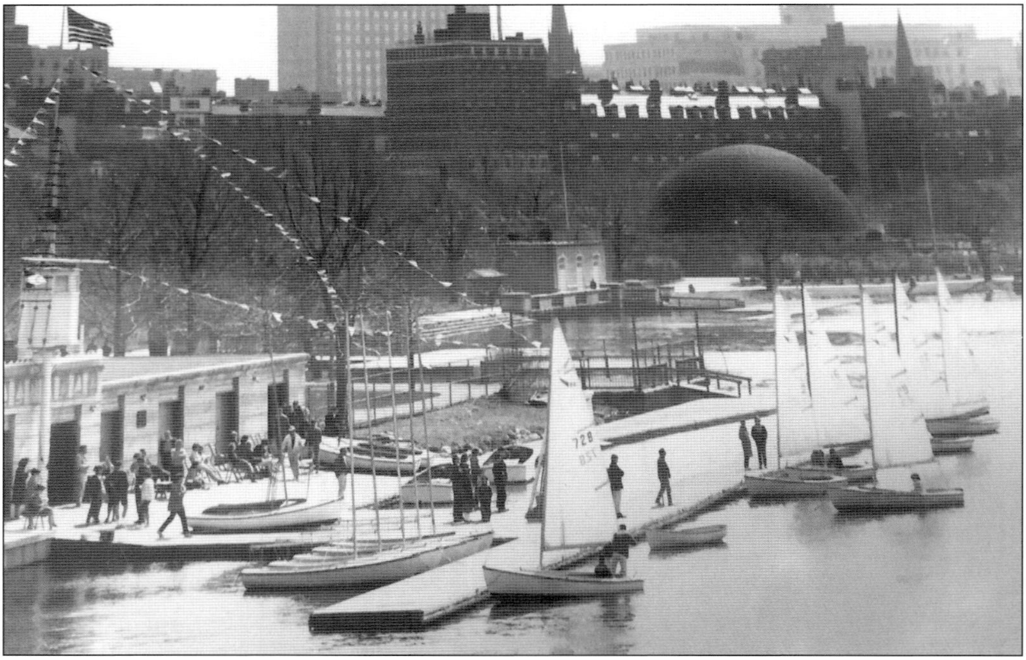

By the 1960s, the festive atmosphere of the Community Boating docks during the summer months was evident with the American flag flying from the flagpole surmounting the crow's nest, with flag bunting fluttering in the wind. Note the large number of people on the dock and the number of sailboats along the wood dock in the foreground.

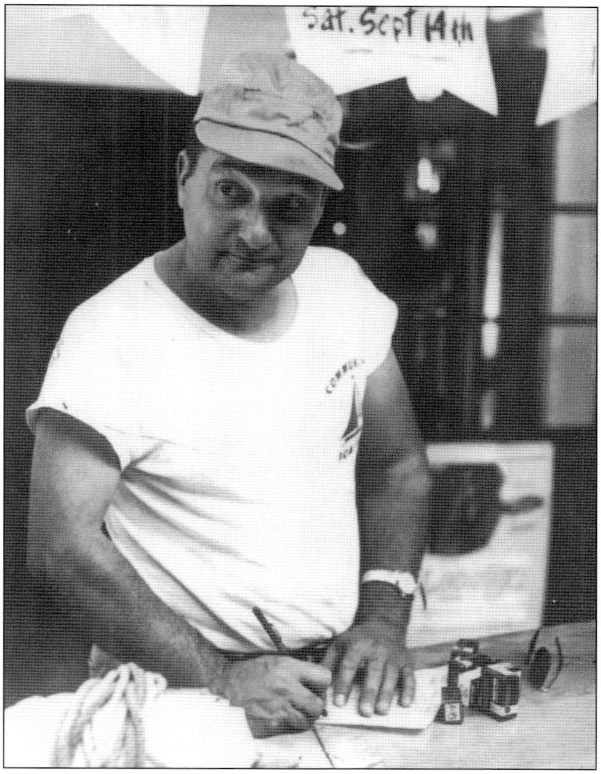

Leon Leonard "Leo" Manfredi was the manager of Community Boating from 1947 to 1972. He lived with his parents, Biaggio and Carmella Manfredi, as well as his five siblings, George, Anthony, Angela, Lucy, and Theresa, at 12 North Anderson Street in Boston's West End. Leo became the manager for a quarter of a century; he worked for 40 years for the City of Boston Parks and Recreation Department and was dedicated to Community Boating. (Courtesy of the Leo and Audrey Manfredi collection.)

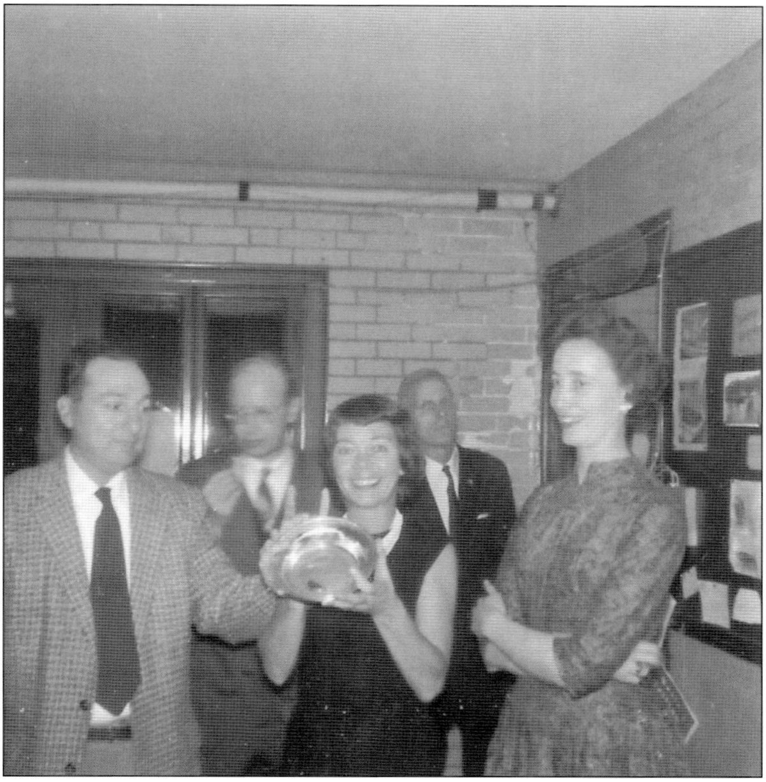

Office staff and volunteers at Community Boating are seen in 1960 with one of the silver trophies awarded at the many sailboat races sponsored on the Charles River Basin for both senior and junior members. Note the many silver trophies in the wall cabinets that were awarded at the many sailboat races sponsored on the Charles River Basin. (Courtesy of the Leo and Audrey Manfredi collection.)

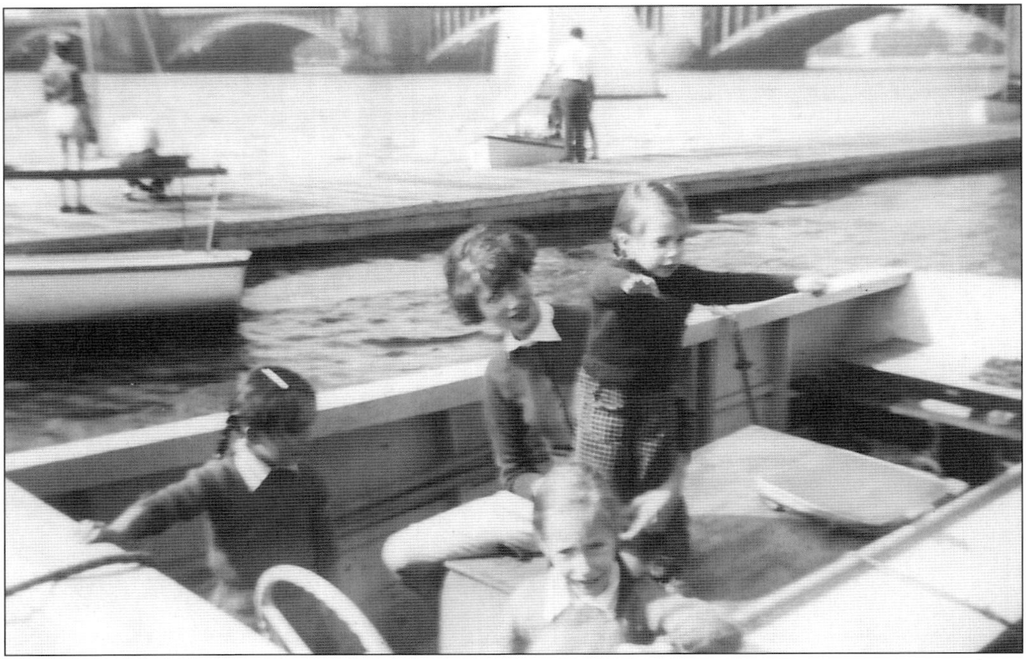

Not everyone was a junior member, let alone an adult member of Community Boating. Seen here is Judith Manfredi with her mother, Audrey MacDuffie Manfredi, sitting in a boat with Martha (left) and Deborah Manfredi in front at the steering wheel. (Courtesy of the Leo and Audrey Manfredi collection.)

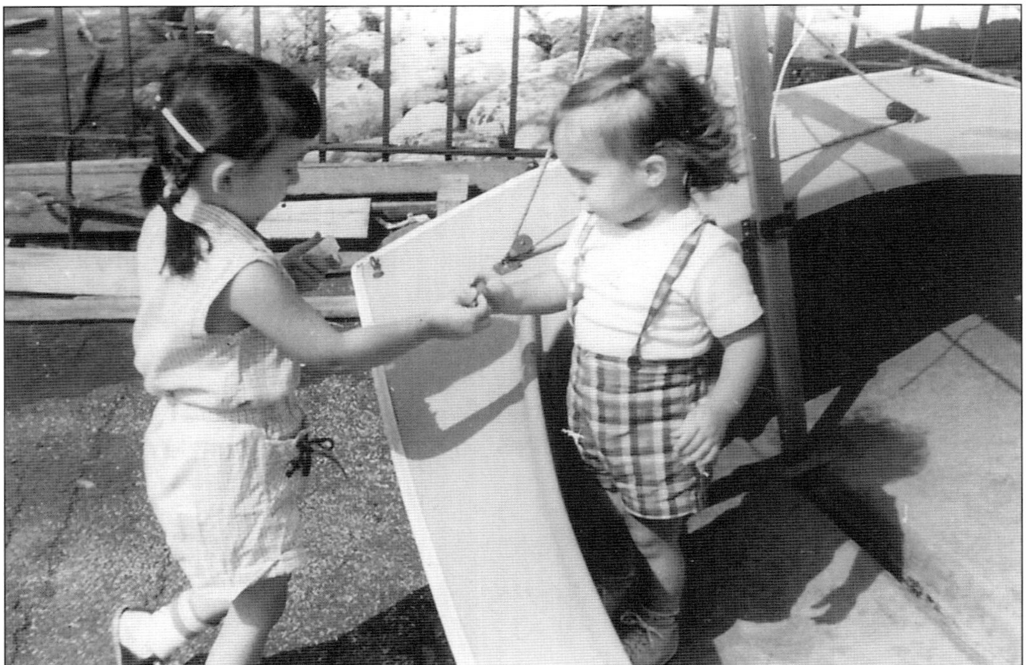

One was never too young to learn how to sail a boat. Judith and Martha (left) Manfredi had probably heard of Joseph Lee's book and had already been out sailing with their parents on the Charles River Basin. (Courtesy of the Leo and Audrey Manfredi collection.)

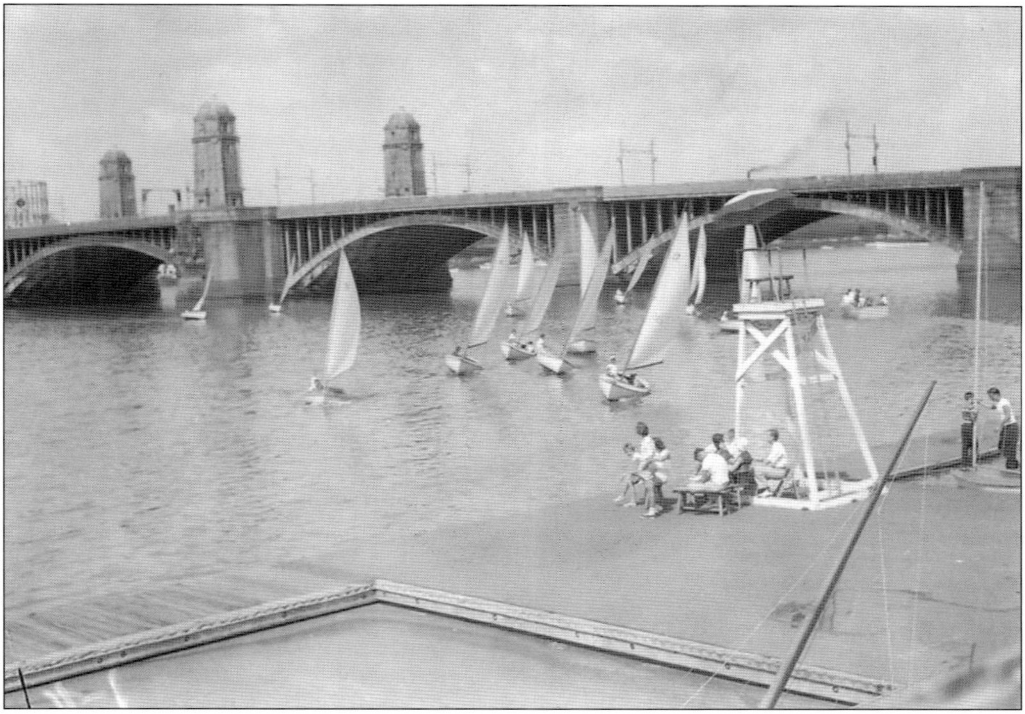

On a picture-perfect summer afternoon in the late 1950s, a group of junior members sit on the dock as a veritable fleet of sailboats sail toward them.

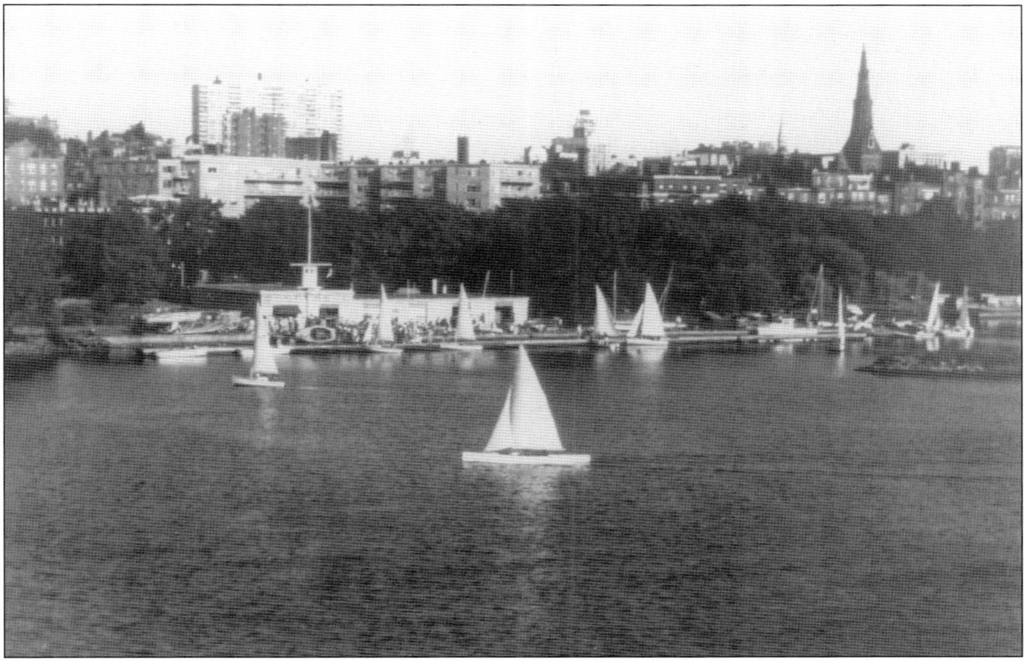

Seen in the early 1970s, the Community Boathouse almost seems dwarfed by the mature trees along the Esplanade. However, the number of people seen on the docks was tremendous. Rising above the boathouse, the River House and high-rise Tremont on the Common, both luxury apartment buildings that subsequently have been converted to condominiums, can be seen.

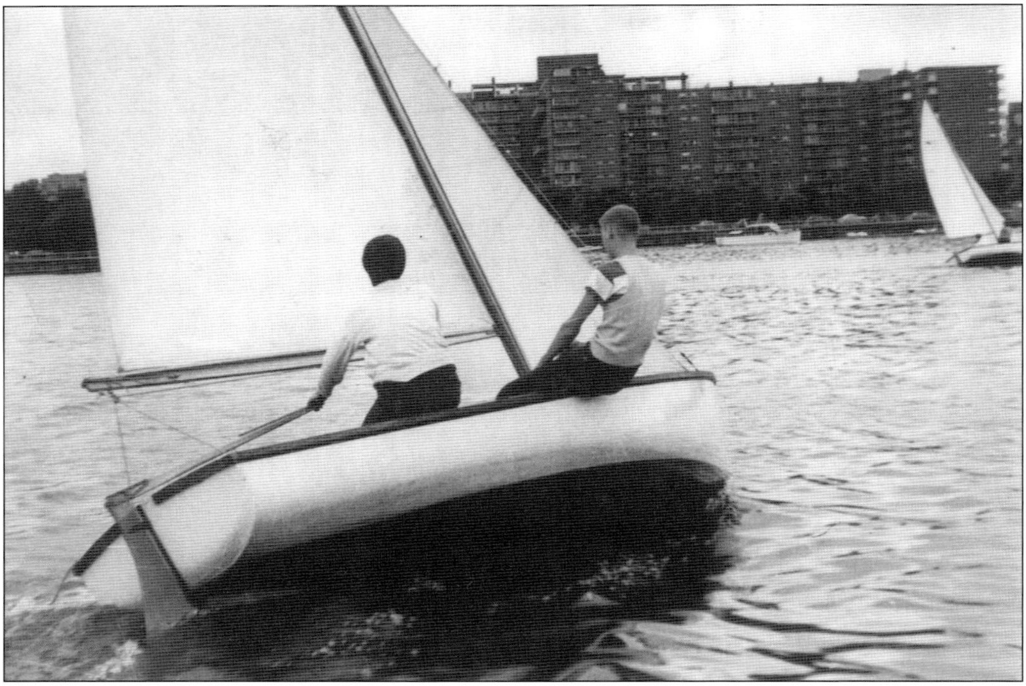

Two men sit on the starboard side of the sailboat as the wind tilts it. They are trying to come about by turning the sailboat to get the wind on the other side of it and point the boat into the wind during the turn.

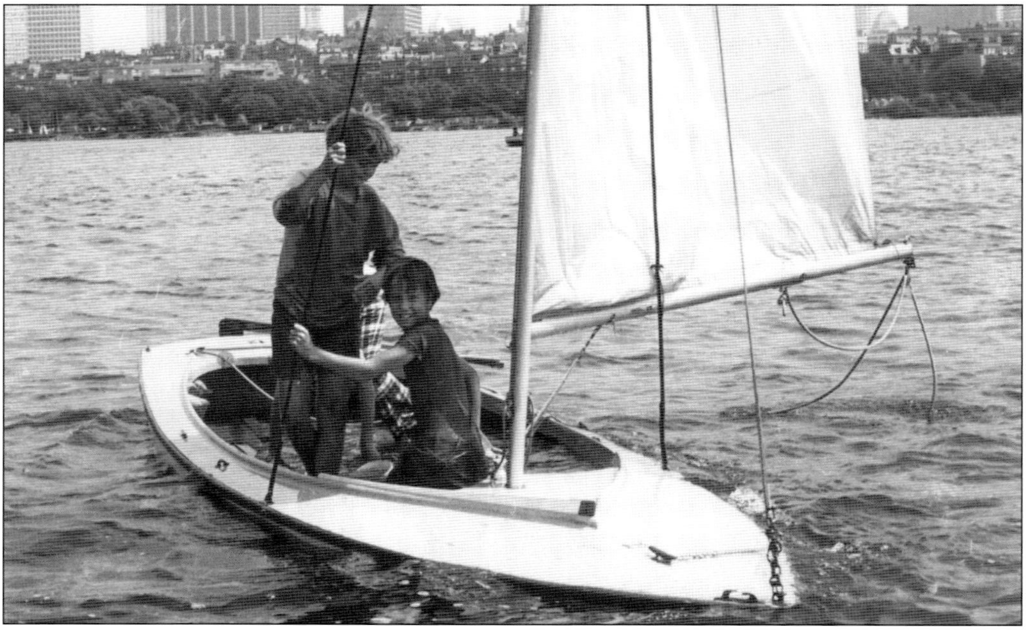

Two young boys are seen sailing on the Charles River Basin in the 1970s, with Boston's skyline framing the scene. High-rise office and apartment buildings dominate the skyline, but in the center, one can see the gilded dome of the Massachusetts State House, and just to the left is the Custom House Tower, once the tallest building in Boston until the Prudential Tower, built in the 1960s.

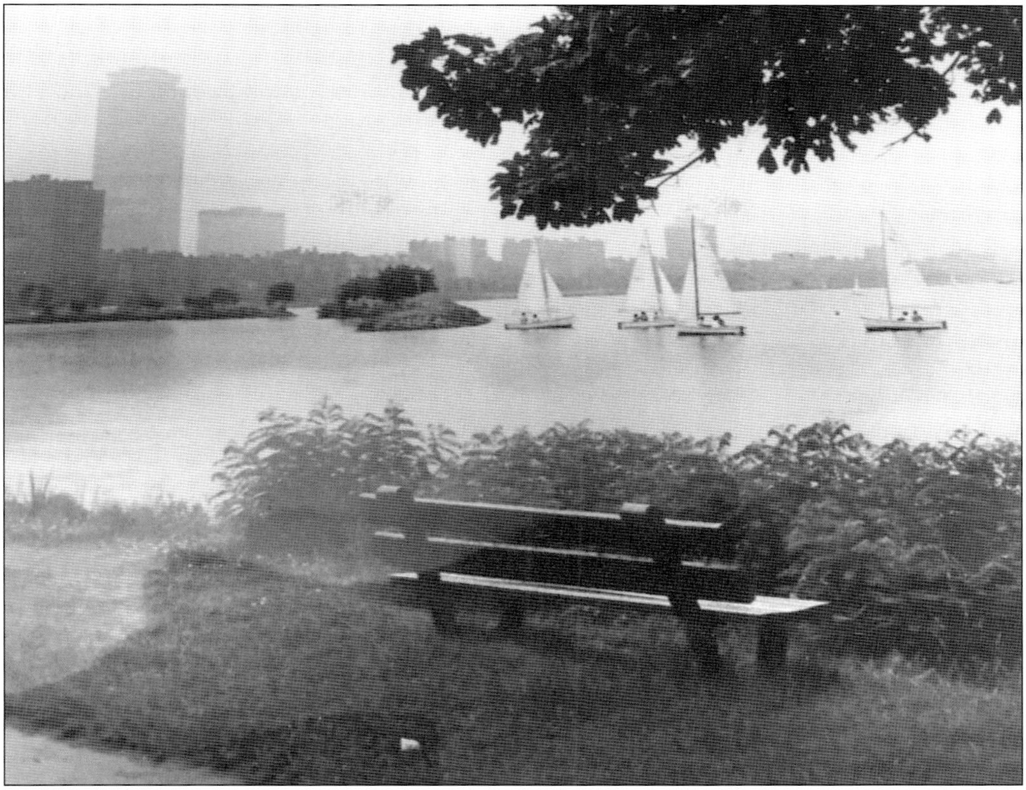

On a slightly foggy morning, the bucolic aspect of the Charles River Basin is obvious from this wood bench overlooking the water. Trees, green space along the Esplanade, and sailboats create a sublime vantage point to watch the scene.

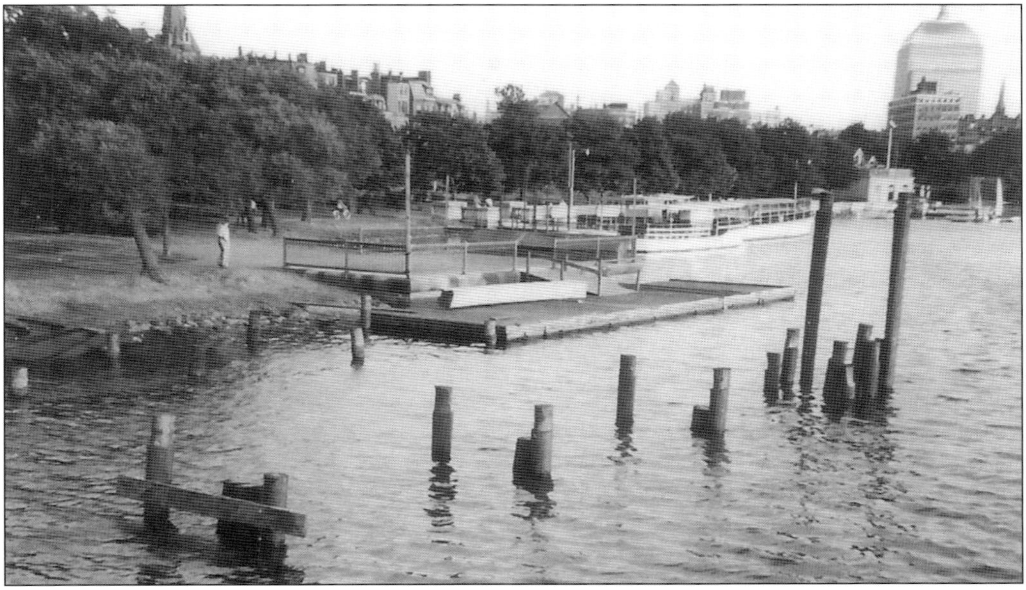

Wood docks were to be rebuilt to ensure safety as well as prevent deterioration to become a safety hazard. These wood pilings project up from the water, awaiting new docks. (Courtesy of the Leo and Audrey Manfredi collection.)

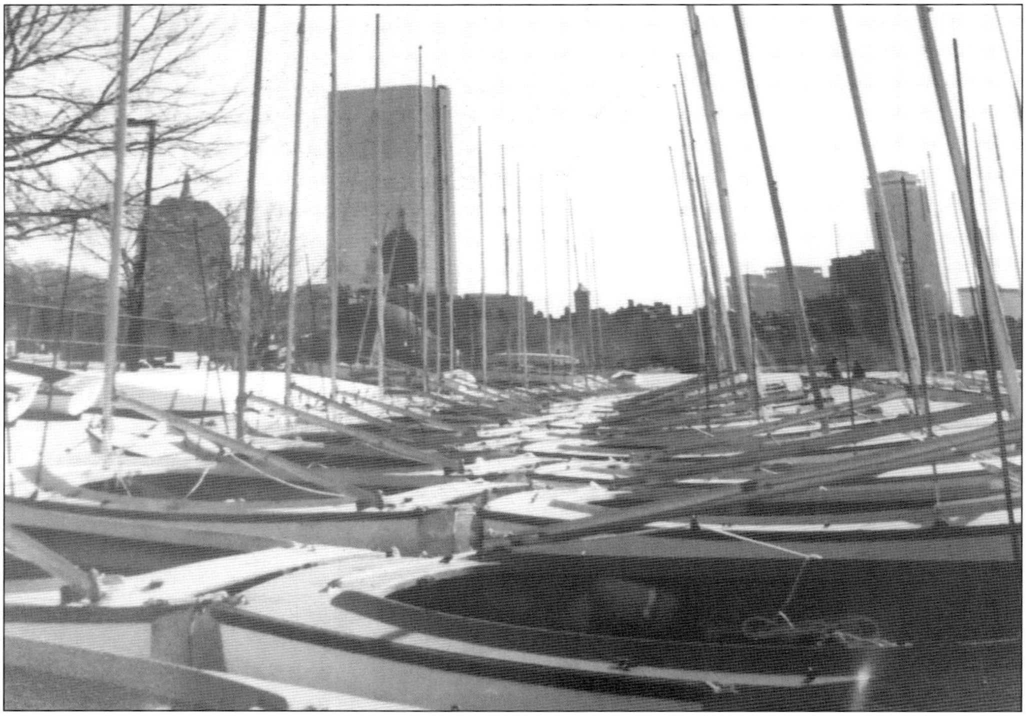

With sailboats lined along the docks with their masts projecting upward, this photograph shows the large number of sailboats in the 1980s.

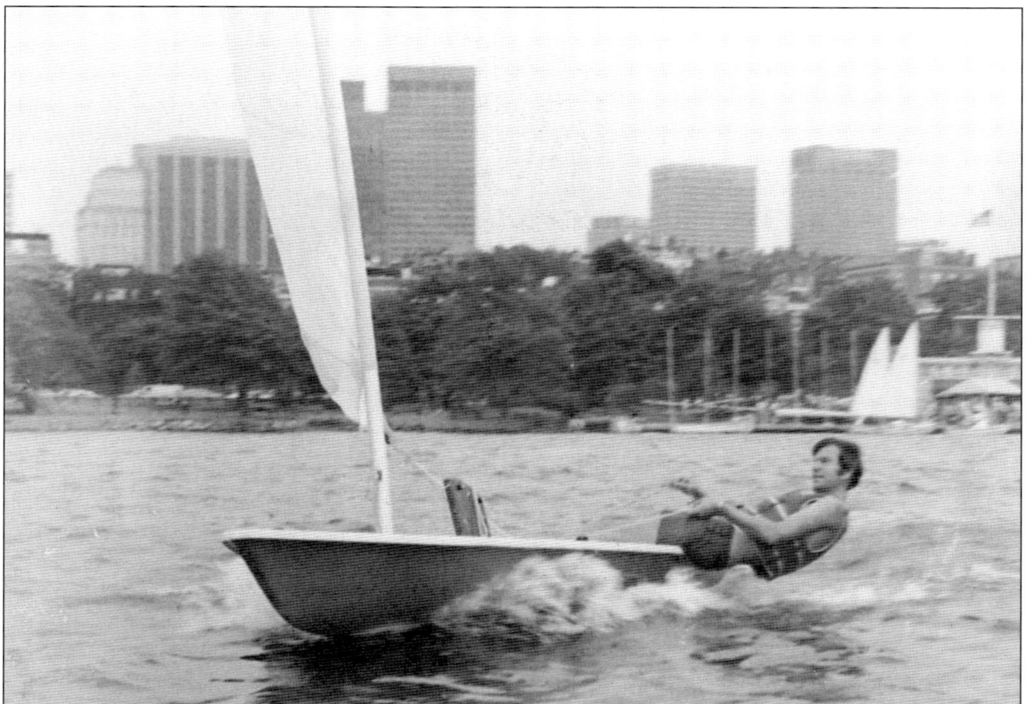

A laser boat is seen with a fearless sailor holding the top taught as he sails on the Charles River Basin in the 1960s.

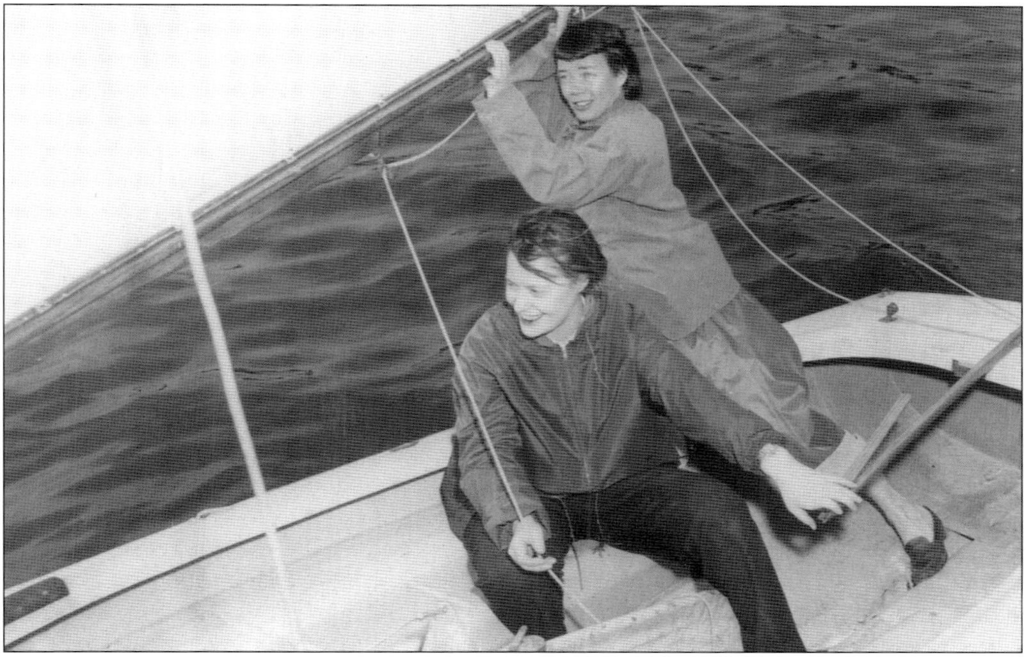

These two windswept women are obviously sailing in difficult circumstances, with one woman holding the wood tiller and the other on the boom under the sail as the wind catches the sail. These sailors need to know how to handle a jib, a spinnaker, the right-of-way rules, and parts of the boat, all of which were learned not just at Shore School but also by sailing.

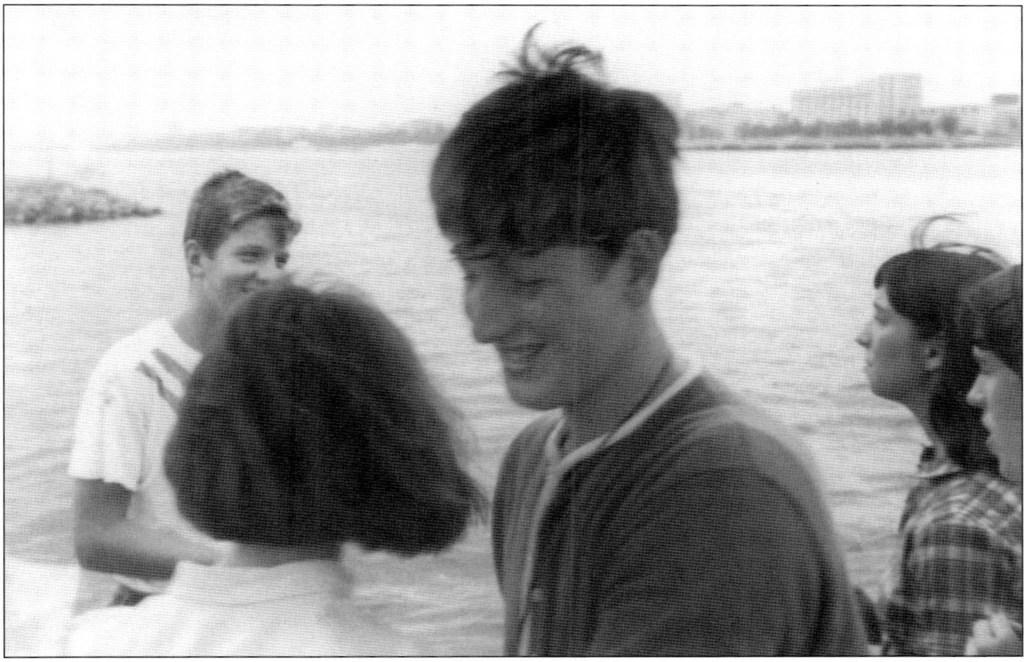

Brendan O'Brien (far left) is seen in the 1960s with (from left to right) Alice Redmond, Dan Winkler, Paula Parkas, and an unidentified Junior Program member on dock at Community Boating. Juniors were encouraged to get involved by offering sailing instructions, all the while enjoying the challenge of sailing. (Courtesy of Brendan O'Brien collection)

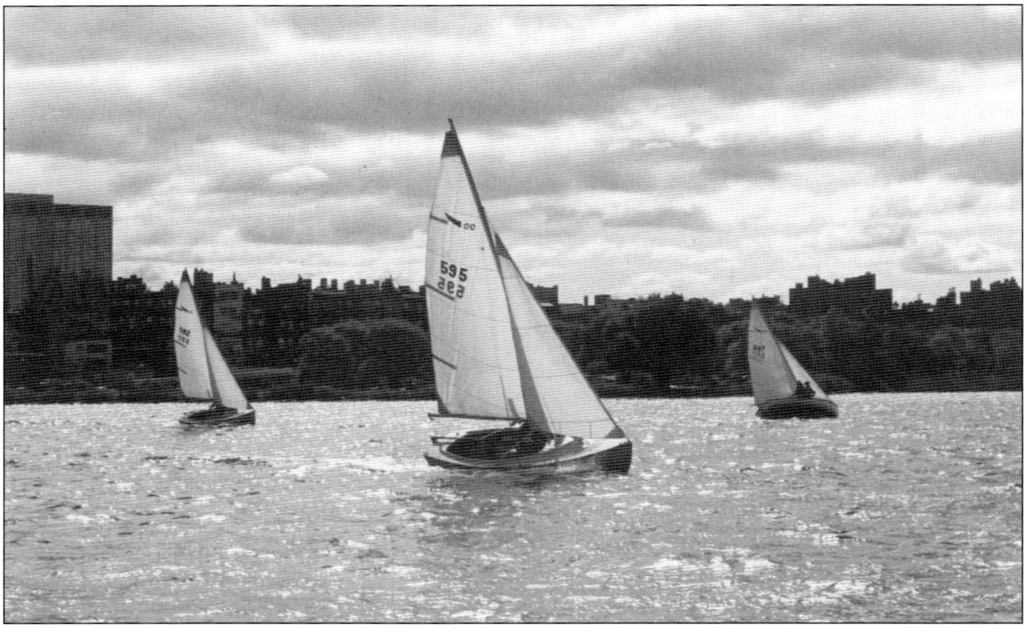

These three sailboats represent the iconic image of Boston's Charles River Basin. Stephen M. Kelleher remembered when he was a member that "Community Boating opened up a world to learn sailing at a minimal cost. It provided an opportunity to not only sail on the Charles but also to meet kids throughout Boston and to participate in a sport that is sometimes viewed only for the affluent."

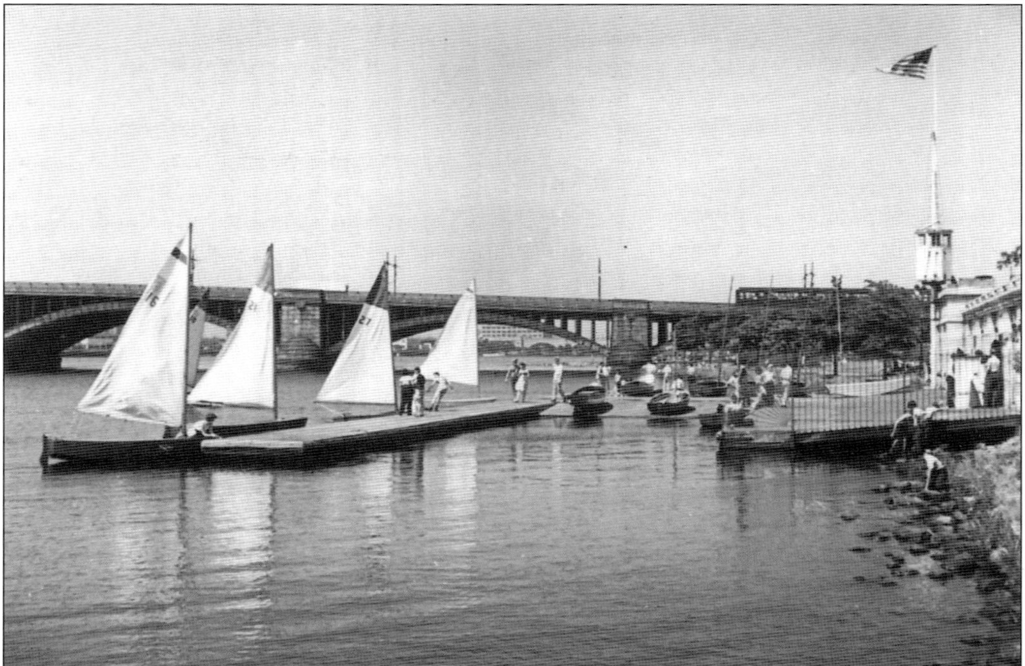

Looking toward the Longfellow Bridge in the 1960s, the sails on the sailboats on the left create an interesting panorama as sailors walk along the wood docks from the boathouse (far right). The daily activity at Community Boating started early in the morning and ended late at night.

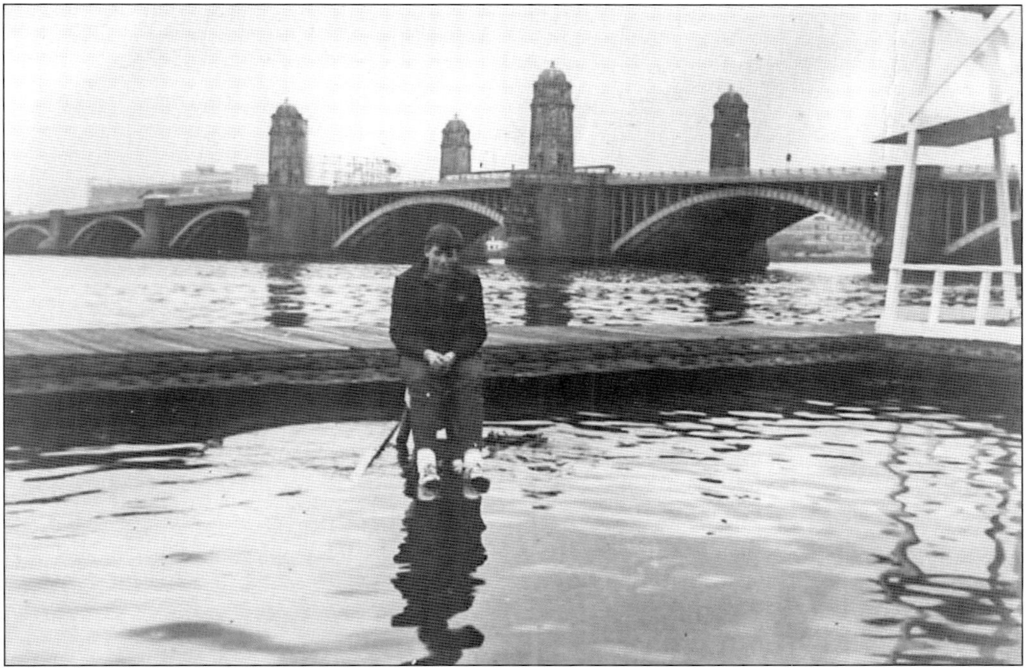

Dan Winkler sits on a buoy, looking like he is literally sitting on water. In all seasons, Community Boating takes on many different aspects, but here in the late fall, just before the winter, the boats have been prepared and stored for the long winter months, and the wood docks are empty of activity. (Courtesy of Dan and Marilyn Farren collection.)

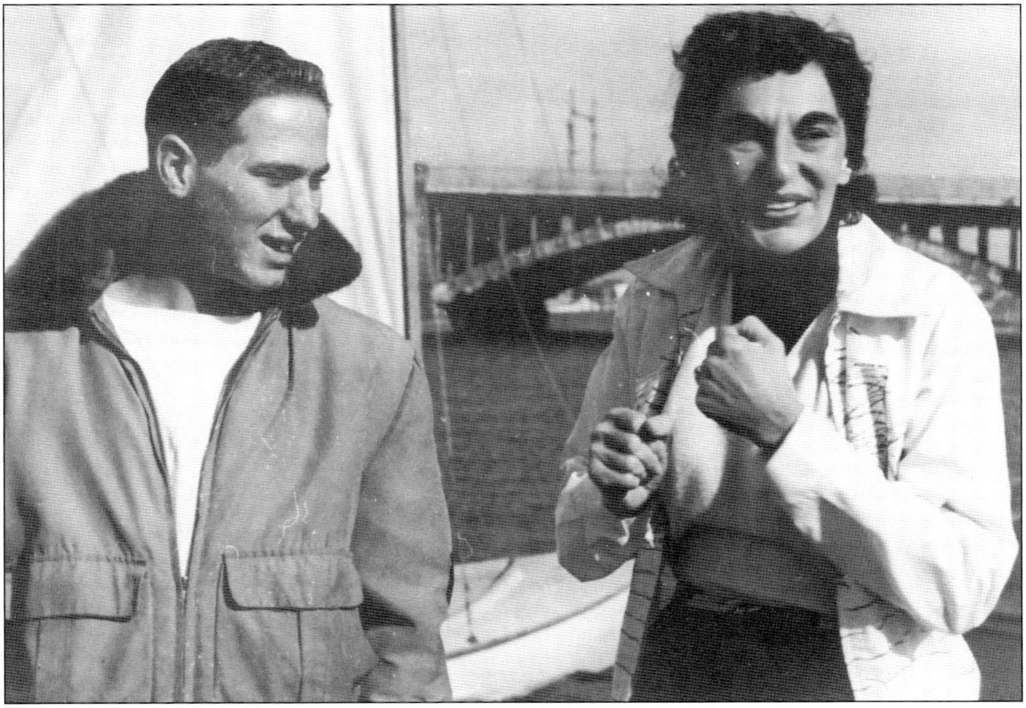

Joe Gordon, seen left, an able dockmaster of Community Boating, is seen here having a conversation with an unidentified member. (Courtesy of the Leo and Audrey Manfredi collection.)

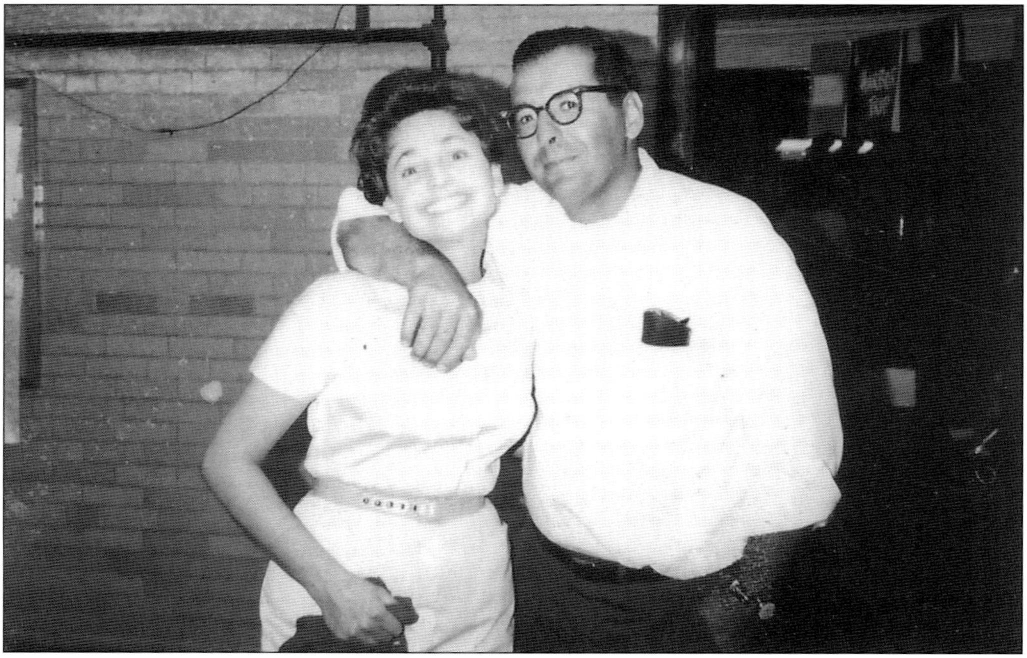

Ellie Rupp and Jack Koffman smile for the camera in the 1960s. Koffman was a popular dockmaster at Community Boating in the 1960s and became an educator in Boston; his personal comment on the Junior Sailing Program was "Heaven help the dockmasters!" (Courtesy of the Leo and Audrey Manfredi collection.)

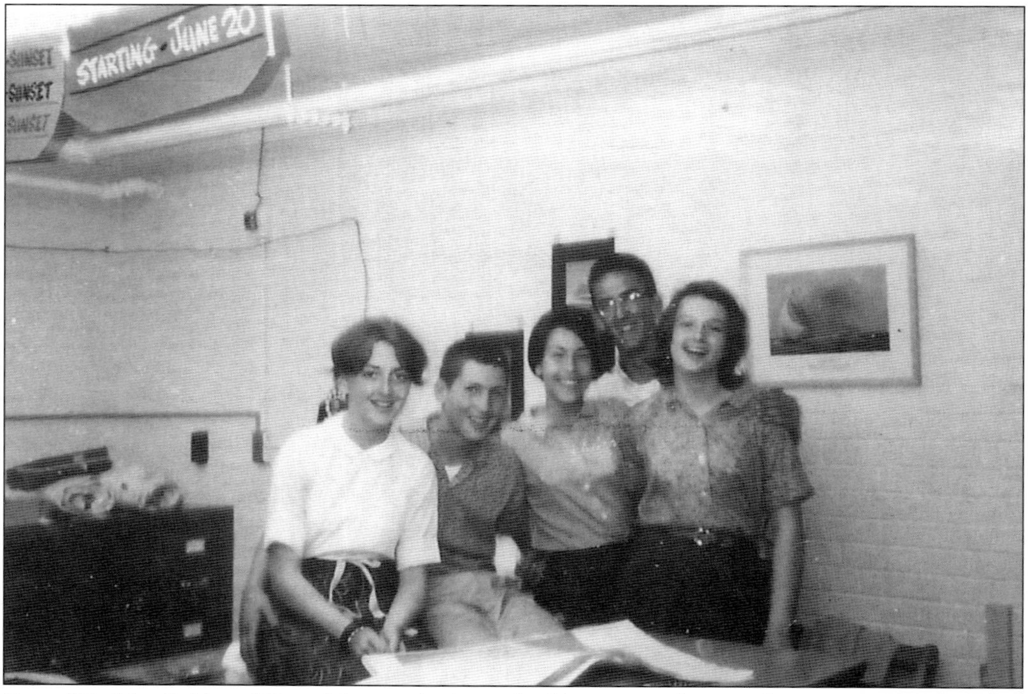

Steve Winkler (left) and Dave Hanson (right, in back) are seen along with a group of unidentified young volunteers in the office of Community Boating in the 1960s. The sign on the upper left says that Junior Program started June 20. (Courtesy of the Leo and Audrey Manfredi collection.)

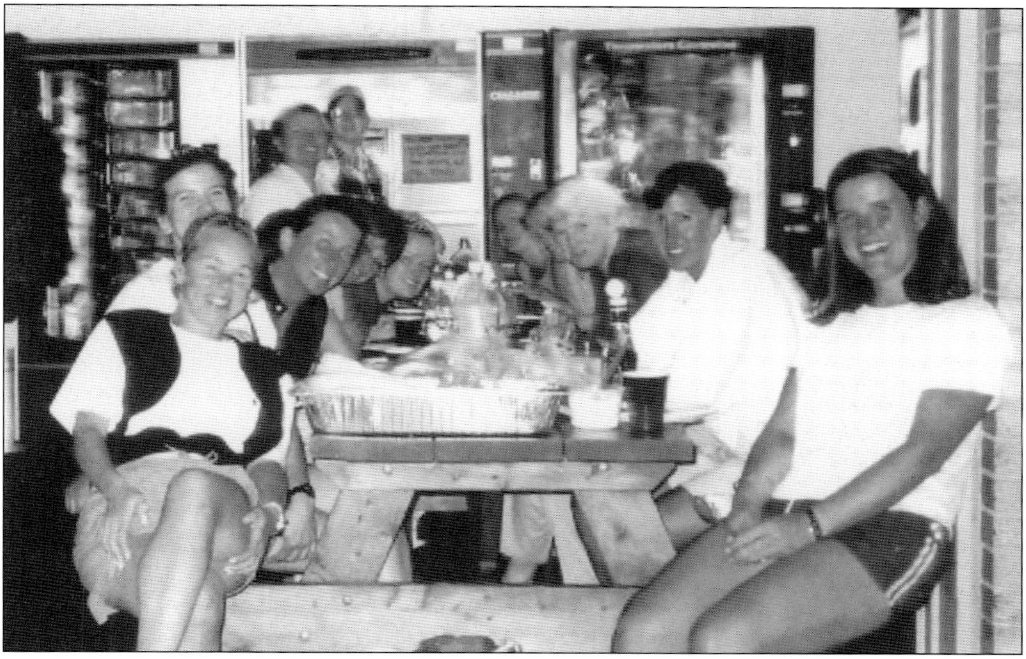

A smiling group of women enjoy an alfresco meal at a picnic table at Community Boating after an early evening sail. Often, the sense of camaraderie and friendship that is derived from being an active member of the boat club is a major reason why so many retain their membership and become supporters of the many programs and activities.

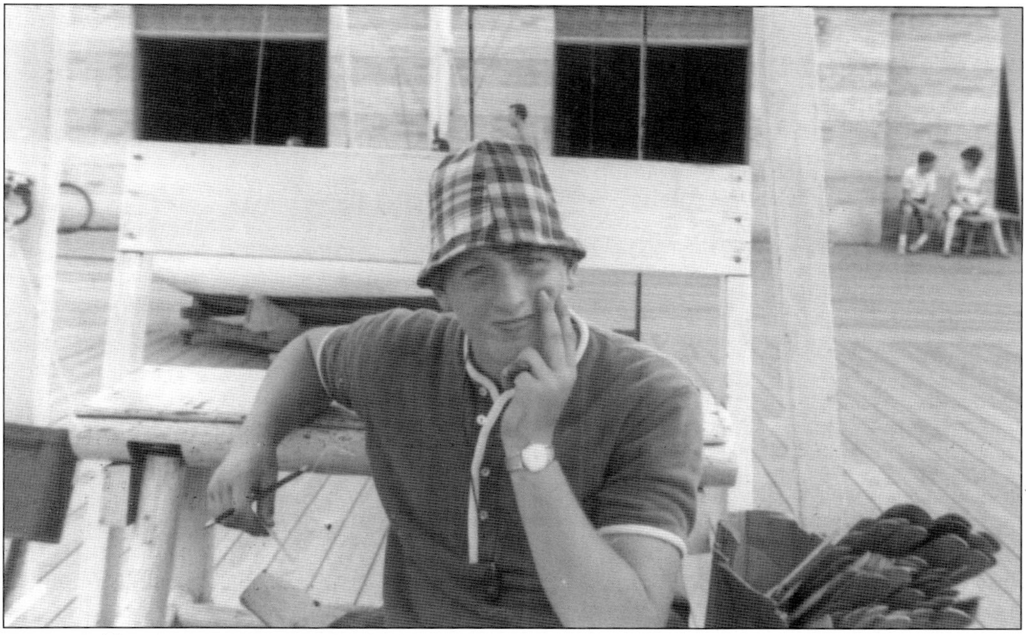

Dan Winkler is seen sitting on the dockmaster's tower at Community Boating as if in deep thought, all the while contemplating his future. A dockmaster, he married Deborah Manfredi, the daughter of Leo and Audrey Manfredi, and became a supporter of this book on Community Boating by loaning numerous candid family photographs of the 1940s through the 1970s. (Courtesy of the Leo and Audrey Manfredi collection.)

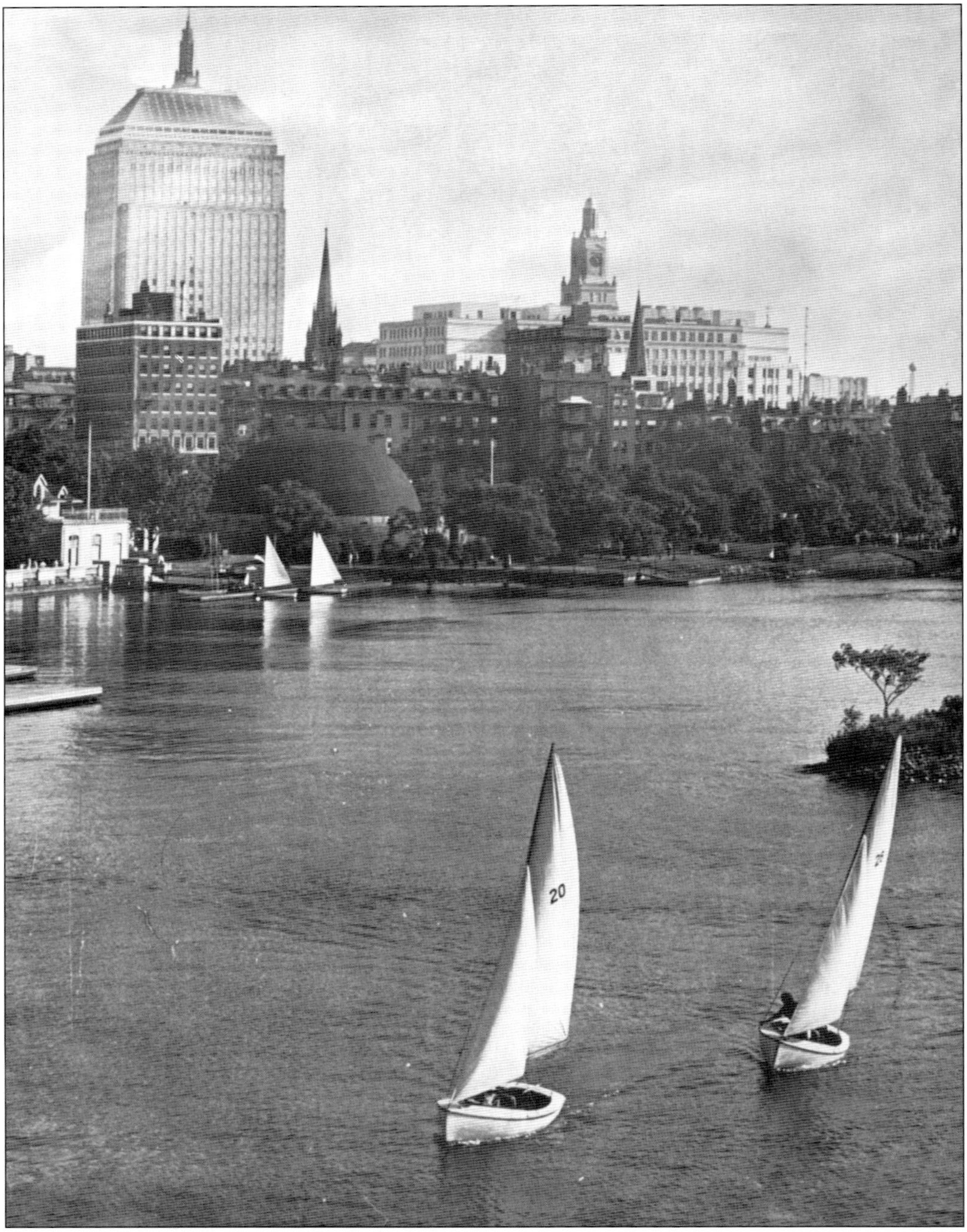

The Charles River Basin, since the late 1930s, has long attracted the attention of Bostonians with its panoramic views of both Boston and Cambridge on both sides of the river. The sailboats in the foreground can be seen on the water from all vantage points, with the Back Bay of Boston skyline in the distance. The boathouse of Community Boating can be seen on the far left.

Eight

THE ICON OF BOSTON

Community Boating opened up a world to learn sailing at a minimal cost.

—Stephen M. Kelleher

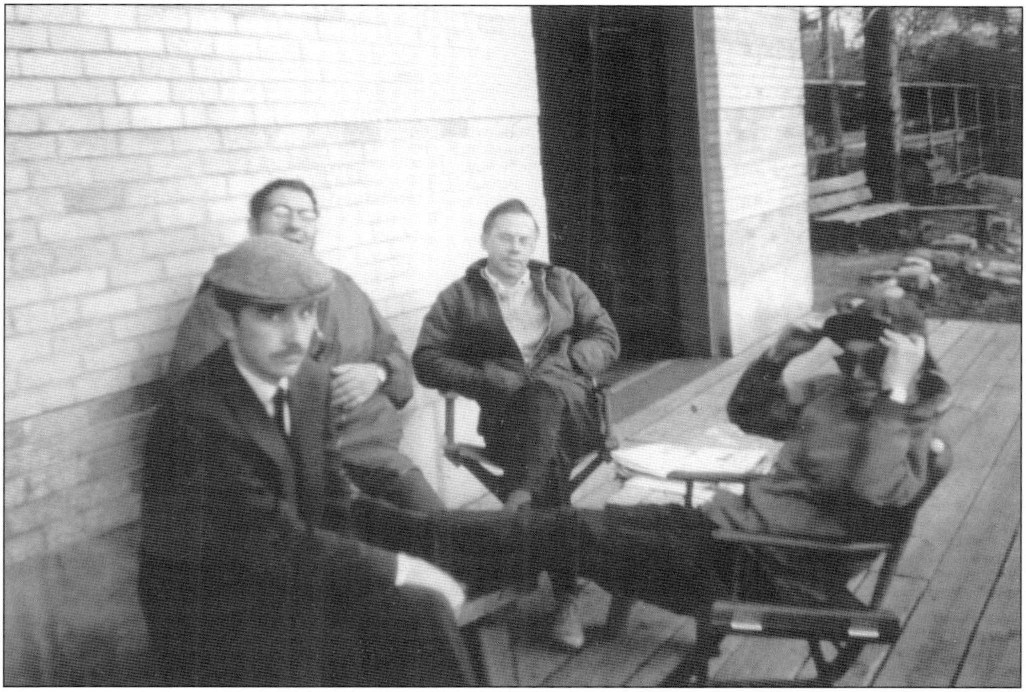

Community Boating has evolved from a sailing club started by Joseph Lee in the 1930s for the youth of Boston's West End but has evolved over the decades to become an inclusive and welcoming club for adults and juniors, offering universal access. Seen relaxing on the dock, from left to right are unidentified (in a scally cap), Marty Nakashian, Bob Brown, and Art Ashley. (Courtesy of the Leo and Audrey Manfredi collection.)

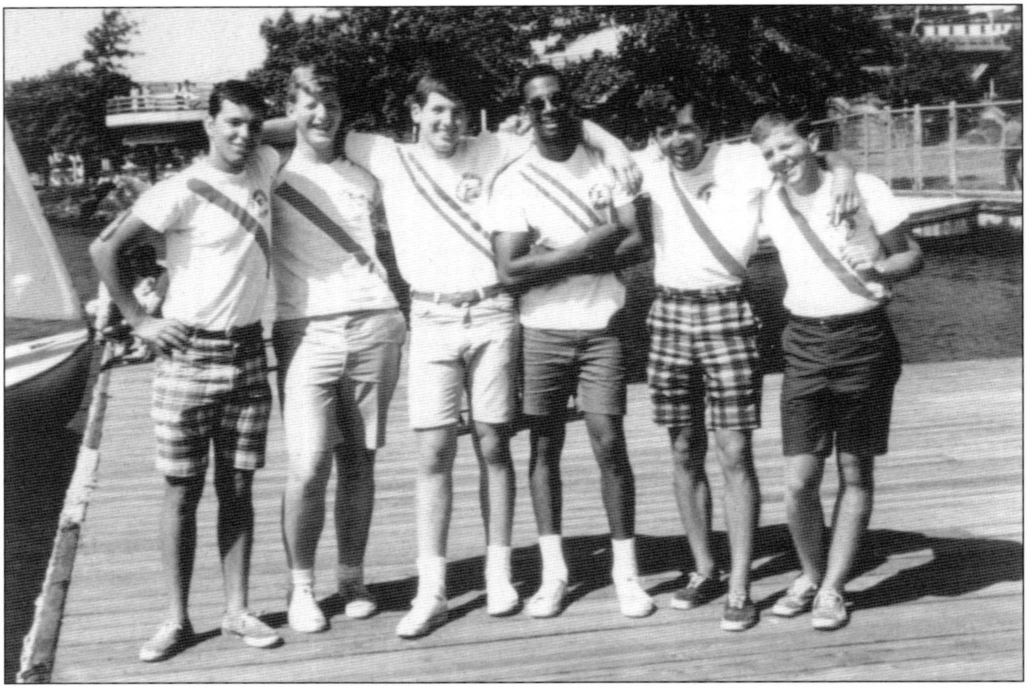

These young boys with a Chicken Stripe on their T-shirts are, from left to right, are Danny Farren, Dan Winkler, Steve Winkler, Bill Hazlewood, Eddie McGovern, and Brendan O'Brien. (Courtesy of the Leo and Audrey Manfredi collection.)

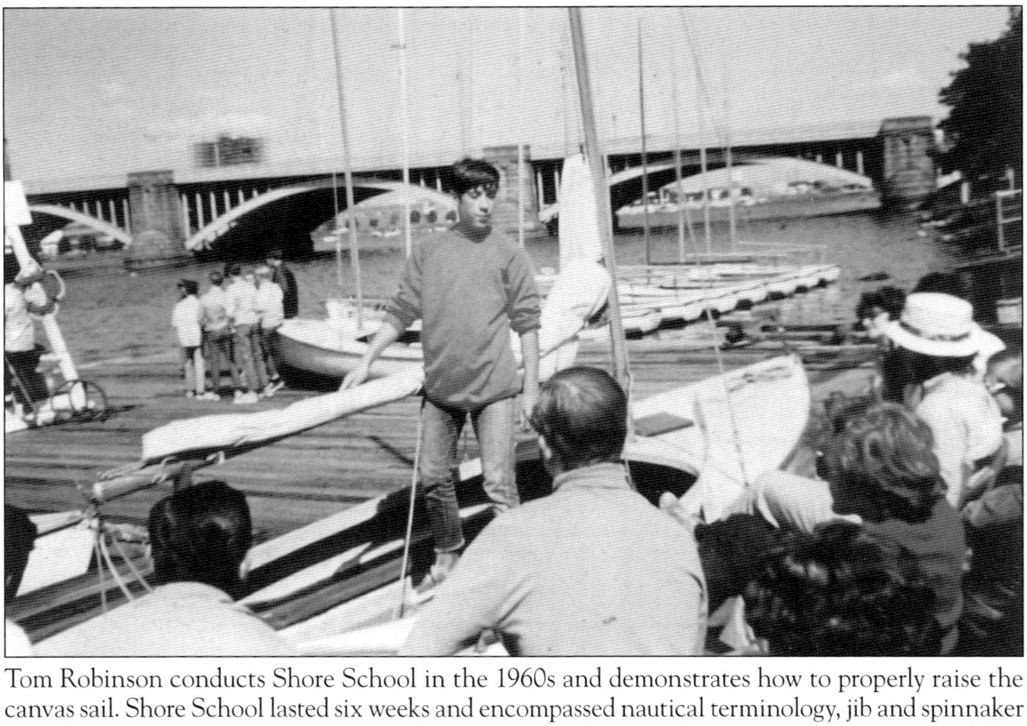

Tom Robinson conducts Shore School in the 1960s and demonstrates how to properly raise the canvas sail. Shore School lasted six weeks and encompassed nautical terminology, jib and spinnaker handling, whipping, knot tying, and splicing. Though daunting for new members, it was said that with their rating comes its privileges. (Courtesy of Brendan O'Brien collection)

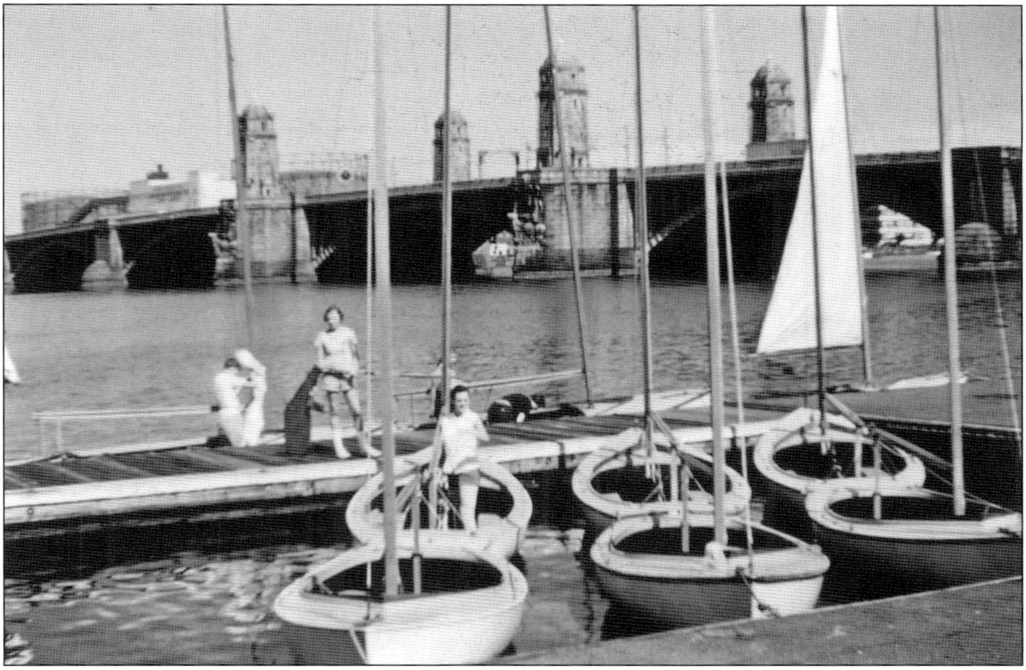

A group of members are seen on the dock as they prepare the sailboats for an afternoon of sailing. The tall masts are seen in front of the pepper pots of the Longfellow Bridge. Designed by Edmund March Wheelwright and dedicated in 1907, the bridge has four large piers that are ornamented with the prows of Viking ships, carved in granite, which refers to a purported voyage by Leif Eriksson up the Charles River. (Courtesy of the Leo and Audrey Manfredi collection.)

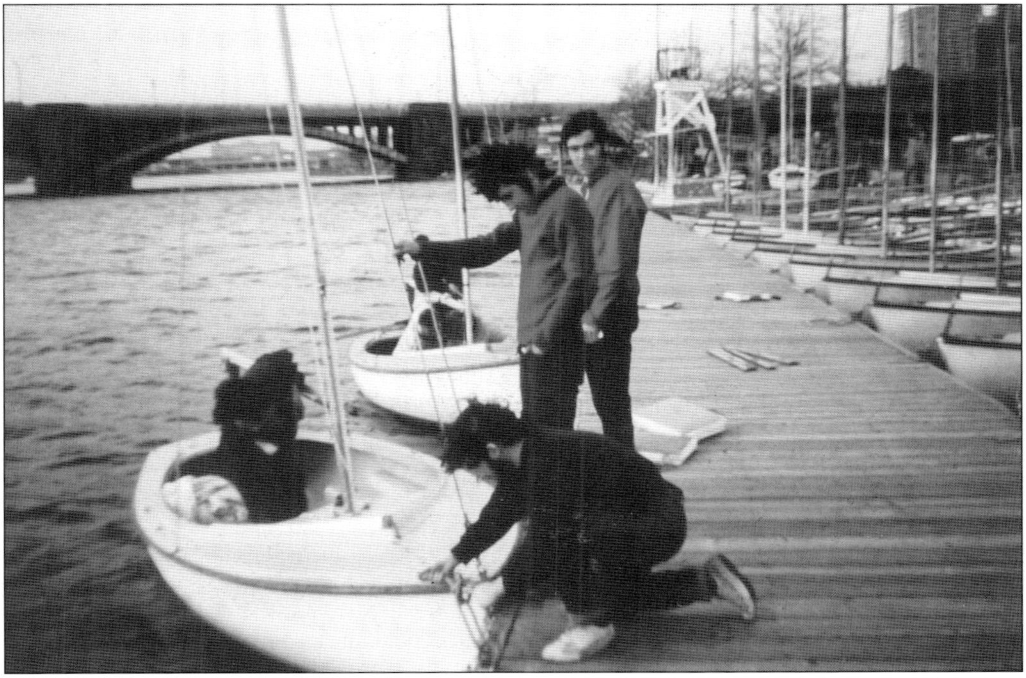

A young instructor explains the sailboat and its components. (Courtesy of the Leo and Audrey Manfredi collection.)

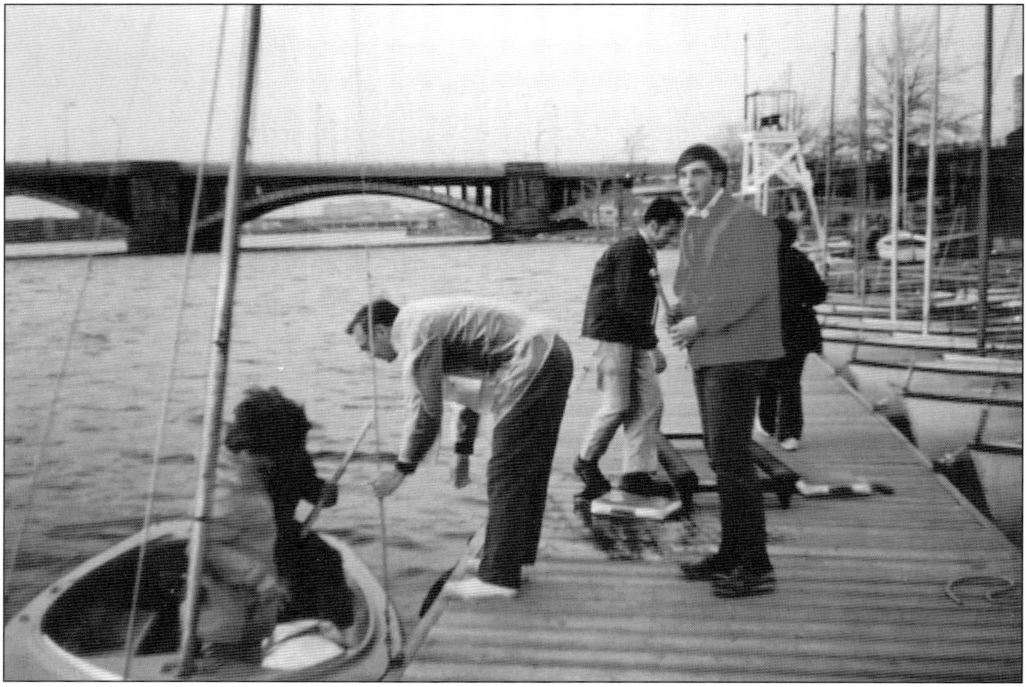

Leo Manfredi said in the early 1960s that "1,500 juniors and between 1,400 and 1,500 seniors are using the club's 44 Cape Cod Mercury Sloops, 15½-footers that have a mainsail, jib and spinnaker." Seen bending toward the sailboat is Danny Farren as Steve Hanaberry faces the camera, with activity on the dock. (Courtesy of the Leo and Audrey Manfredi collection.)

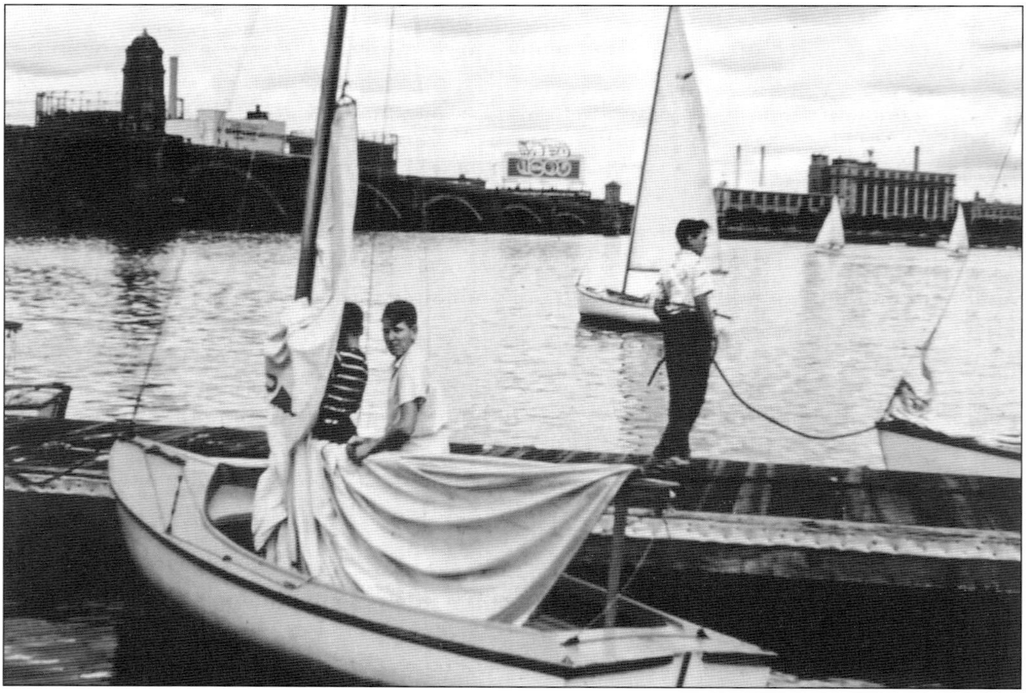

Looking toward the top of the mast, Junior Program members pull the rope that raises the canvas sail, allowing him to sail. (Courtesy of the Leo and Audrey Manfredi collection.)

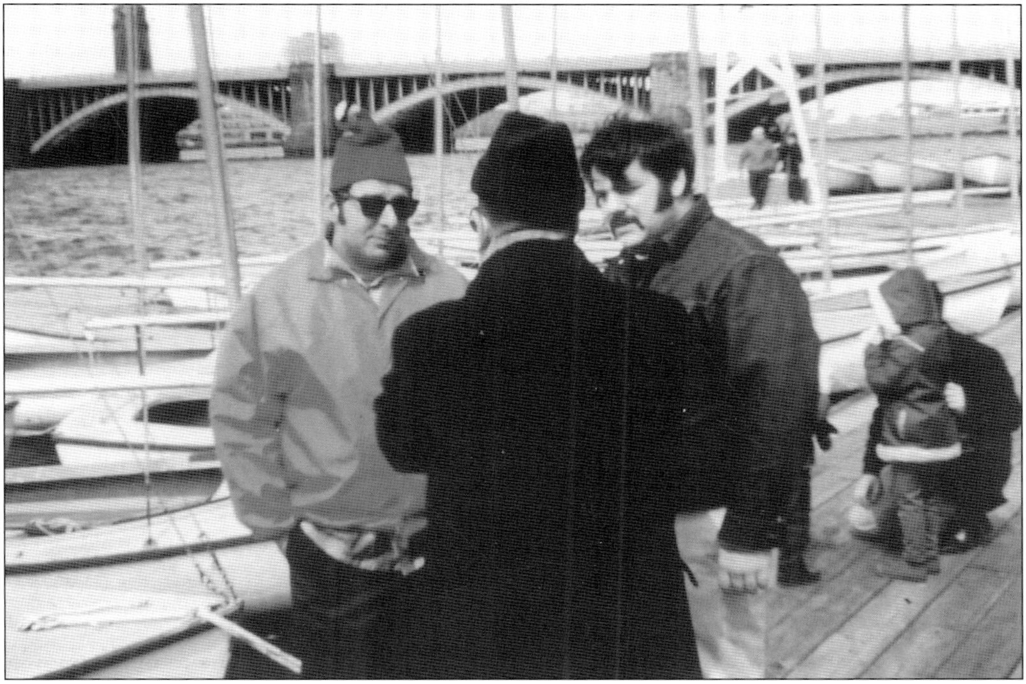

Having a conversation on the boat dock in the 1960s are Jack Koffman (left) and Louis Goldstein on the right. College professor Dan Rudman has his back to the camera. (Courtesy of the Leo and Audrey Manfredi collection.)

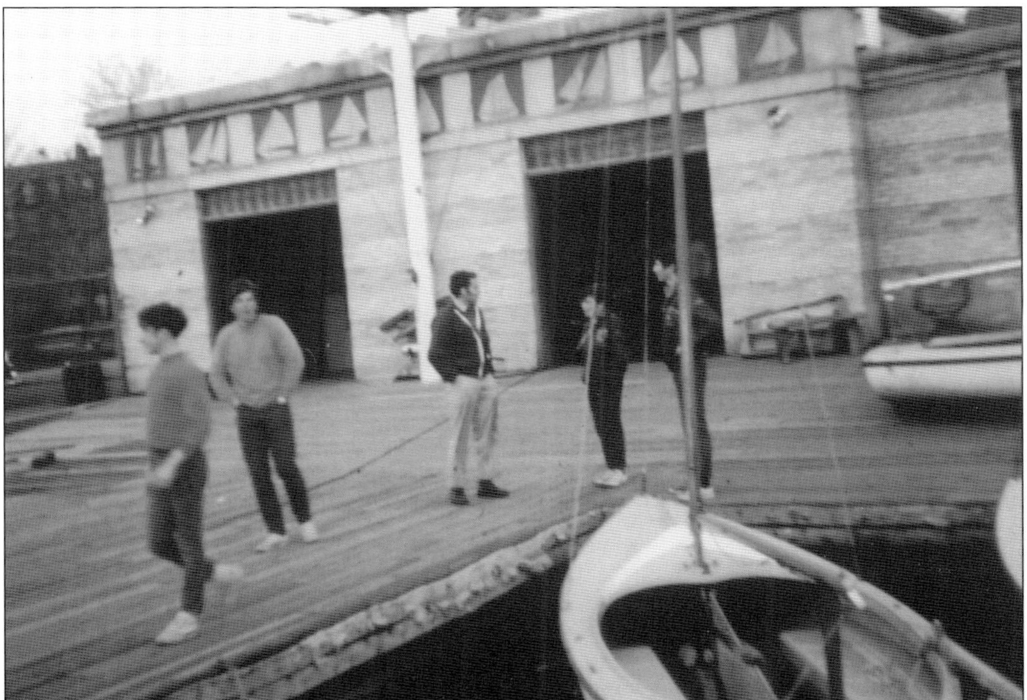

A group of members walk along the dock with a sailboat moored at the edge in the 1960s. (Courtesy of the Leo and Audrey Manfredi collection.)

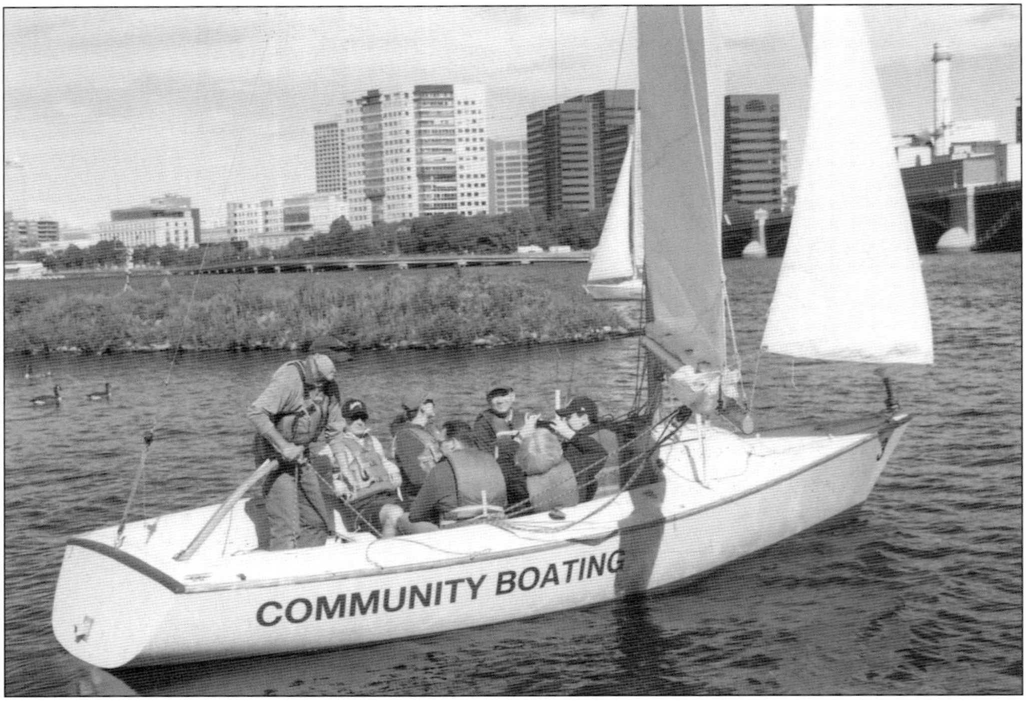

A group of Community Boating members sail into the Charles River Basin, with the leader manning the tiller on the left. They often had a thoroughly enjoyable time but were unhappy when "Bunna Bob's mellow tomes announced the end of sailing" at the end of the day.

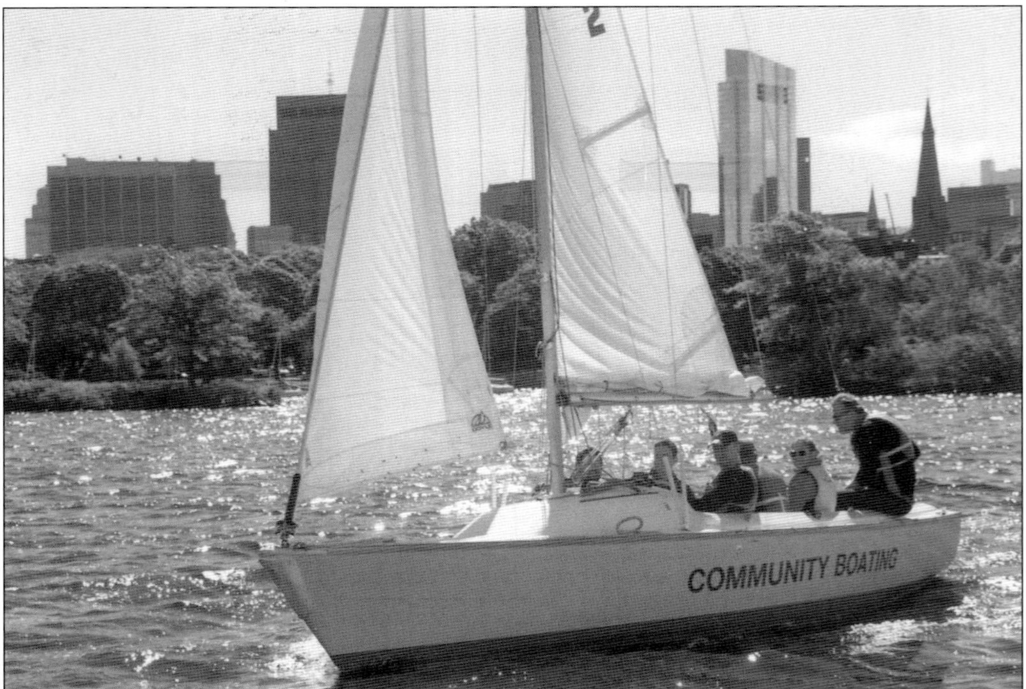

Seated in a sailboat are members of Community Boating on a perfect summer afternoon with sparkling water.

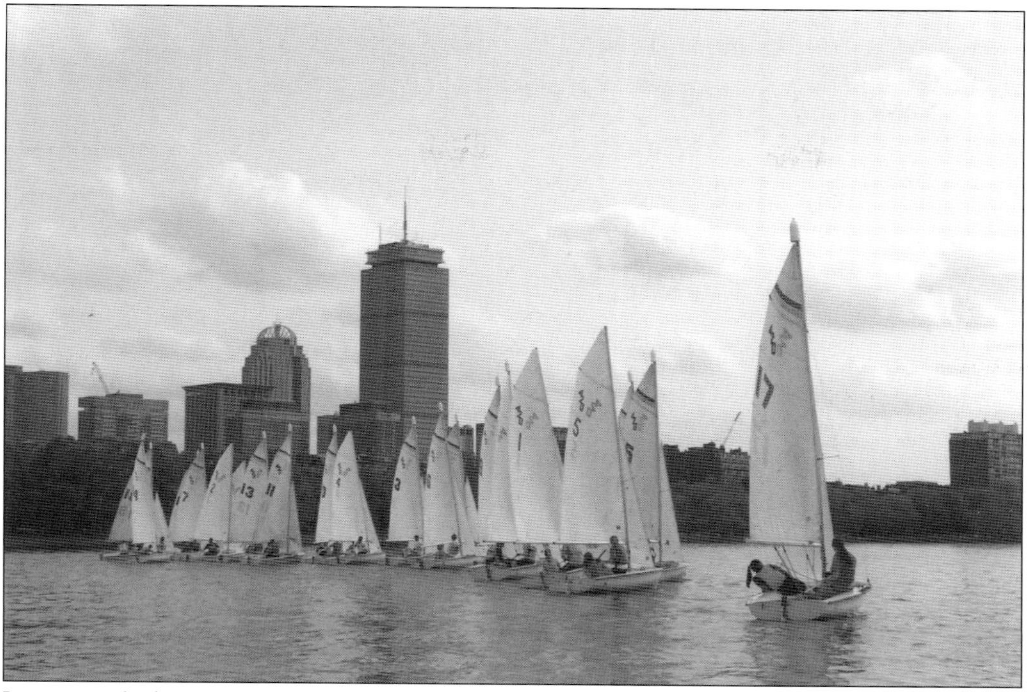

Leon Manfredi is quoted as saying that "there are races for juniors on Saturday mornings and seniors Sunday morning" and that the racing skipper's rating is only given to prospective members after a stiff written examination.

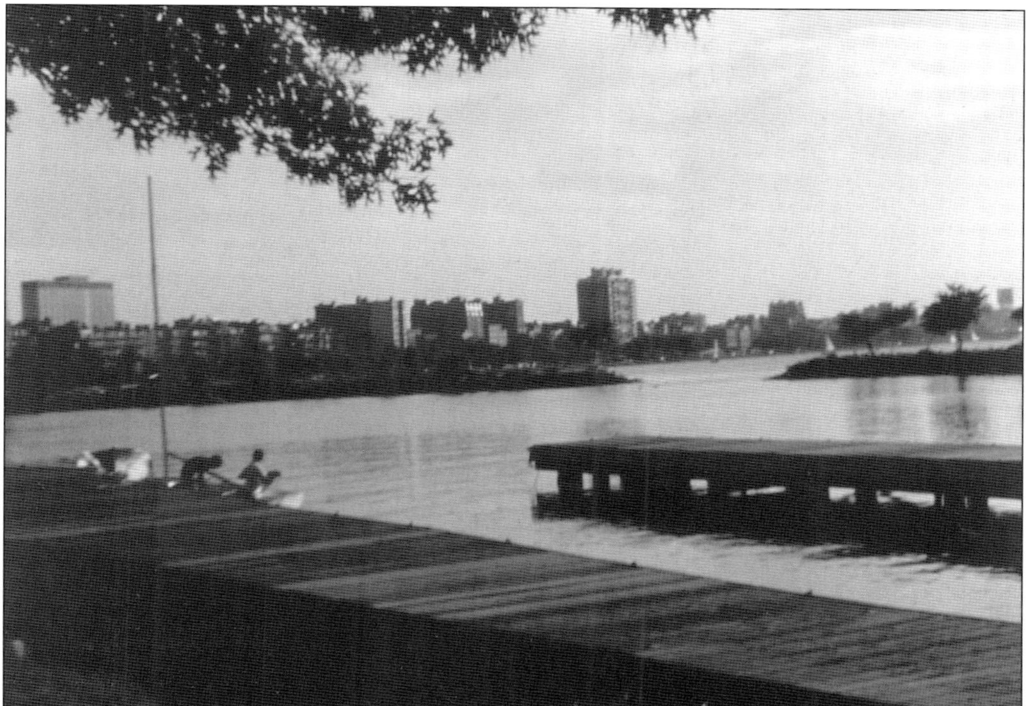

This bucolic early evening photograph shows two sailors coming in from a sail on the Charles River Basin as the sun sets. (Courtesy of the Leo and Audrey Manfredi collection.)

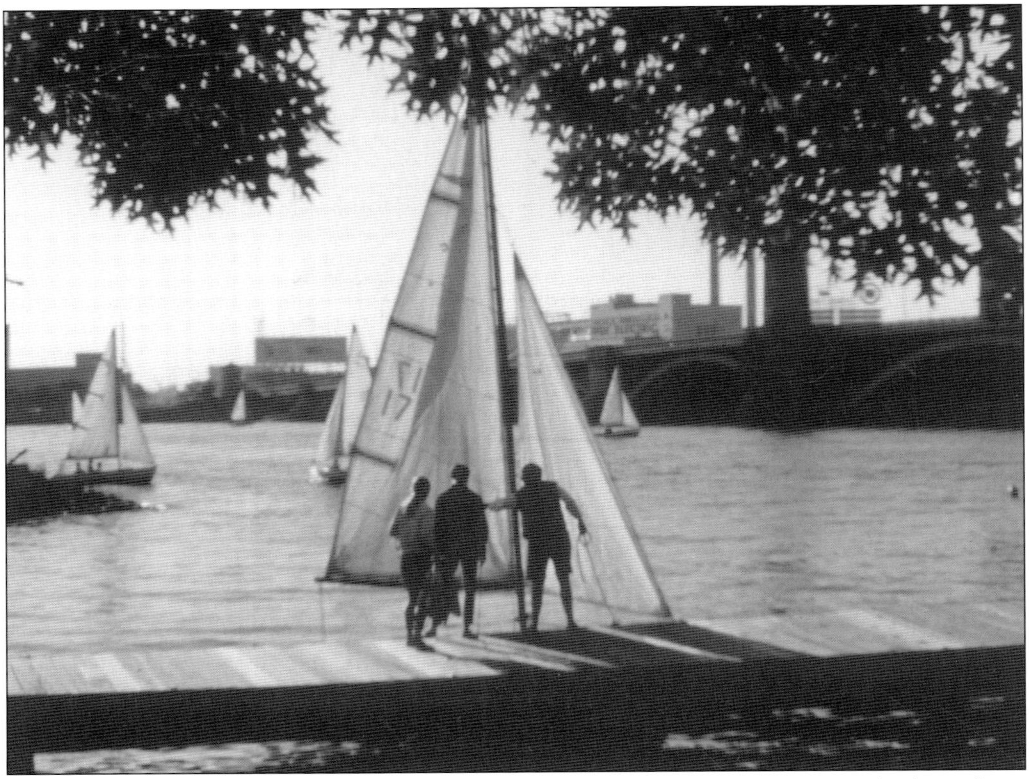

Three Junior Program members are seen in the early morning as they prepare to sail. The sailboat is being rigged before they take the Mercury sloop out for a sail. By 1963, there were 1,287 Junior Program members. (Courtesy of the Leo and Audrey Manfredi collection.)

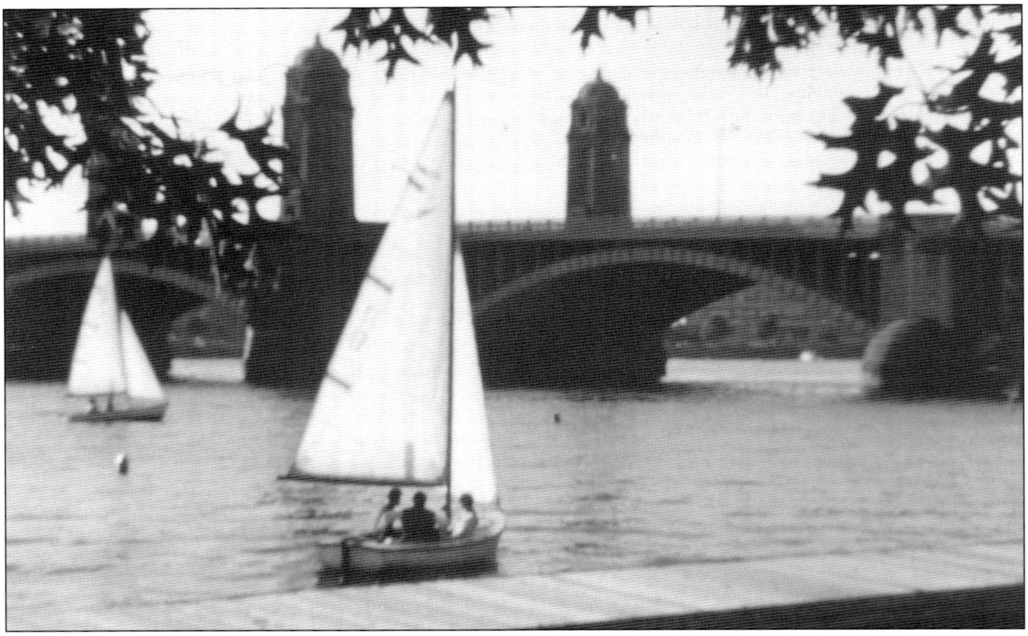

After having rigged the sailboat and prepared the sail, the three Junior Program members set out for a sail. (Courtesy of the Leo and Audrey Manfredi collection.)

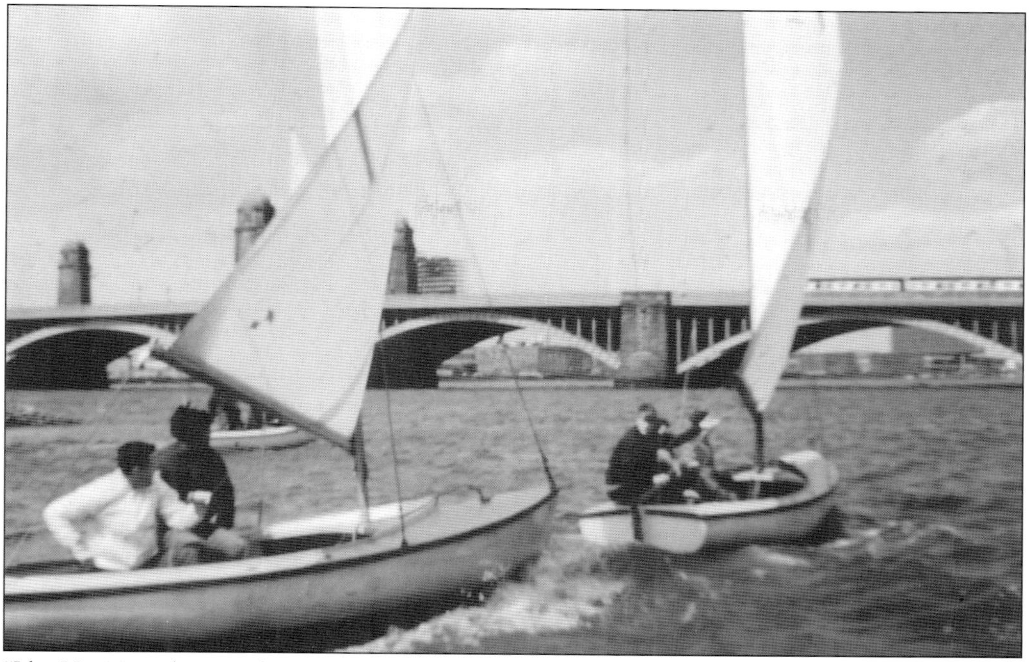

"Jibe Ho!" In other words, duck as the boom swings around during a tack. (Courtesy of the Leo and Audrey Manfredi collection.)

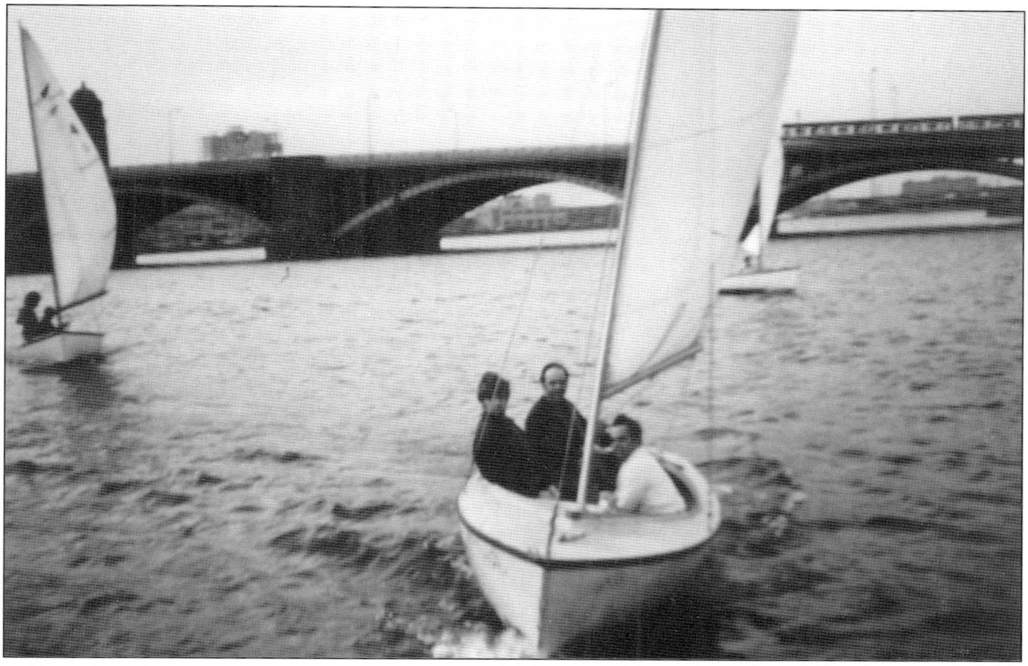

Sailing for all really meant that anyone could handle a mainsheet and tiller. Teaming up with a qualified member who instructs the novice sailor not only allows the novice to gain confidence but also fosters sociability among the members. (Courtesy of the Leo and Audrey Manfredi collection.)

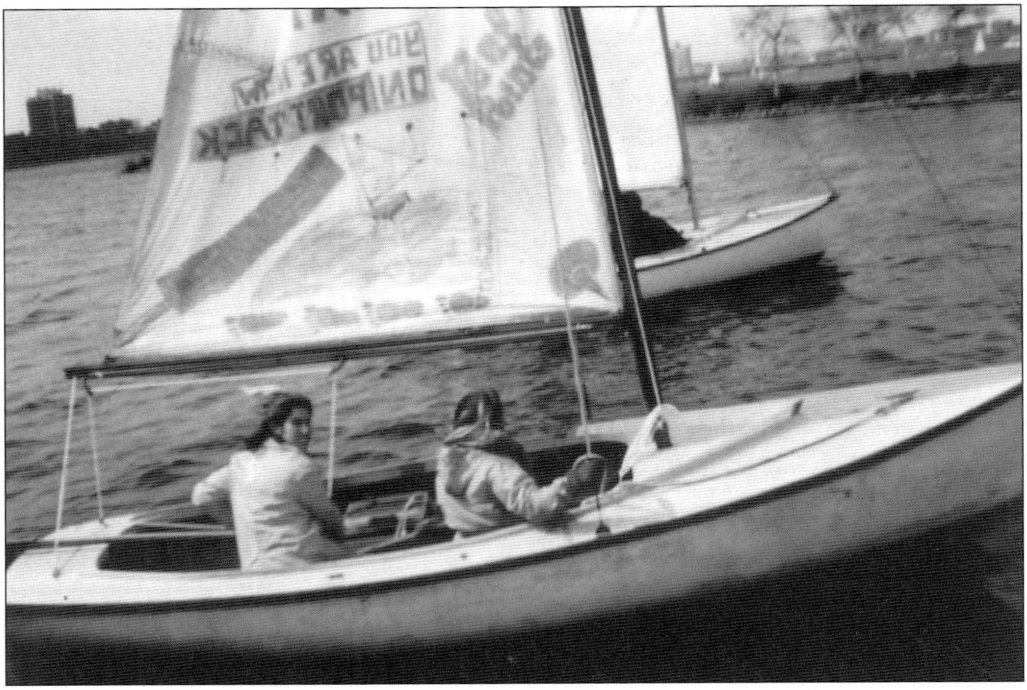

Two women sail with ease on the Charles River Basin with a breeze seemingly tailored neatly for their sail. (Courtesy of the Leo and Audrey Manfredi collection.)

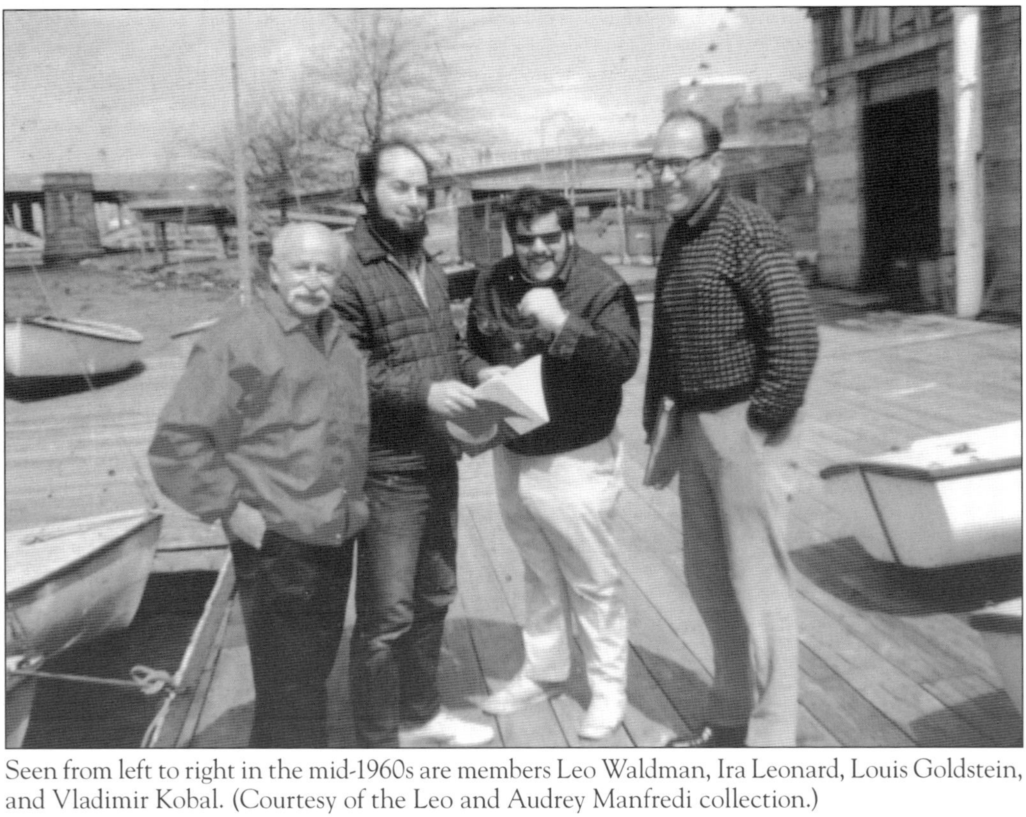

Seen from left to right in the mid-1960s are members Leo Waldman, Ira Leonard, Louis Goldstein, and Vladimir Kobal. (Courtesy of the Leo and Audrey Manfredi collection.)

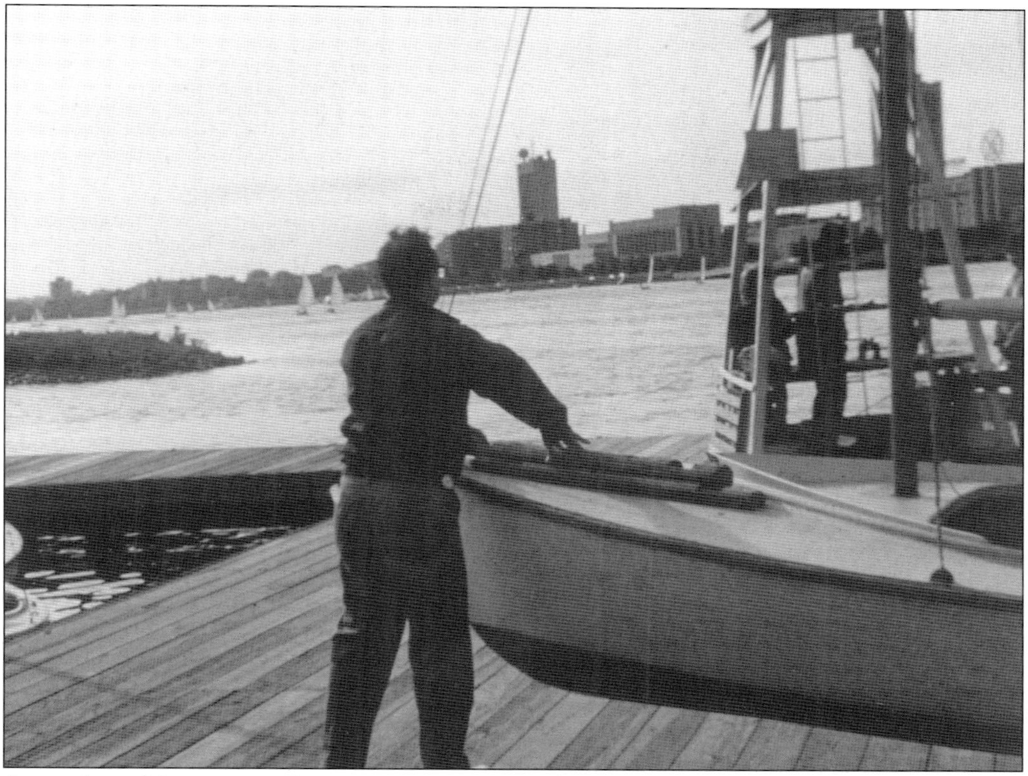

A member of Community Boating prepares his sailboat before it is launched into the water. After caulking, sanding, and painting the sailboats in the early spring, they are ready for another season of providing joy to former landlubbers who have become sailing aficionados. (Courtesy of the Leo and Audrey Manfredi collection.)

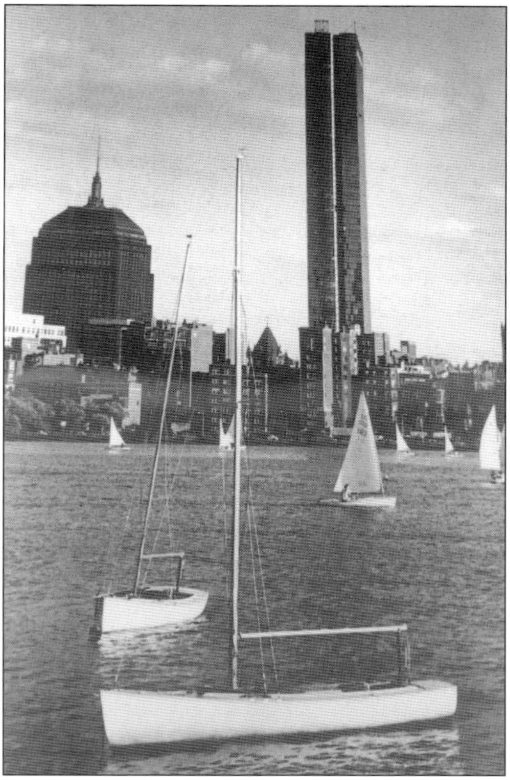

This bucolic 1970s scene of the Charles River Basin shows sailboats awaiting members and others out for an afternoon sail. The backdrop of the Back Bay of Boston has the two John Hancock Towers; the one on the left was designed by Cram & Ferguson and built in 1947, and the one on the right was designed by Henry Cobb of I.M. Pei & Associates and completed in 1976. (Courtesy of the DCR.)

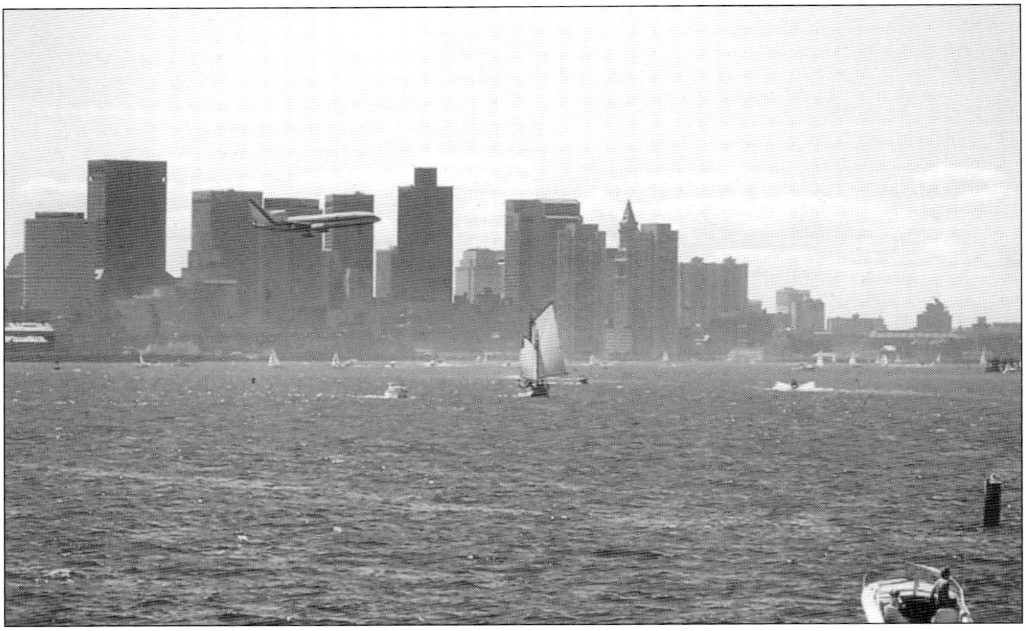

The activity on the Charles River Basin and above it is incredible. An airplane is seen approaching Logan International Airport in East Boston as sailboats, a motorboat, and all sorts of recreational activity makes for a busy afternoon in the 1970s. The skyline of Downtown Boston can be seen in the distance. (Courtesy of the Leo and Audrey Manfredi collection.)

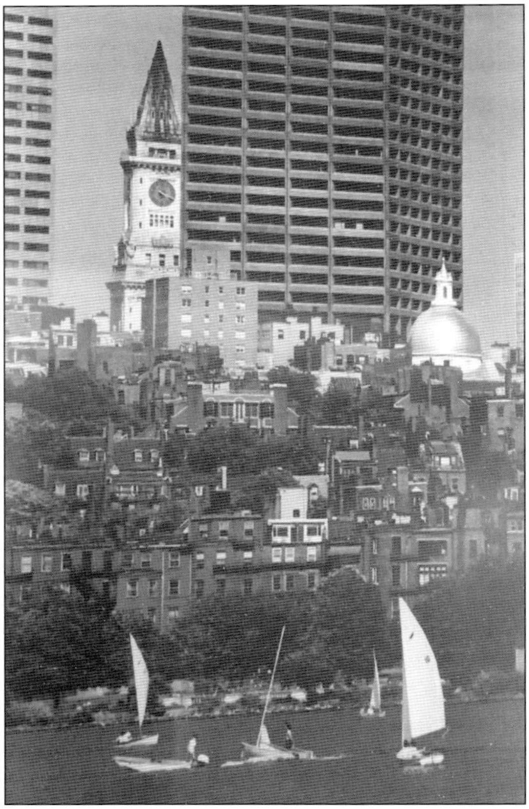

One of the more impressive views of Boston is this scene with Community Boating sailboats in the foreground, with the gilded dome of the Massachusetts State House and the Custom House tower, once the tallest building in Boston until 1965, flanked by the new high-rise office buildings that transformed the skyline of the city. (Courtesy of the DCR.)

Nine

JUNIOR PROGRAM AND UNIVERSAL ACCESS PROGRAM

These Community Boating programs are among the hidden gems of Boston.

—Steve Kelleher

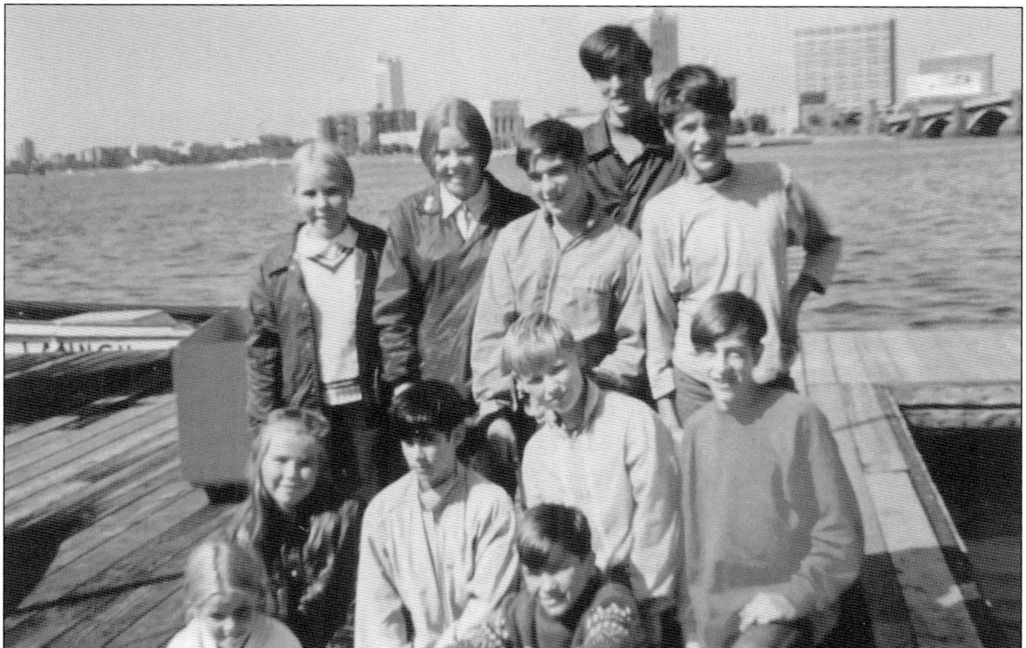

A group of Junior Program members pose on the Community Boating dock in the early 1960s. What makes Community Boating so special is the open nature of the Junior Program, whose members have the freedom to choose what they want to do and how to spend their time. Community Boating provides a safe and nurturing environment while giving kids a sense of freedom and responsibility that they do not often experience. (Courtesy of the Dan and Marilyn Farren collection.)

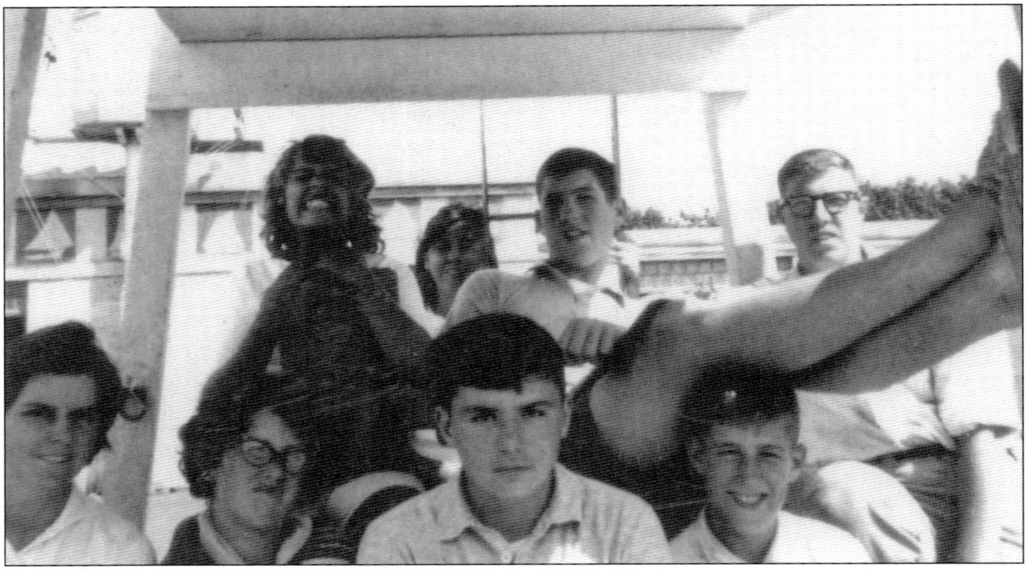

A group of young Junior Program members pose for a group photograph in the early 1960s on the tower, with Steve Winkler in the center. They often became stalwart friends over the summer months as they sailed and enjoyed shared camaraderie, all the while learning to sail and kayak and enjoying the Charles River. Note the crow's nest on the left. (Courtesy of the Dan and Marilyn Farren collection.)

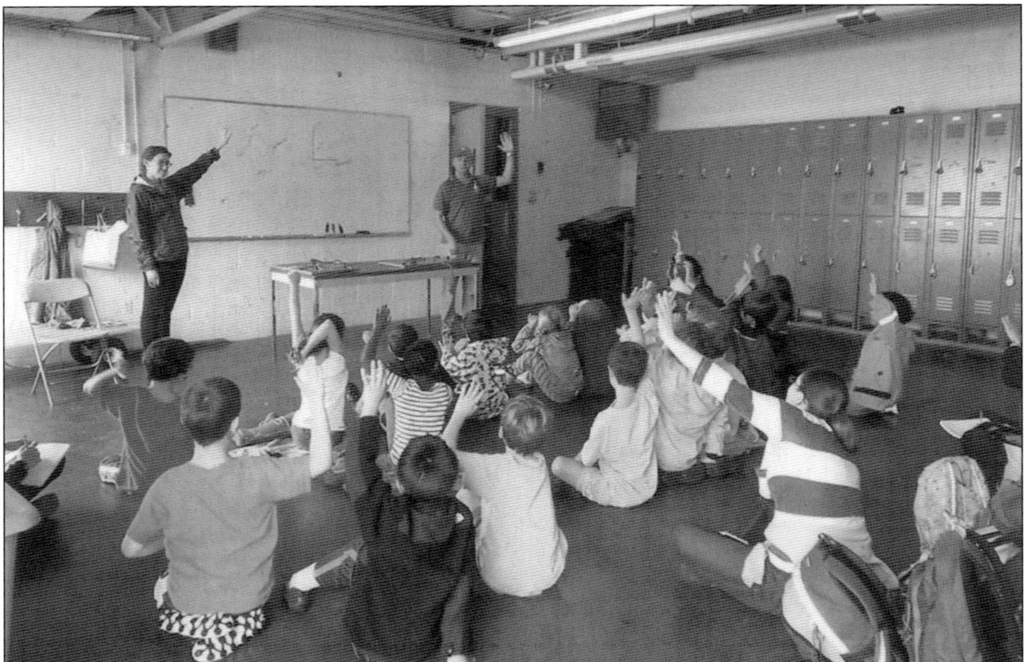

Classes were held for members of the Junior Program in the boathouse, as it was vitally important that they understand not just how to properly sail a boat but also the rules of the sea and how their actions were impacted by it. Joseph Lee's book *How to Sail a Boat* is a practical manual on how to sail a boat for anyone stepping into a boat for the first time, but it is the hands-on learning with safety first that offers sustained growth.

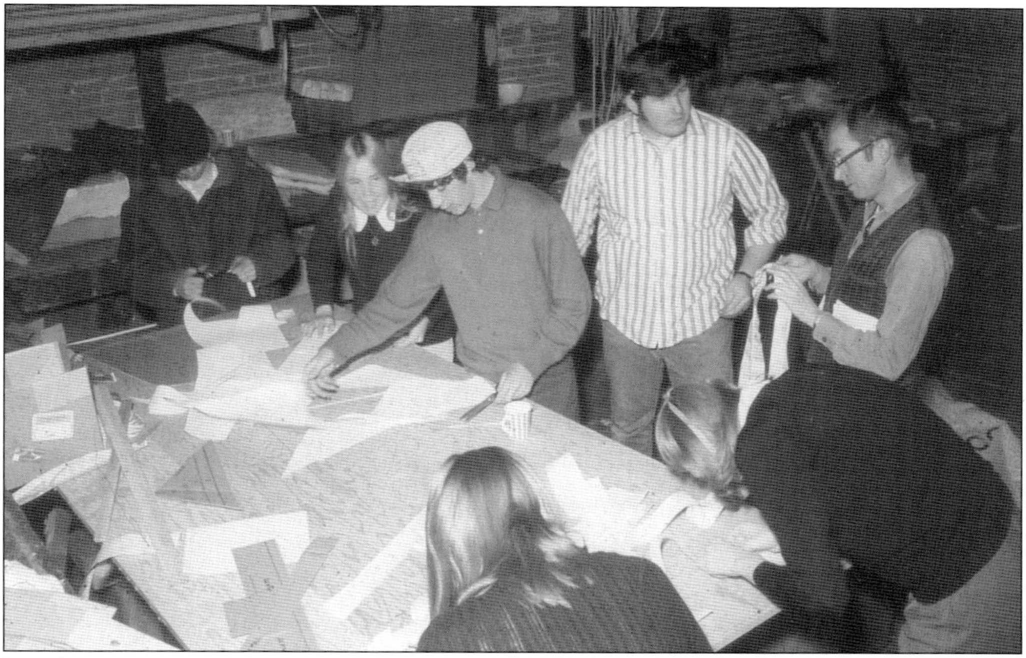

Hands-on experience was important for the members of the Junior Program, whether it was cutting out patterns, helping to sew canvas sails, or maintaining the sailboats by caulking, sanding, and painting. One of the premises of the Junior Program was to instill a sense of independence and the value of volunteerism.

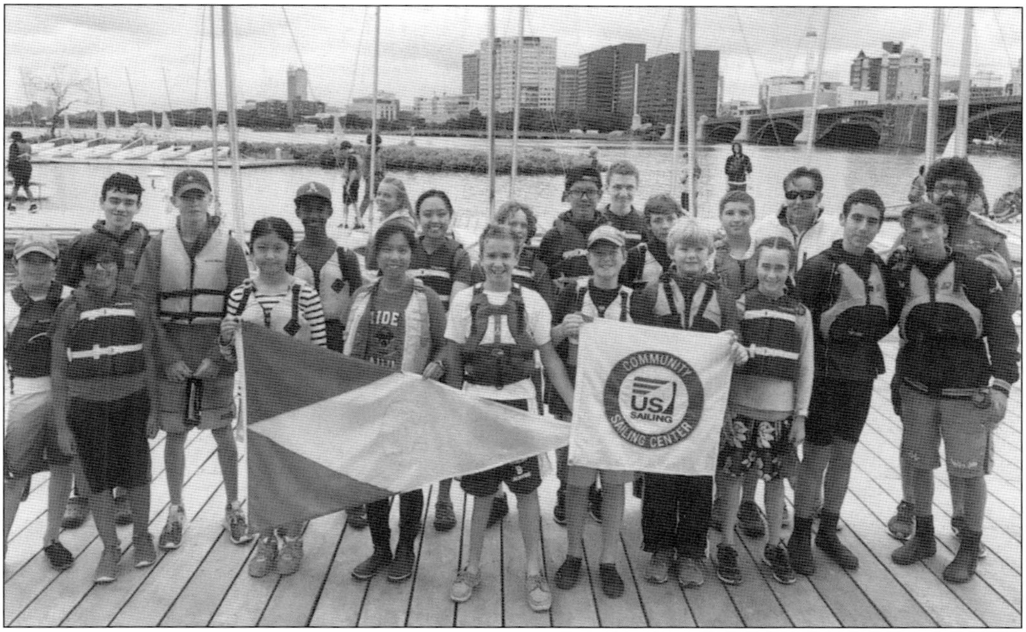

Holding the Community Boating pennant-shaped burgee and seal on a square flag, members of the Mascalzone Latino Youth Regatta pose on the dock in their life jackets for a group photograph before they set out for a sail. The smiles on their faces show how very proud they are of being a part of this regatta that allowed them to not just gain confidence but also learn to captain their own vessel in a safe and nurturing environment.

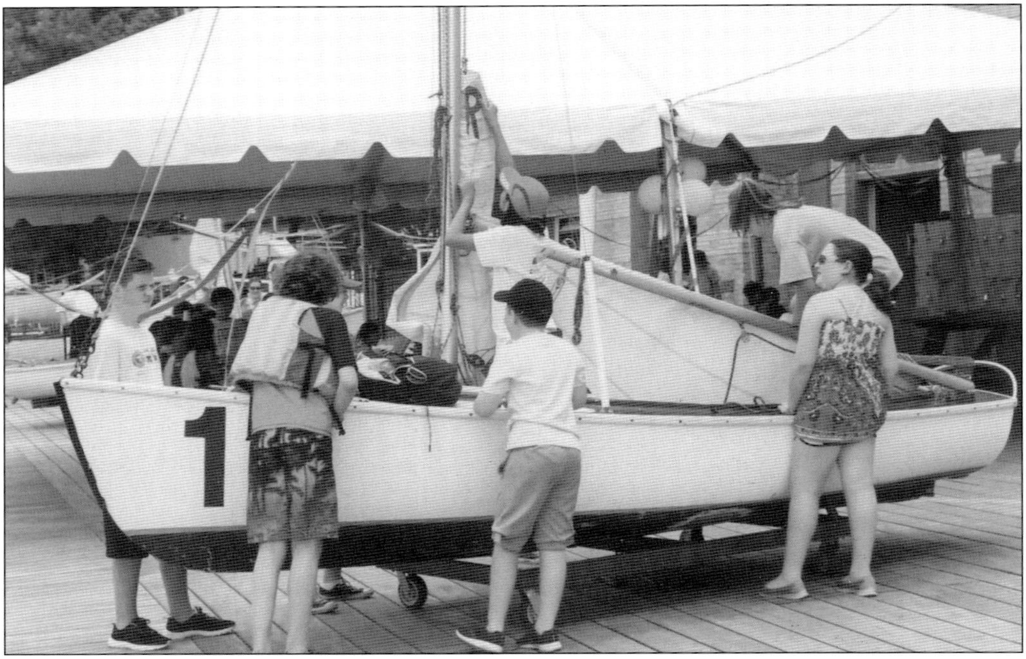

A group of Junior Program members practice how to raise the canvas sail, move the boom, and prepare the sailboat before it can be made ready to sail. Practice really does make perfect, and in this case, they get an important hands-on experience while still on the dock that they can translate to when they begin sailing.

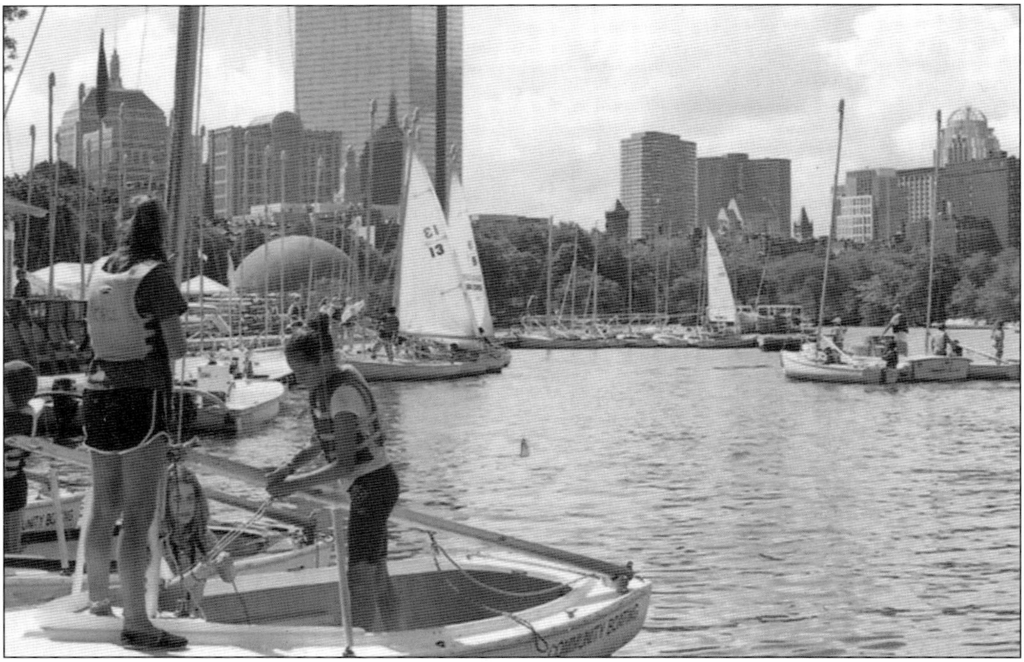

The Junior Program has long been a wonderful and accessible program that attracts kids from diverse backgrounds learning to become independent and developing long term friendships. One parent said about this Community Boating program: "I am really happy to have such a high value program around for kids."

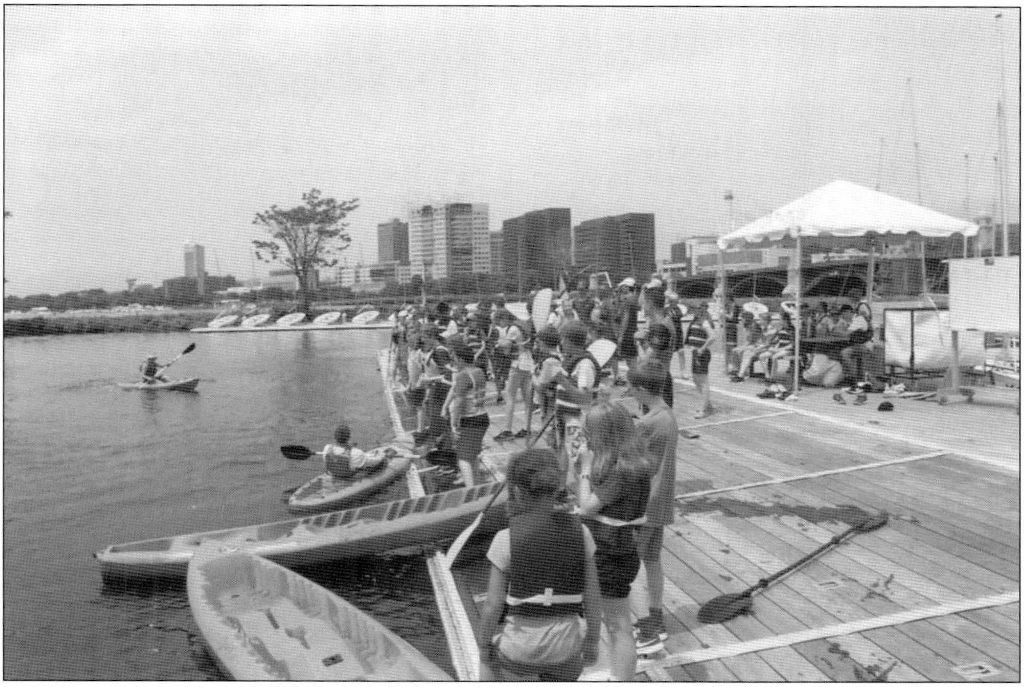

Since 1946, Community Boating has been a place where the youth of Boston are encouraged spend their summers learning to sail as well as kayak and enjoy the banks of the Charles River. Community Boating's unique Junior Program offers sailing classes, as well as membership with access to the water for youth participants, at a low membership cost.

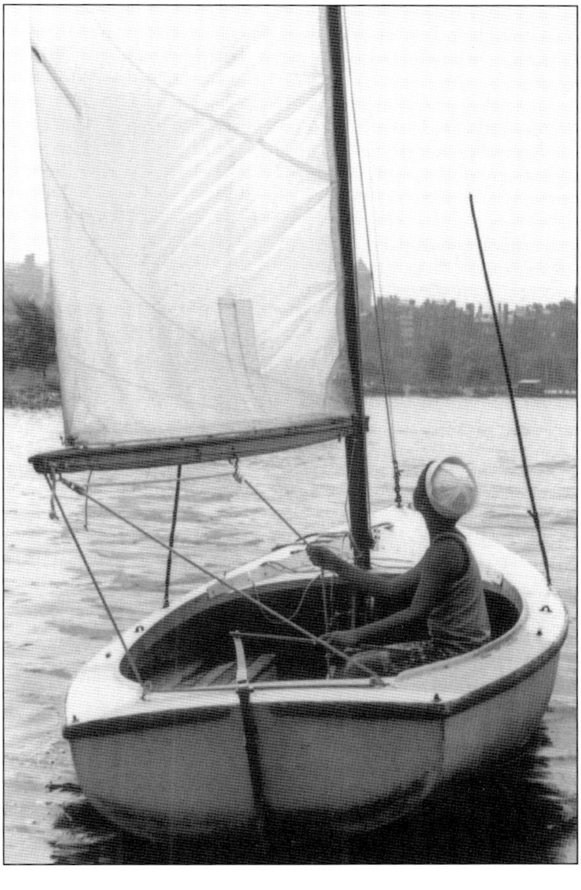

A sailor-hatted boy holds the rope to pull the sail taught to keep it from flapping in the wind. This young man is gaining confidence by learning to captain his own vessel in a safe and nurturing environment, all the while having fun on the Charles River Basin.

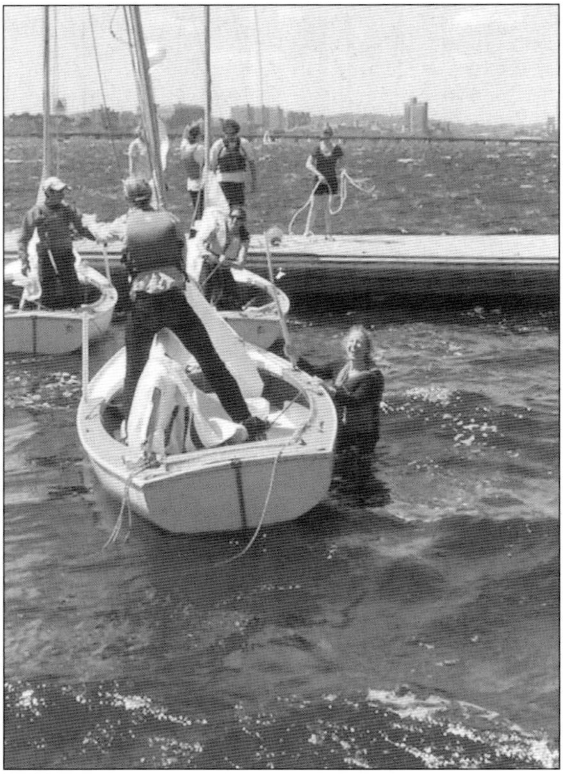

Developing a sense of sailing skills, independence, and confidence over the 10-week program during the summer months, these Junior Program members lend a hand when needed, whether helping to dock a sailboat, assisting on taking a sail down, or just being there when needed.

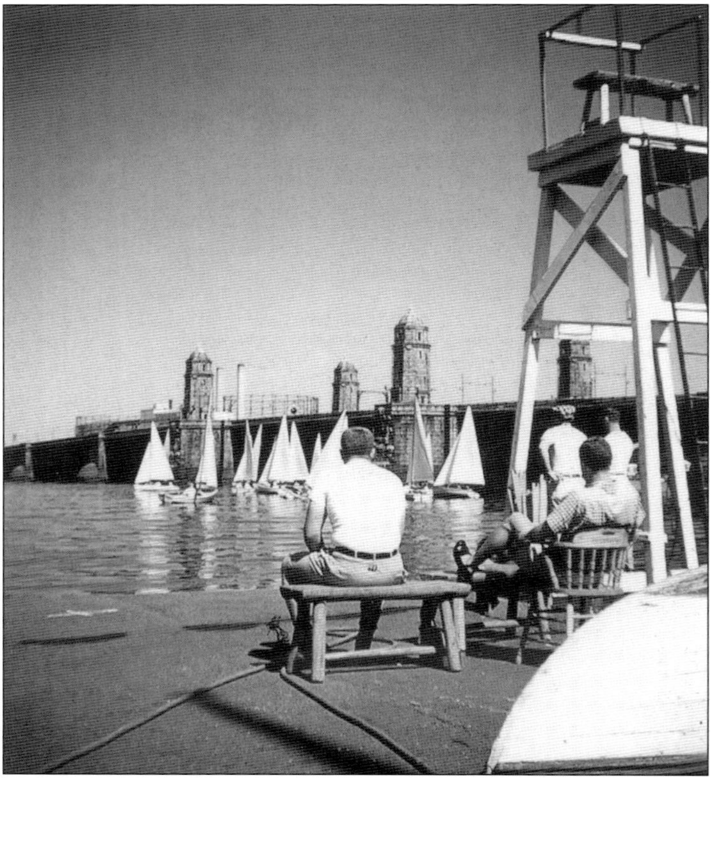

These instructors intently watch members of the Junior Program sailing on the Charles River Basin. As one parent said of Community Boating, it "offers the best summer activity for my 14-year-old. He was not quite an outdoor teenager until he started in June at Community Boating. He loves it and goes back week after week this summer! He had a blast learning sailing, wind surfing, and all other activities! Thumbs up!"

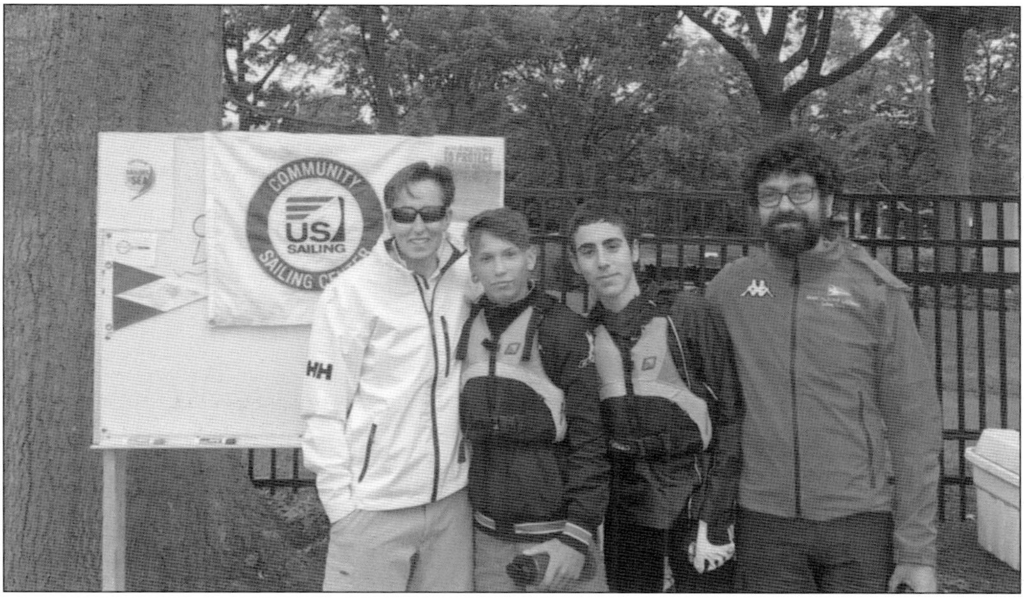

In 2017, Professionisti Italiani a Boston hosted two Italian students from the nonprofit sailing school Scuola Vela Mascalzone Latino. Laura Canzanella and Salvatore Pistone, both 13 years old and seen in the center, visited Boston, where they discussed motivational personal stories with local Italian professionals and competed against young sailors from Community Boating. On the left is Antonio Dell' Omo Beneduce, and on the right is Giovanni Abbadessa, who praised the kids' efforts.

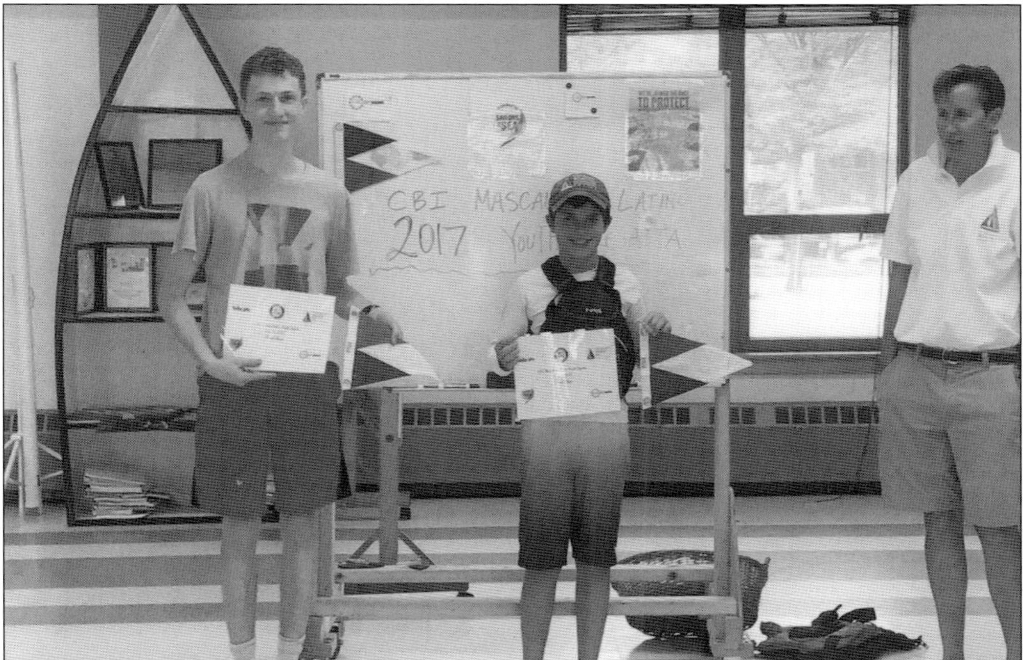

The Mascalzone Latino Youth Regatta was an exciting sailboat race. Two of the young sailors received awards as well as Community Boating burgees from instructor Antonio Dell' Omo Beneduce (right) for their part in the regatta.

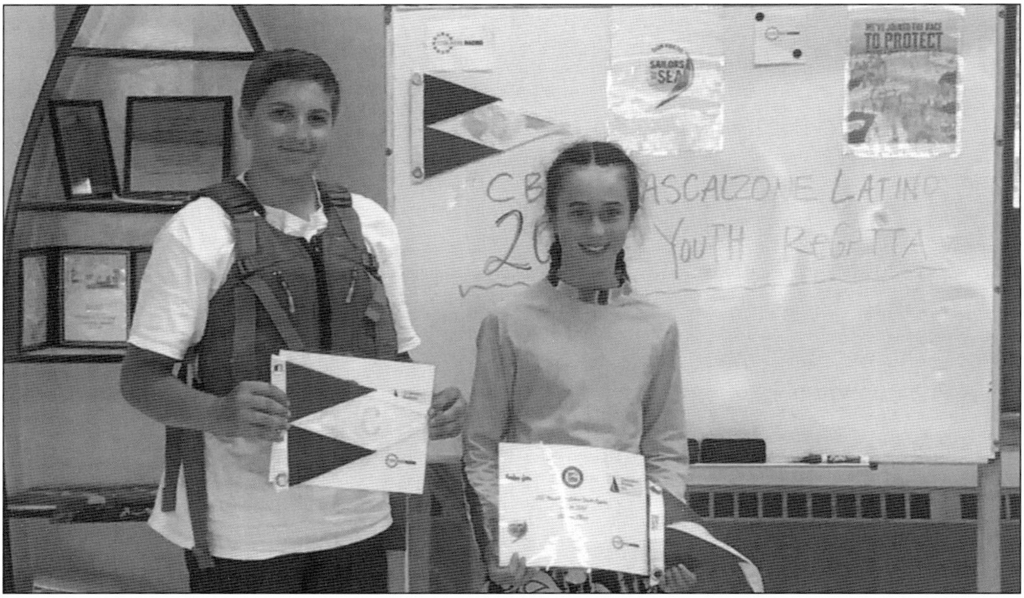

These two teens receive awards and Community Boating burgees in the Mascalzone Latino Youth Regatta. "It was the best experience of my life," said Laura, on the right, who finished the competition with the best time. There had been three regattas held, which took place at the Courageous Sailing Center, the MIT Sailing Center, and Community Boating. The Professionisti Italiani a Boston partnered with Mascalzone Latino to give teenagers from underprivileged neighborhoods in Naples, Italy, the chance to sail on the Charles River.

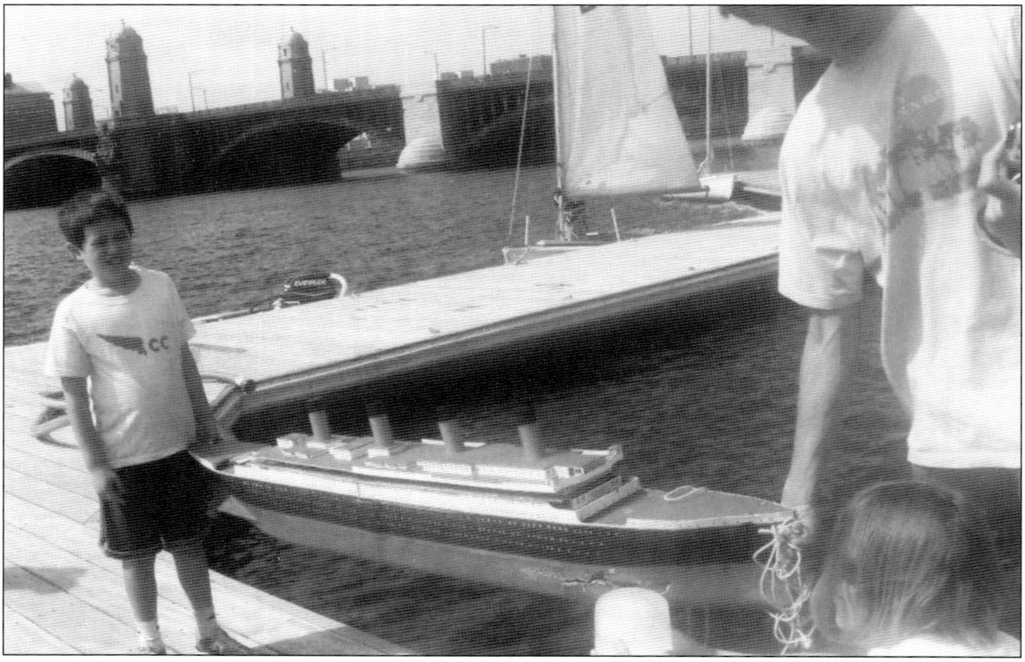

In commemoration of the 100th anniversary of the sailing of the RMS *Titanic*, this scale model of the doomed ocean liner was launched from the Community Boating dock in 2012. It was an interesting and historic lesson on how to apply the safety of a sailboat—or in this case an ocean liner—to one's ability.

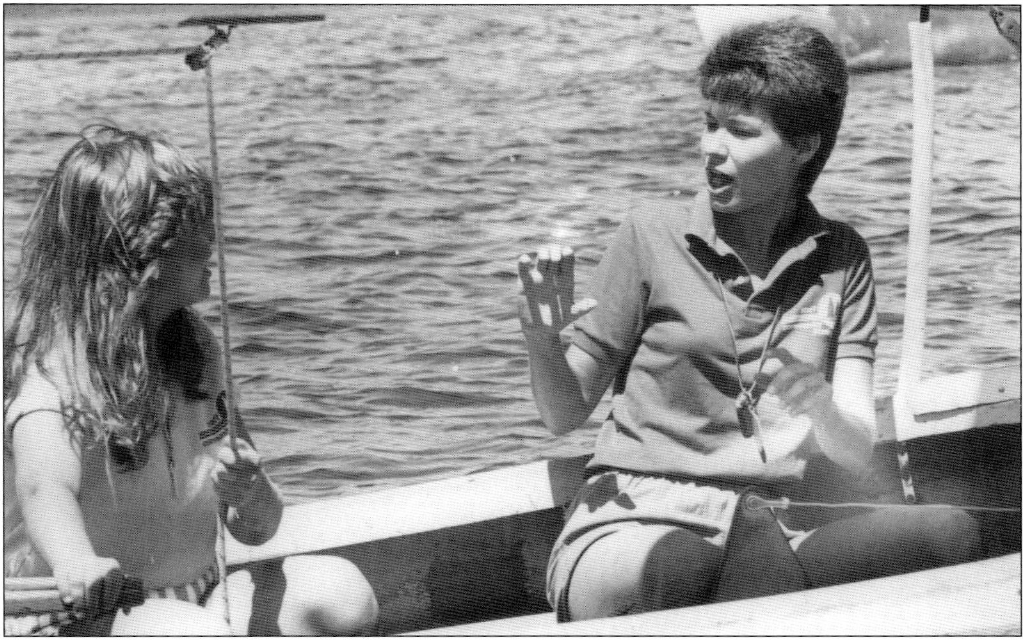

The Universal Access Program was an award-winning program started by Community Boating to allow people with learning, developmental, and physical challenges to participate in the programs and learn how to sail. Here, an instructor tutors a young woman who is hearing impaired on how to properly operate the rope to allow the sailboat to proceed. She is probably instructing her to pull the rope to stop the sail's flapping in the wind. Even students from the Perkins School for the Blind were encouraged by Leo Manfredi to learn sailing.

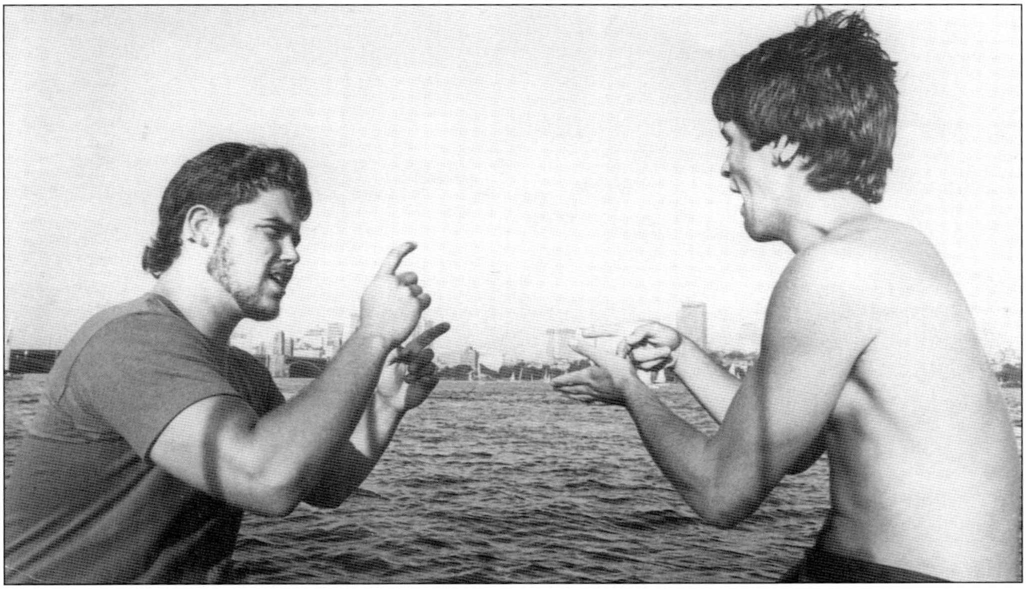

Hearing impairments should never deter anyone from enjoying the benefits of sailing at Community Boating. Using sign language, these two men discuss sailing techniques on the Charles River Basin. In 2007, working with the DCR Universal Access Program, the Executive Office of Environmental Affairs Office of Public Private Partnerships, and Genzyme Corporation, the Universal Access Program at CBI was started to great acclaim and widespread public approval.

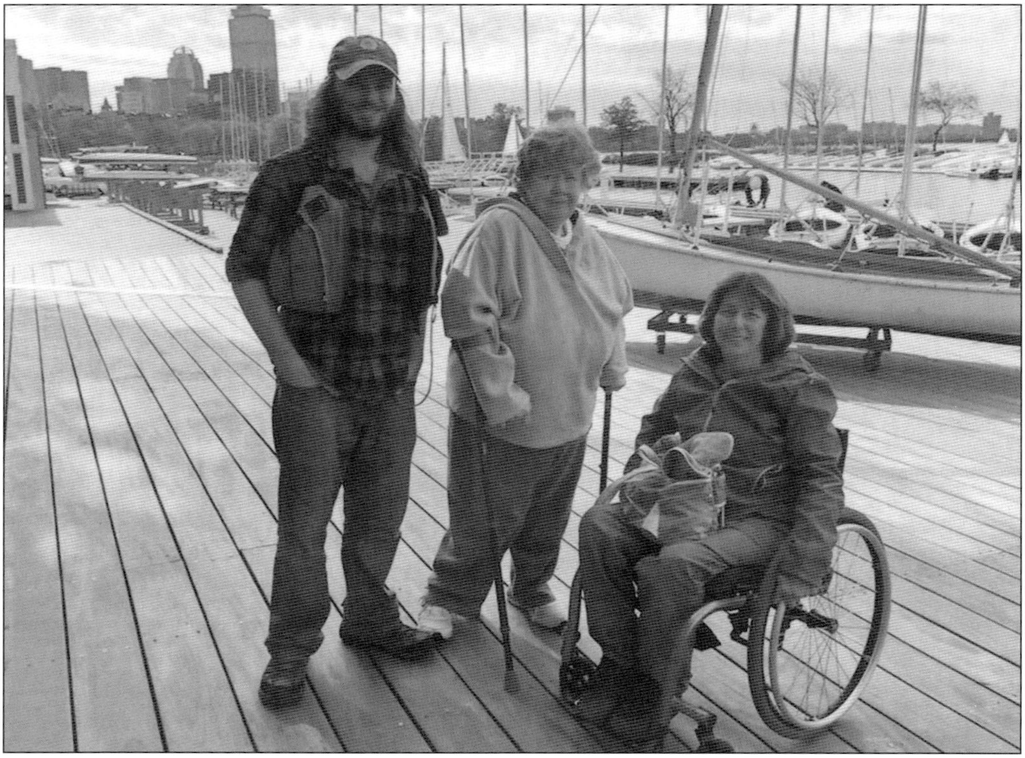

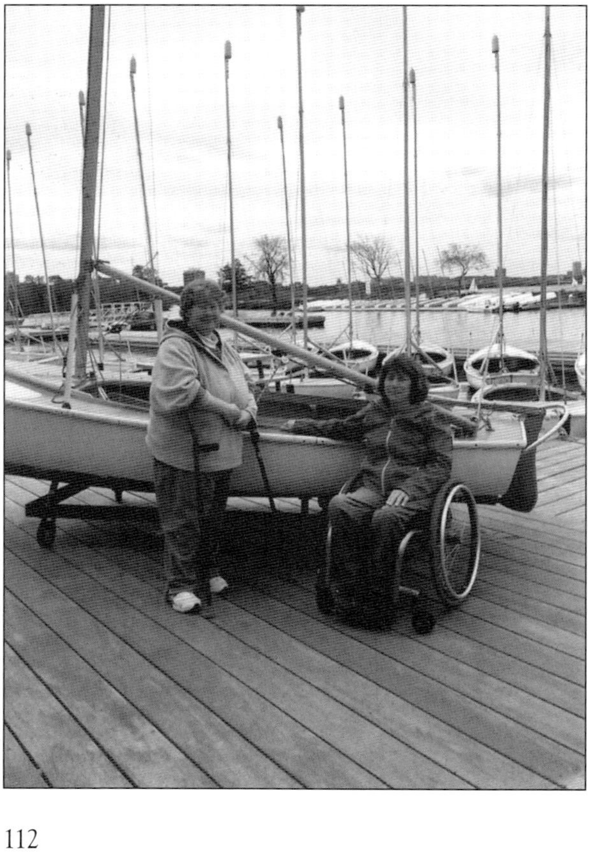

Physical limitation challenges have long been daunting for those who seek to be a part of any activity, but at Community Boating, there is a concerted effort to allow everyone, even those with disabilities, to fully participate through the Universal Access Program. One can only imagine the sense of achievement that people attain through this program, which is partially funded by the Cheers4Chairs Campaign.

Posing by the sailboat on the dock, the award-winning Universal Access Program is a credit to the inclusiveness of Community Boating. Persons with disabilities have the use of specially adapted sailboats and transfer equipment, dedicated staff assistance to get in and out of the boats, and sailing instruction, all for an affordable annual membership fee. This makes the slogan "Sailing for All" a fitting one.

Ten

Community Boating Today

Sailing for All! The nation's oldest public sailing center—incorporated in 1946 on the Charles River Esplanade. Learn to sail, kayak, paddleboard and windsurf.

—Community Boating

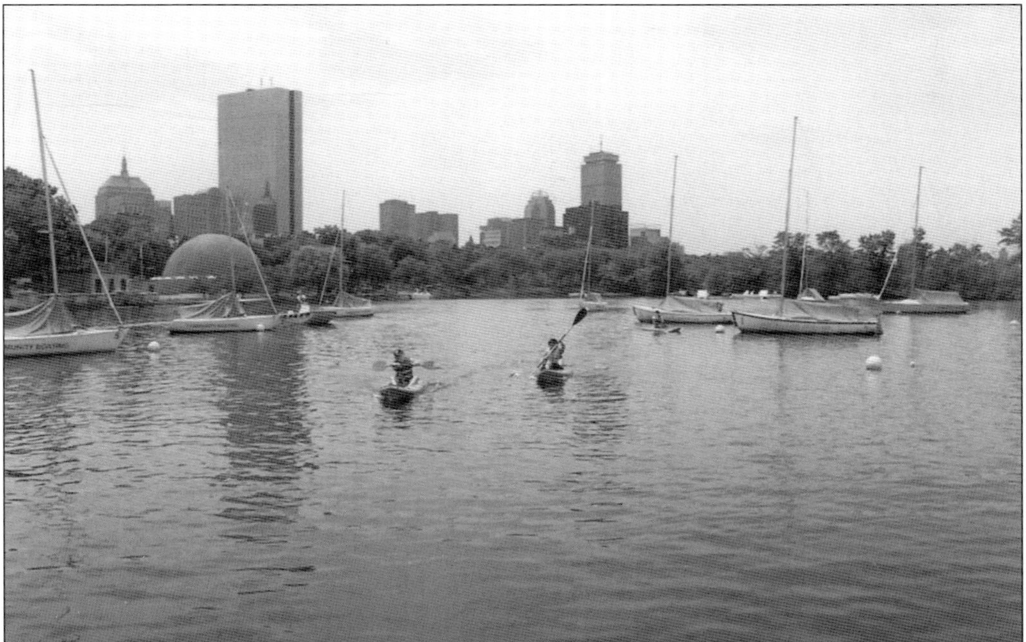

Two kayakers paddle on the Charles River Basin between the sailboats of Community Boating with their protective tarp covers. The river has long been used for water sports, and the graceful sailboats with their stiff sails have become a beloved icon of Boston in the 21st century. On the left, the Hatch Shell and the modern skyline of Boston's Back Bay can be seen.

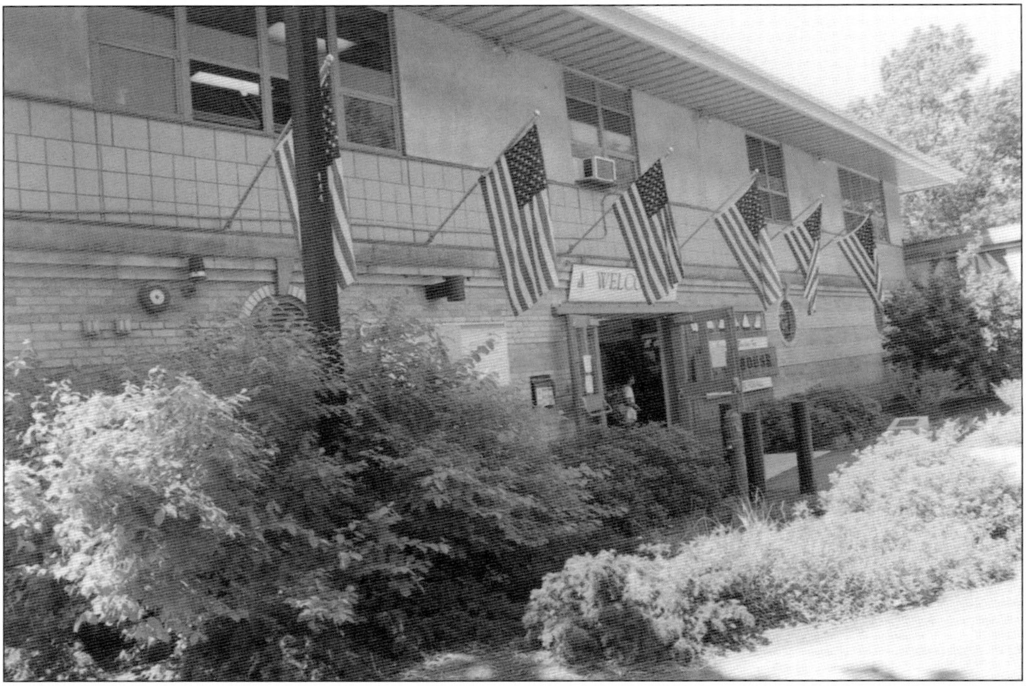

The entrance to Community Boating on David Mugar Way, named for the well-known Boston philanthropist and heir to the Star Market fortune, is bedecked with American flags along the façade as well as a large "Welcome" sign above the doorway. The boathouse has welcomed people of all ages and walks of life who wished to sail on the Charles River and become part of one of the oldest sailing clubs in the country.

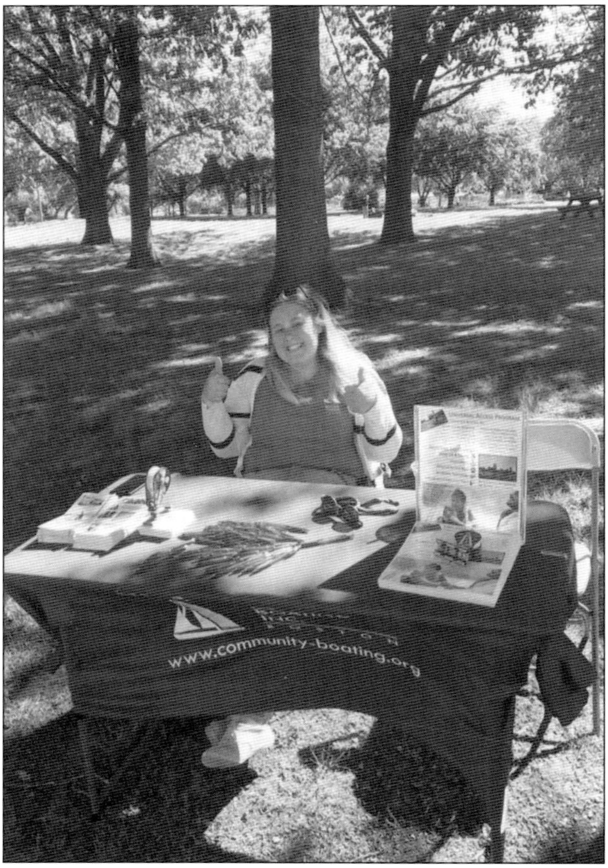

Assistant program director Keala Winer encourages walkers on the Esplanade to stop and look at promotional items on Community Boating and possibly learn and ask questions about the many programs offered throughout the year from the Adult Program, the Junior Program, and the Universal Access Program for people with disabilities. These DCR Adaptive Recreation fairs bring throngs of Bostonians to the Esplanade.

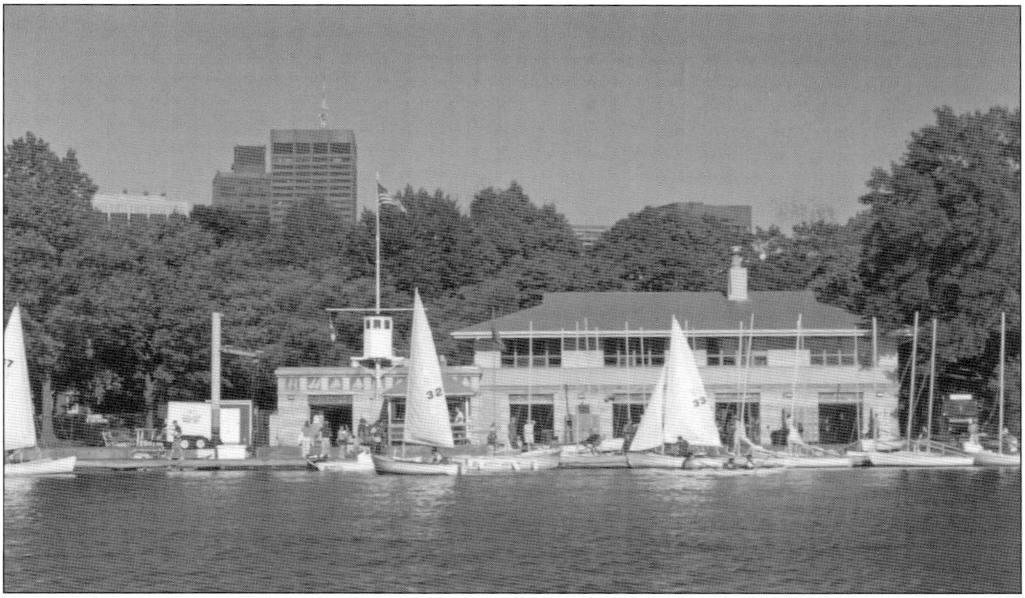

The Community Boating clubhouse has been greatly enlarged since it was originally designed by William R. Greeley of Kilham, Hopkins & Greeley and opened with great éclat in 1941. It has become a mecca for people of all ages that begin to learn to sail and become an integral part of the programs, often in turn teaching a new generation of sailors on the Charles River Basin. Though the Department of Conservation and Recreation owns the land and the building, Community Boating operates its programs under a permit with the DCR.

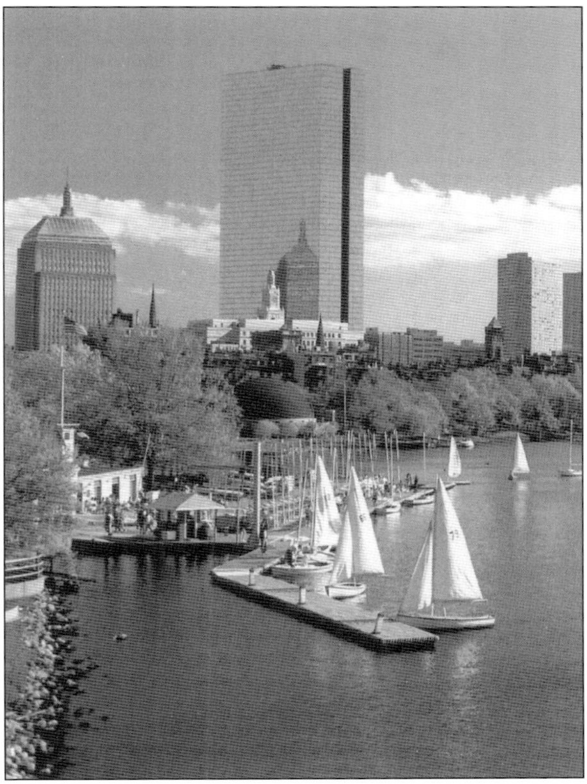

This bucolic photograph shows the boathouse of Community Boating situated along the tree-lined Esplanade of Boston with its wood docks projecting into the Charles River Basin. With the two John Hancock skyscrapers in the distance, on the left is the Cram & Fergusson–designed Berkeley Building tower, completed in 1947, and the sleek mirrored tower, designed by Henry Cobb of I.M. Pei & Partners and completed in 1976. Community Boating is an accessible and popular destination for many Bostonians.

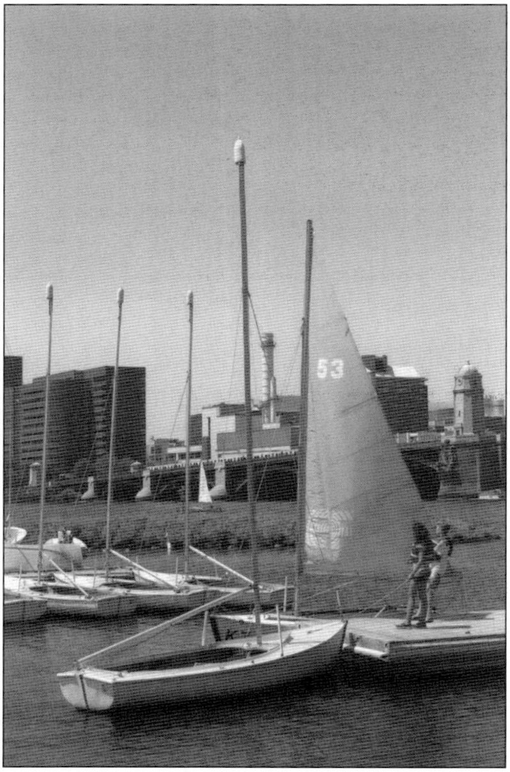

Two young sailors are standing on the dock, getting ready for an afternoon sail on the Charles River Basin. Holding the painter, which is the rope that secures the boat to the dock, they check the jib before beginning their sail.

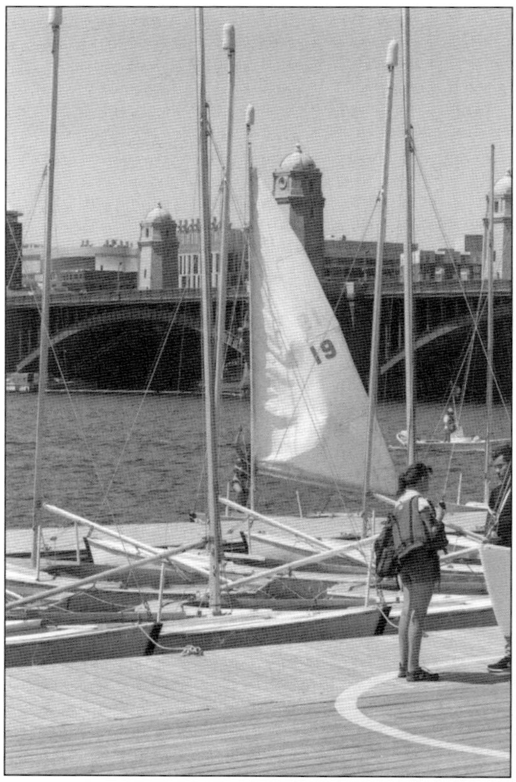

A young sailor discusses safety tips with an older mentor on the dock prior to taking a sailboat out for a sail. In her backpack, she might have included what Joseph Lee suggested in his detailed book *How to Sail a Boat:* a compass, chart, lights, knife, oilskins, water, chocolate, and cotton waste in addition to, hopefully, a level head, detailed prudence, and a sinuous disposition.

The young sailor is seen on the Charles River Basin, with its sail catching the wind. As Joseph Lee wrote in *How to Sail a Boat*, "Except at the moment of turning about or coming into the landing, you sail slanting, more or less to and fro, across the wind. The wind will always be a little broadside to you." If one understood the general concept of his book, Lee made sailing understandable for generations of Boston youth.

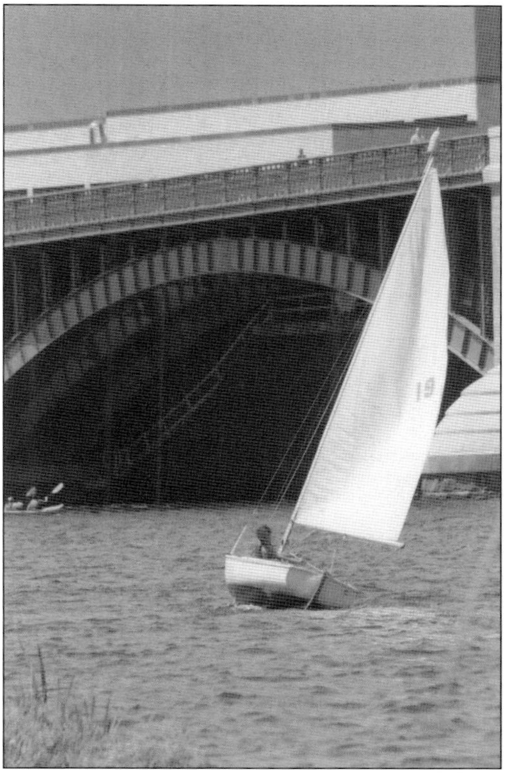

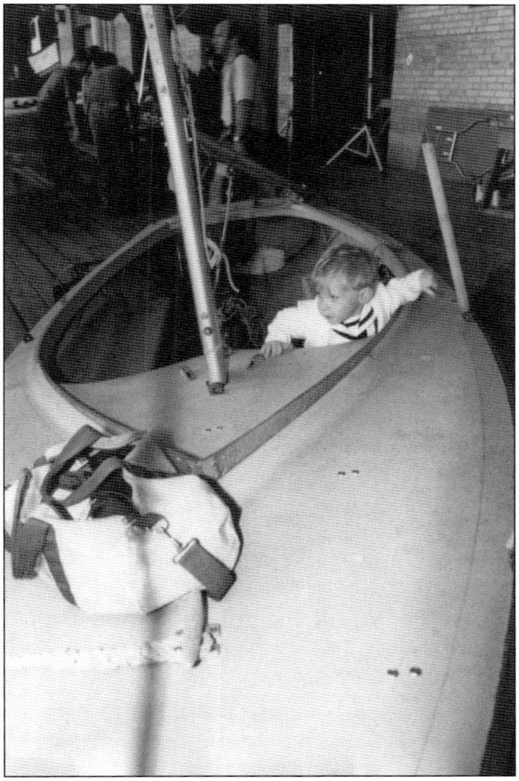

Ethan Lee, the son of Douglas and Kenwyn Lee and grandson of Ariel and Joseph Lee Jr., sits in a sailboat on the dock at Community Boating in his dapper sailor top. Three generations of the Lee family have been stalwart supporters of Community Boating. A portrait of Joseph Lee Jr. was painted by the noted Beacon Hill artist Patricia Marshall Tate and presented to Community Boating in 1987 to commemorate his founding and long association with Community Boating. (Courtesy of Douglas Lee.)

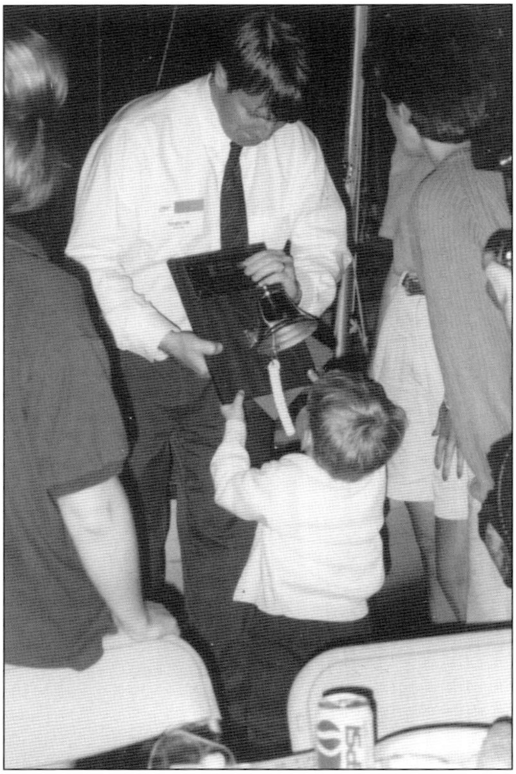

Douglas Lee shows the bell award he had been presented in honor of his father's founding and involvement with Community Boating over the years to his young son Ethan Lee. The ship's brass bell, mounted on a mahogany plaque, has long been used to indicate the time aboard a ship and hence regulate the sailors' duty watches; it was an appropriate marine memorial to Joseph Lee Jr. (Courtesy of Douglas Lee.)

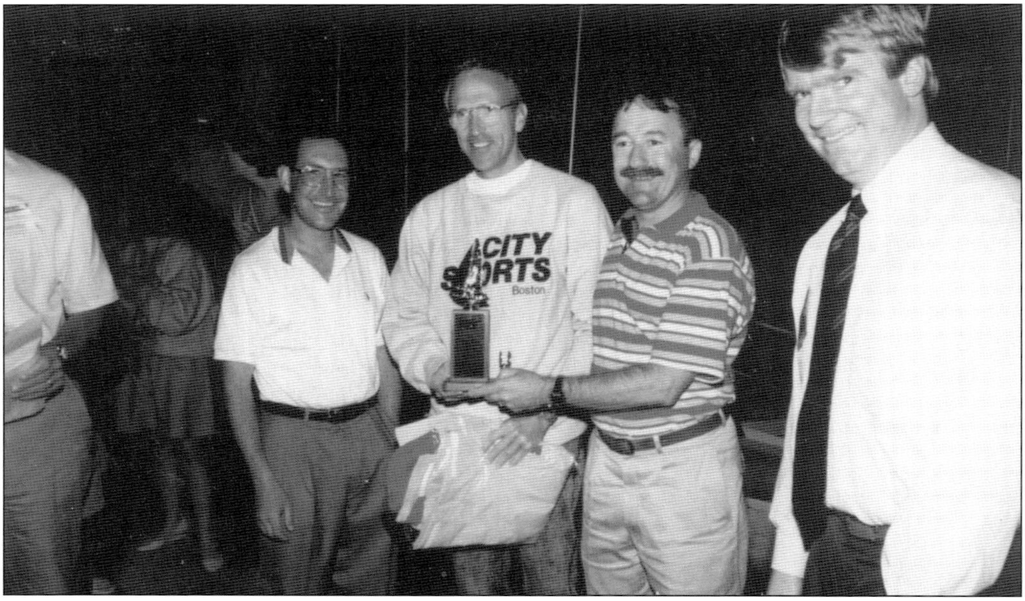

The Joseph Lee Memorial Trophy was testimony to the memory of Joseph Lee, who founded, in 1936, the Community Service Association, which was to become Community Boating in 1946. The first-place winner in the Corporate Regatta was the Pensions and Investment Company, with three of the sailors seen holding the brass sailboat award that had been presented to them by Douglas Lee (far right), the youngest son of Joseph Lee Jr., at an awards evening at the boathouse. (Courtesy of Douglas Lee.)

Eleven

The Fourth of July Sailabration

The SAILabration is probably the best family event around for Independence Day. Everyone is welcome to attend this very secure and adventurous event.

—WBZ 4 CBS Boston

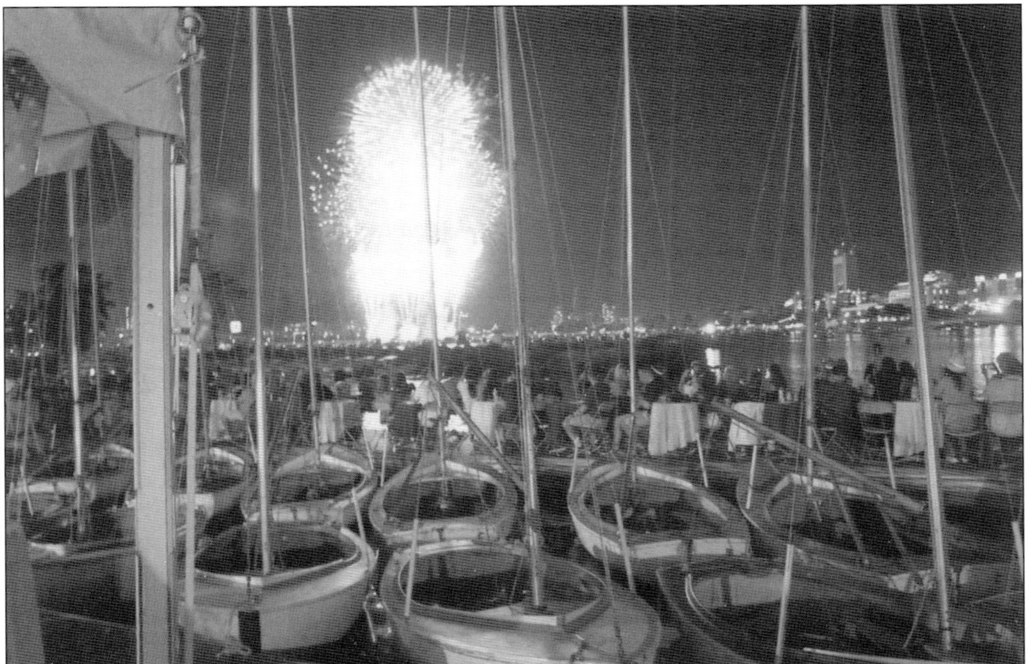

For decades, the Fourth of July has been celebrated with great aplomb in Boston, with a concert at the Hatch Shell playing "The Star-Spangled Banner" and other popular songs and culminating with the rousing "1812 Overture" being played by the Boston Pops as spectacular fireworks light up the sky above the Charles River Basin. Seen here with the sailboats of Community Boating in the foreground and revelers along the dock, a burst of a fireworks explodes to the delight of spectators.

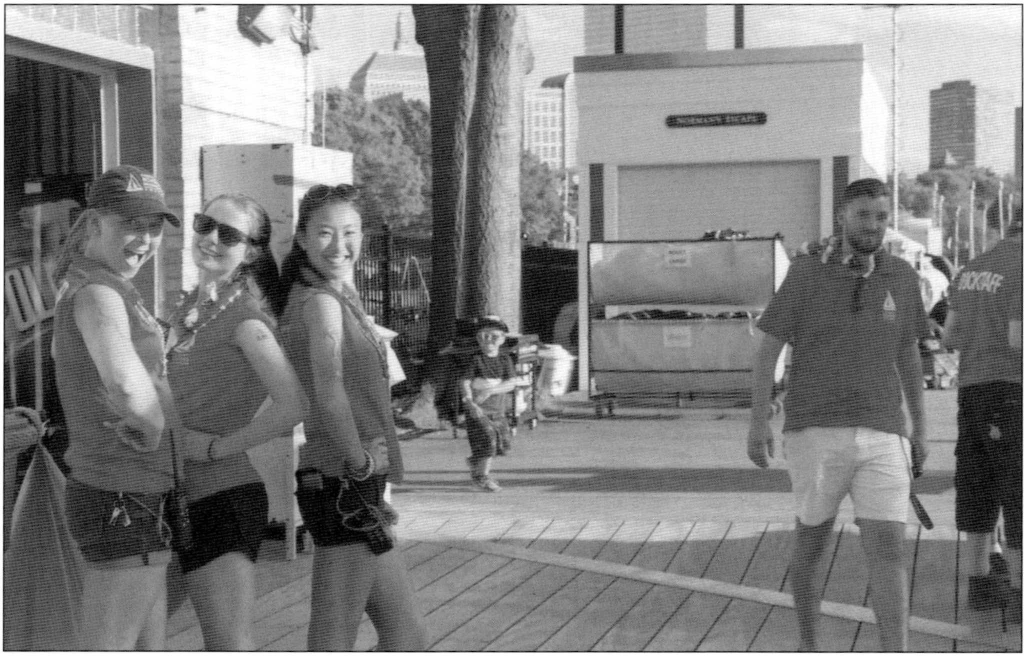

Young volunteers of Community Boating prepare for the Fourth of July celebration, awaiting the guests who arrive in the late afternoon to enjoy camaraderie as well as the panoramic views. The three young ladies on the left all sport airbrushed tattoos that enhance their summer dock attire.

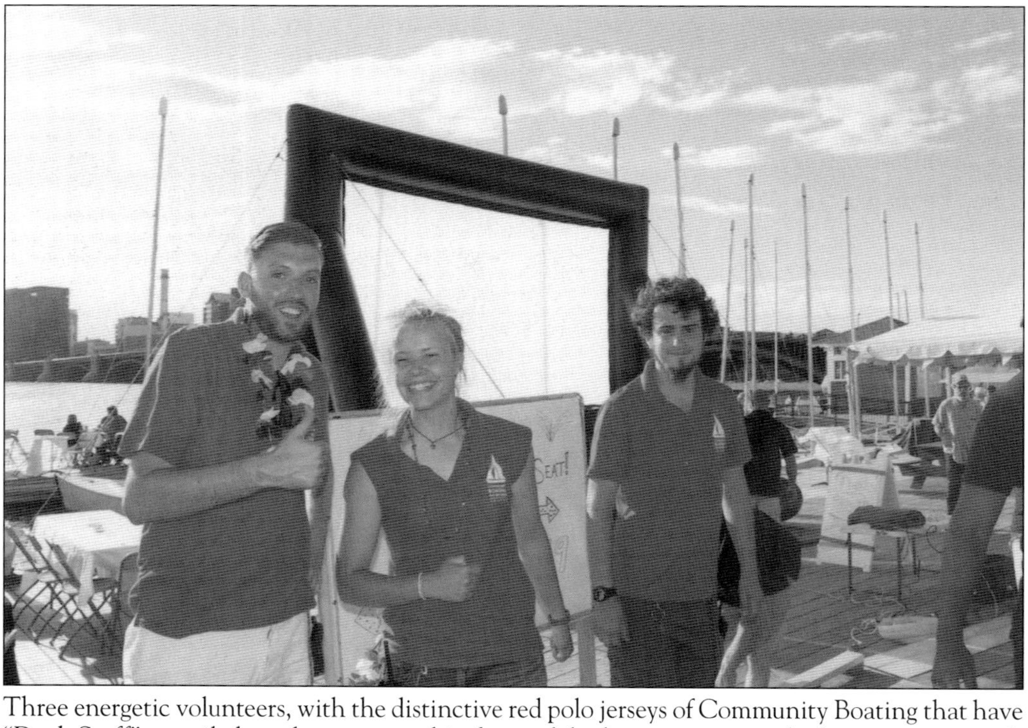

Three energetic volunteers, with the distinctive red polo jerseys of Community Boating that have "Dock Staff" stenciled on the rear, stand in front of the huge screen on which guests can watch the Boston Pops concert.

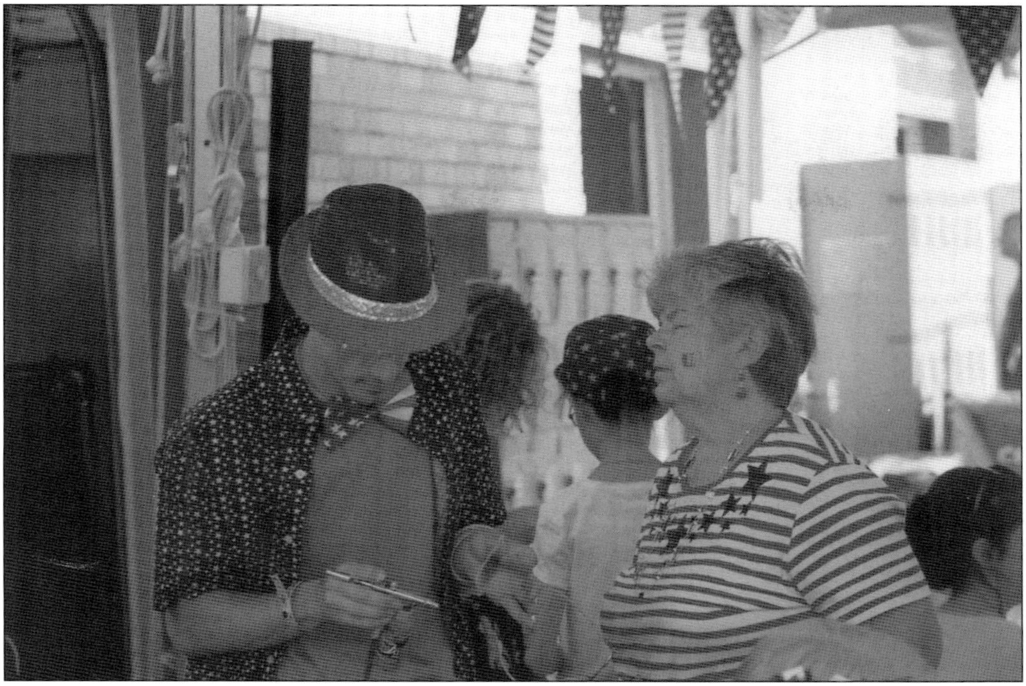

Under a bunting and flag bedecked tent, a volunteer prepares airbrushed tattoos that were applied on arms, chest, or in this case, the cheeks of a guest for an extra festive holiday revelry. This guest at Community Boating's Sailabration is having "USA" stenciled on her cheek to offset her patriotic red-and-white striped blouse with blue stars.

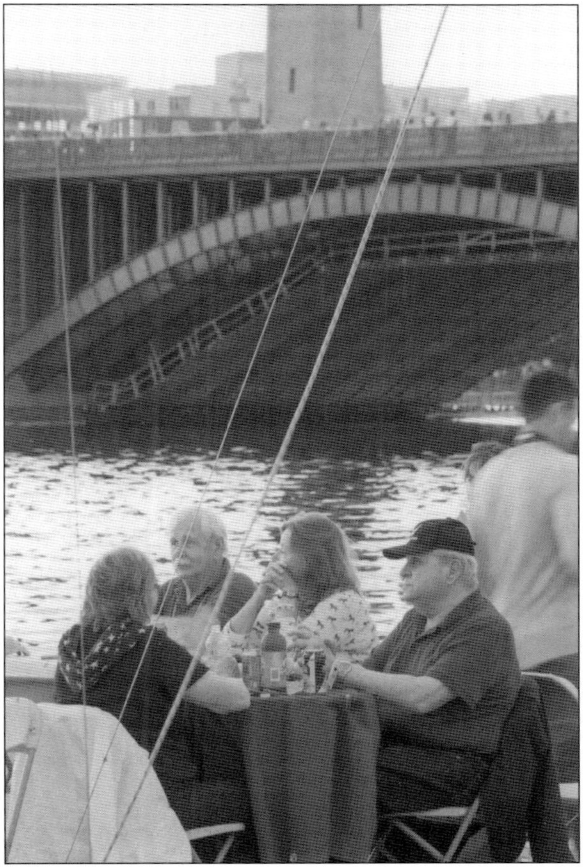

Two couples enjoy not just one another's company and conversation but also the views from the dock and the gentle cool breezes from the Charles River. Note the people beginning to flock to the Longfellow Bridge in the distance, where they, too, would have uninterrupted views of the fireworks.

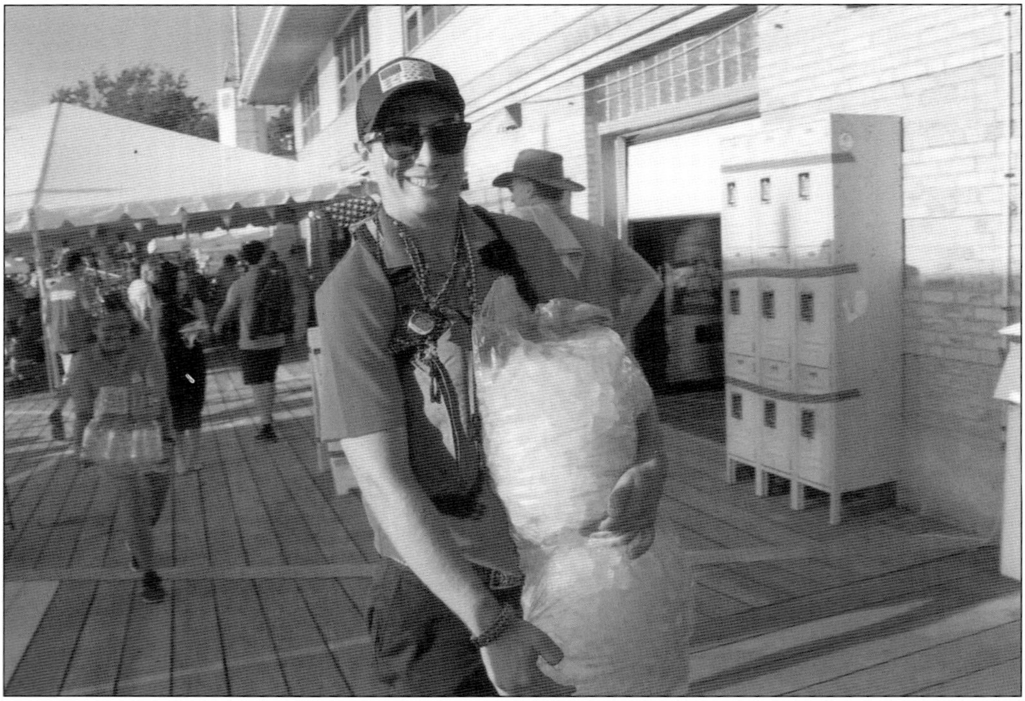

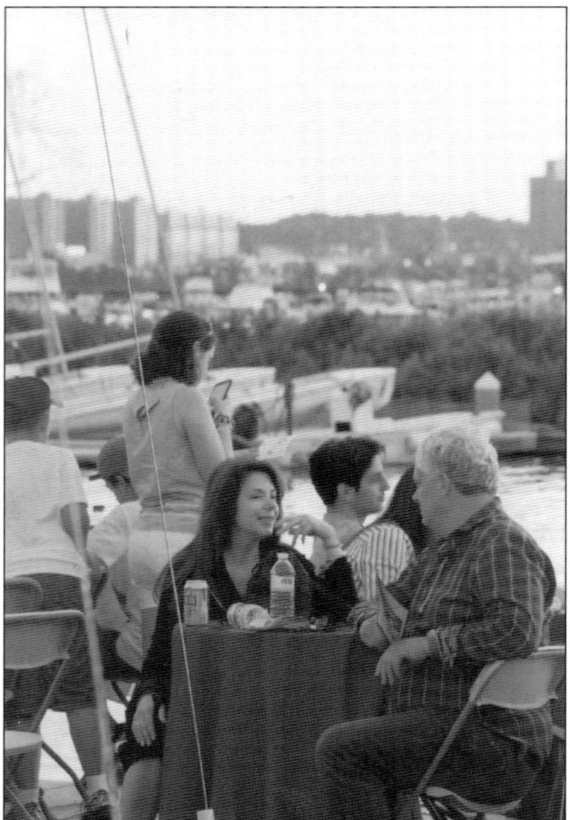

A young volunteer totes huge bags of ice along the boat dock that will be used at the bar for guests. The volunteer to the left in the background carries bottled water.

This charming photograph shows a couple in conversation amidst people of all ages who come to the dock of Community Boating for the Sailabration.

By early evening, the guests are seated at tables that line the boat docks along the Charles River. At this point, excitement is mounting, and the railing along the Longfellow Bridge is becoming lined with people as a Red Line train passes across the bridge.

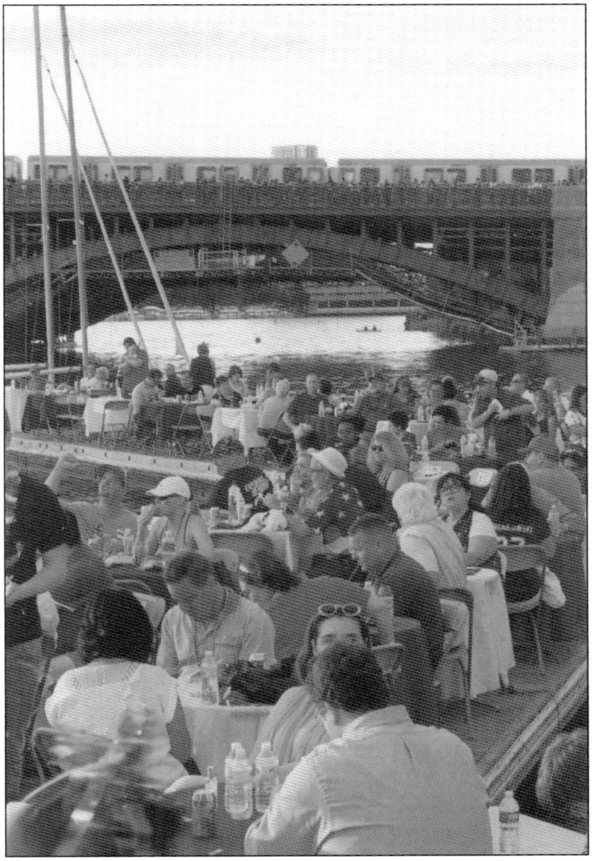

The guest seen right is served cool water by two young volunteers who are an important part in making this event a success as well as ensuring that guests are happy and safe.

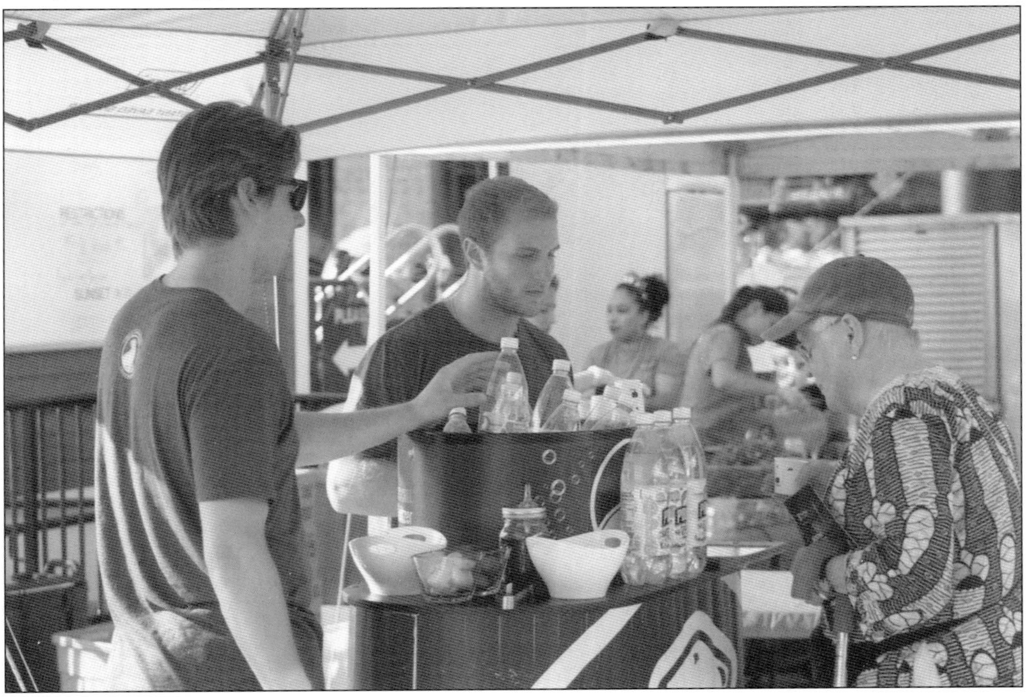

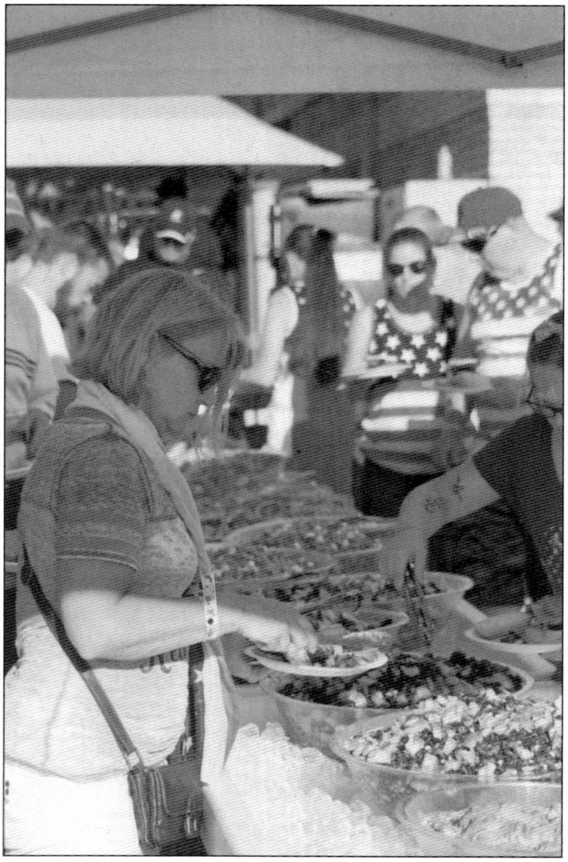

Guests enjoy a wonderful buffet set under the tent on the boat dock. The traditional New England clambake includes hard-shell native lobster, barbecue bone-in chicken breast, and a grilled veggie plate with hot dogs and hamburgers for the kids. This is accompanied by clam chowder with fresh rolls and butter; Cape Cod steamer clams, mussels, and linguiça; red bliss potatoes, corn on the cob, and homemade coleslaw and watermelon. Note the two guests on the right who sport patriotic tank tops for the Fourth of July.

After the buffet dinner, many guests take a seat on folding chairs facing the Charles River Basin, where the fireworks will be set off. In the center distance, the Hatch Shell with the two John Hancock Towers rising above it can be seen, as can the Prudential Tower on the far right. The panoramic view of Boston's Back Bay is incredible from this vantage point.

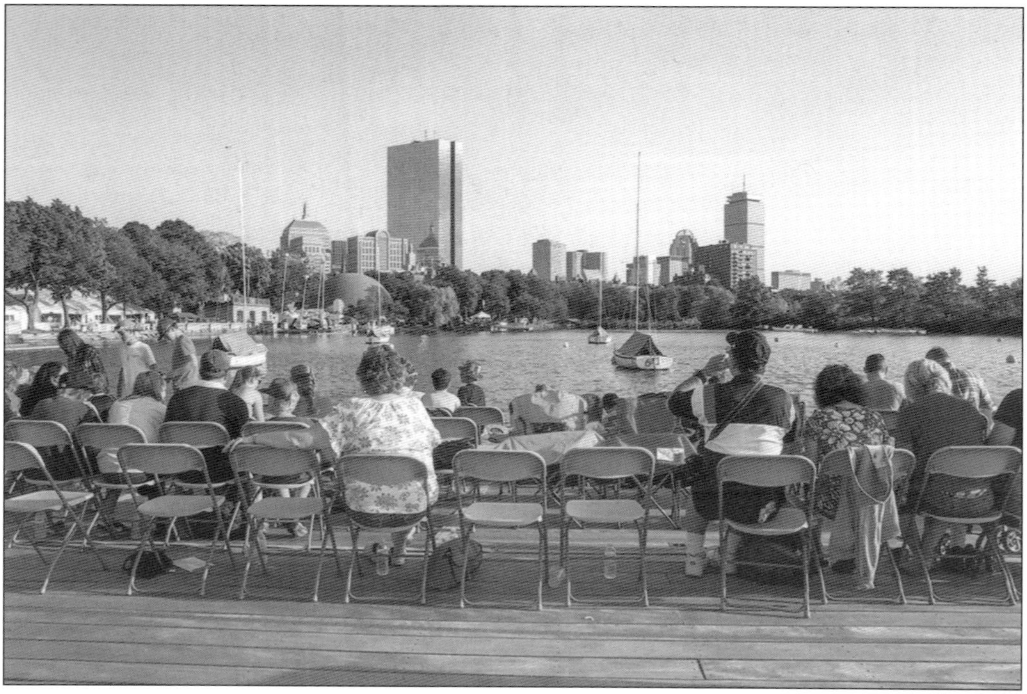

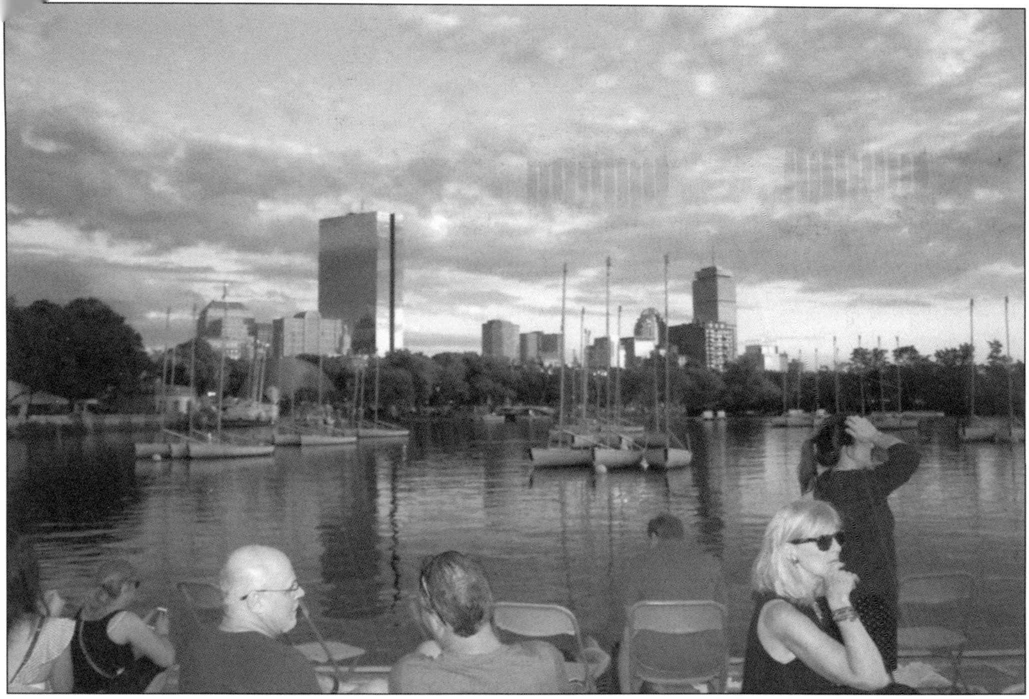

This view from the boat dock shows sailboats moored on the river with the gentle light of the early evening.

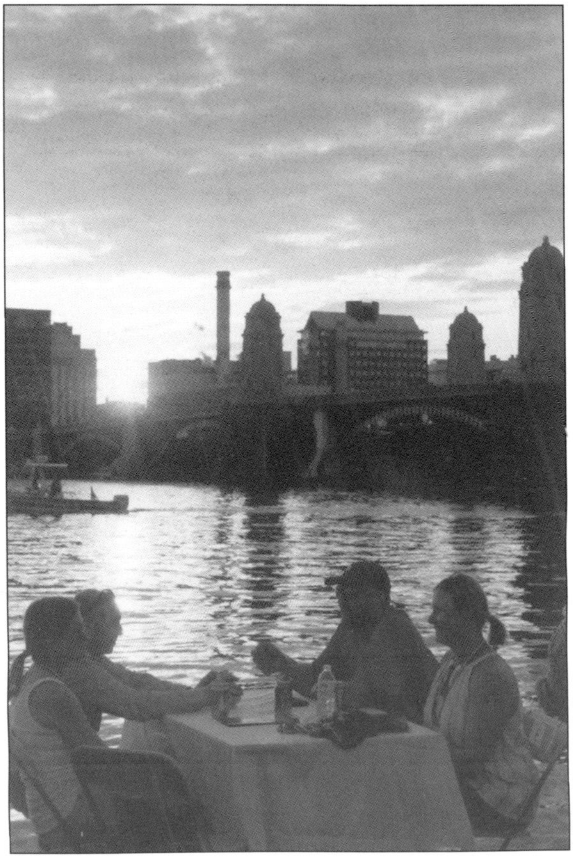

At dusk, guests and the buildings along the Cambridge side of the Charles River are silhouetted as they sit at the tables overlooking the river. At this point, the excitement of not just listening to the Boston Pops but also watching it on the massive screen is heightened.

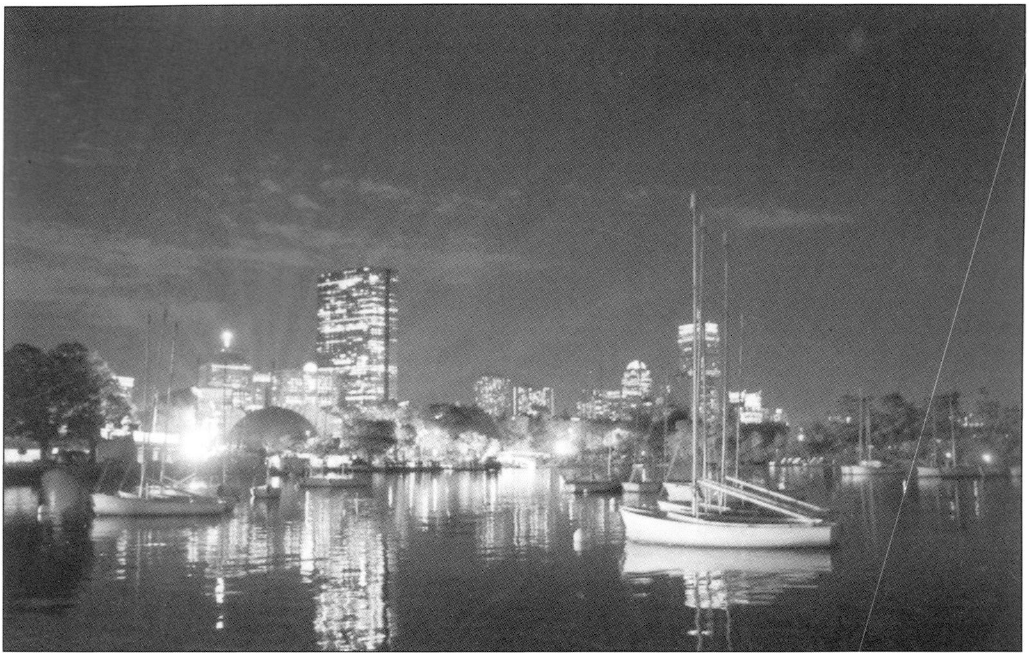

The many seasons and many times of the day are all charming at Community Boating, but there is something special about the water and how Boston is reflected in it. The sailboats, with their tall masts, are on the Charles River Basin awaiting another day of sailing, but the scene here is ethereal and a Boston icon.

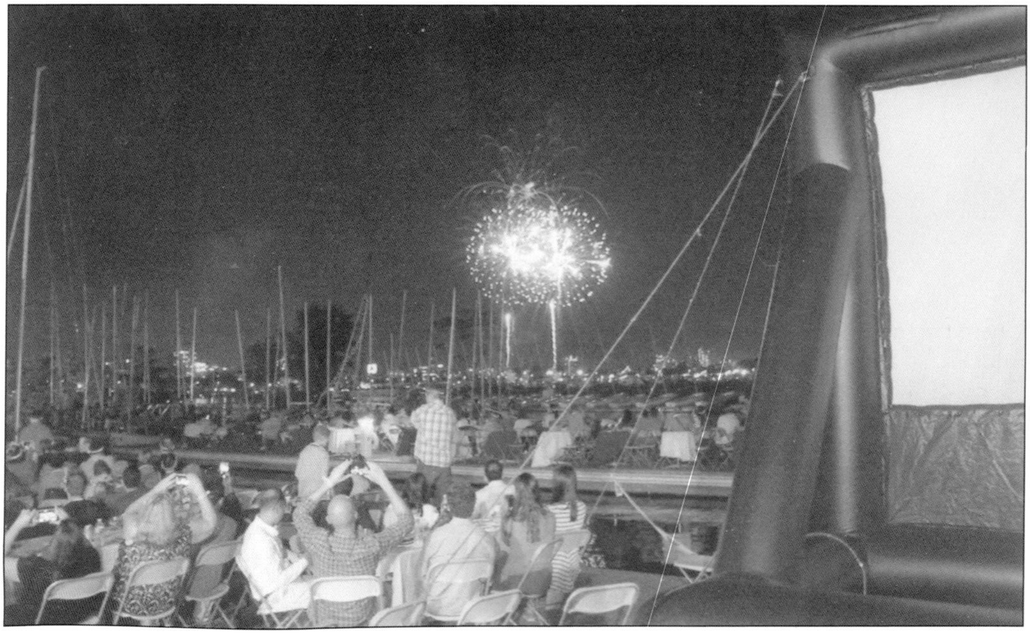

The 20-minute fireworks show has, in recent years, been designed by Grucci Fireworks to explode high over the Charles River Basin to the delights of the guests at the Community Boating docks, along the Esplanade, from the Longfellow Bridge, and every building and rooftop with a view of the Charles River Basin. The shared pride and joy of the Fourth of July Sailabration makes everyone a part of this festive annual event.

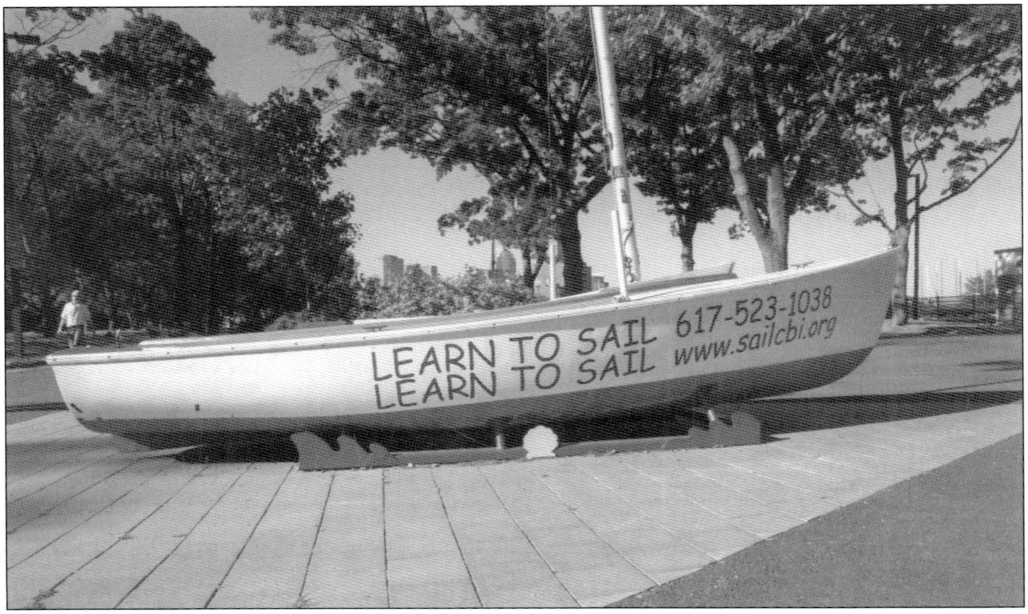

A sailboat is purposely land-locked in front of the entrance to the Community Boating boathouse on the walkway along the Esplanade of the Charles River Basin. It attracts walkers with its "Learn to Sail" sign along with the telephone number and the internet contact www.sailcni.org. For decades, Community Boating has offered adults, as well as the youth, of Boston the joys of sailing.

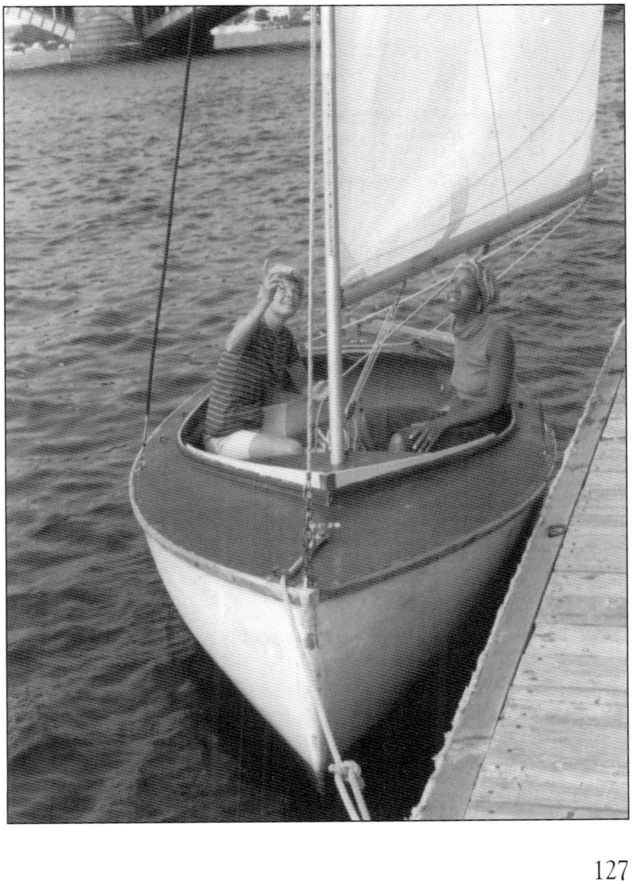

These two women sit in a sailboat, awaiting the wind that will allow them to set out on an afternoon sail on the Charles River Basin. As the woman on the left gestures to the sail, she might be following Joe Lee's guidance in *How to Sail a Boat*: "You first let go of the rope in your hand which holds the outer corner of the sail. This lets the sail flap like a flag in the wind. . . . Pull in the sail with the rope in your hand enough to stop its flapping. This will pull you ahead."